Motorcycle Electrical Manual 2nd edition

by Tony Tranter

THE BOOK

(446 – 11S1) ABCDE FGHIJ KLMNO PQ

Haynes Publishing
Sparkford Nr Yeovil
Somerset BA22 7JJ England

Haynes Publications, Inc
861 Lawrence Drive
Newbury Park
California 91320 USA

Acknowledgements

Many people from the motorcycle world were consulted during the preparation of this second edition and much gratitude is expressed for their time given and interest shown. Companies which gave copyright permission to reproduce their material are acknowledged below; if a source has been unknowingly omitted, apologies are tendered.

Boyer Bransden Ltd; Roy Bacon (author and publisher); AO Services; BMW AG Ltd and the staff of the BMW Technical Institute, Bracknell; Honda Motor Europe Ltd and the staff of the Honda Technical Training department, Chiswick; Honda Motor Co Ltd, Tokyo; Old Bike Mart; Kawasaki Motors (UK) Ltd; Mitsui Machinery Sales (UK) Ltd (Yamaha); Heron Suzuki PLC; Robert Bosch Ltd; British Standards Institution; Champion Sparking Plug Co Ltd; Gunson Ltd; NGK Spark Plugs Ltd; Joseph Lucas Ltd; Edward Arnold Ltd, for permission to reproduce illustrations from *Lamps and Lighting* by Hewitt and Vause; FKI Crypton Ltd; Rists Ltd; 'Radco' (Frank Farrington) for information on rotary magnetos; Drive Publications Ltd; Yuasa Battery Co Ltd, Japan; Feridax (1957) Ltd; 3M UK PLC; Datatool Alarms; Delta Press Ltd.

Thanks must also go to Rose Finch, who coped with a temperamental word processor to produce the text in fine style, and Penny Cox, who steered the editorial work.

A book in the **Haynes Owners Workshop Manual Series**

Printed by J. H. Haynes & Co. Ltd., Sparkford, Nr Yeovil, Somerset BA22 7JJ, England

ISBN 1 85010 823 4

Library of Congress Catalog Card Number 93-77339

British Library Cataloguing in Publication Data
A catalogue record for this book is available from the British Library

Contents

Preface

This book has been written to meet the needs of the practising mechanic, both professional and amateur, together with the increasing flow of student mechanics at Further Education colleges in the UK, and in the US in technical institutes running motorcycle mechanics courses. In the UK it will be of particular relevance to those preparing for the City and Guilds of London Institute examinations (C and G 389/7).

The reader will not find here a catalogue of electric circuits for all machines, but rather a book dealing with the principles of how and why things work. Armed with an understanding of fundamentals it will be easier to follow developments which will surely take place in electrical equipment design.

Modern motorcycles are remarkable examples of high technology and much of it is due to the electrical equipment designs of recent years. Electrical power requirements now demand generators of greatly increased output and because of the sensitivity of on-board electronic units, voltage regulators of high stability are needed. Not surprisingly these are also electronic!

Readers are introduced to the transistor, Zener diode and thyristor (silicon controlled rectifier) for these vital rugged devices lie at the heart of most electronic circuits found on the motorcycle. The on-board computer which finds so many applications in engine ignition and fuelling systems is now essential reading and is described in sufficient detail for most purposes.

For all this, it would be folly not to include an account of older electrical equipment for there are still many earlier motorcycles on the road; a description of dc dynamos and magnetos is therefore included.

Finally, a word to those who think that electricity is too difficult to understand – start at the beginning with an open mind and it is surprising how simple it all is when taken a little at a time.

Tony Tranter

Guildford 1993

Chapter 1 The Complete system

Contents

1 An overall view

1   In tackling the workings of motorcycle electrics, it is best to look first at the whole system and then to study the separate parts. It is interesting to see that the fuel provides the power to drive motorcycle and rider, and also all the electrical system. Take the case of the road machine shown diagramatically in Fig 1.1.

2   The generator provides power to the electrical components and also charges the battery so that the electrical circuits will work when the engine and generator are stopped. Essentially the generator must be of sufficient power output to run all electrical circuits simultaneously, with the exception of the starter motor – this being a job for the battery.

2 Charging and storage

1   All road-going motorcycles will normally have a battery to store electrical energy. The battery will work only on direct current (dc) and the generator which charges it will need to provide a direct current for this purpose.

2   A dynamo is a generator which produces a direct current output

(see Chapter 7) and was used on older machines until about 1954 and in some East European types until recently. Most motorcycles however are fitted with an alternator, this producing alternating current (ac) which is converted into a form of direct current suitable for battery charging (see Chapter 12) by a rectifier.

3   The direct current dynamo has a lower output than an alternator of the same size and requires more maintenance. The alternator has the advantage of being able to charge the battery even when the motorcycle engine is at tickover, but the dynamo needs to run at a higher speed before it starts to charge. With the heavy city traffic of today, engines run at tickover speeds for significant periods. A dynamo-equipped machine would soon suffer a flat battery, whereas a machine with an alternator can keep the battery charged.

3 Ignition

1   Petrol (gasoline) engines require a spark to ignite the compressed charge of turbulent air and fuel vapour. The spark must be accurately timed so that the resulting burning of the compressed vapour will give maximum power output consistent with economic fuel consumption.

2   **Magneto** – An engine-driven generator designed to give a high voltage of up to 30,000 volts (30 kV) at the instant of ignition.

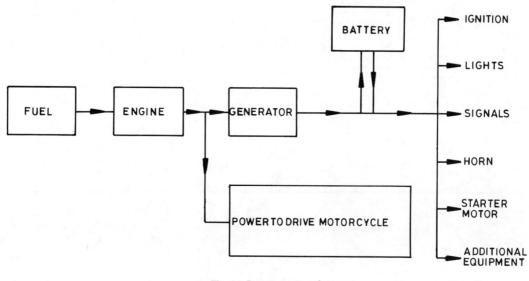

Fig. 1.1 Power conversion   H.22863

3   **Coil ignition** – An ignition coil, used as a transformer to step up the input voltage to that needed to produce a spark at the plug gap. This is achieved by altering rapidly the current in the primary winding; traditionally this has been done by cutting off the current with an engine-driven switch (the contact breaker) but is today by electronic control.

4   Lighting and signals

1   The provision of front and rear lighting together with some form of horn is a legal requirement for road machines in most countries. Headlamps have a main beam and some means of beam dipping to avoid dazzle to oncoming road users. The taillight is most important for rider safety and usually it is housed with a brake stop light.

2   Flashing turn signals are now almost universal on all modern motorcycles; in the UK and US the colour is amber. To warn the rider that the turn signals are working, a low wattage warning light is fitted in the instrument cluster.

5   Starting (engine cranking)

1   Many motorcycles are equipped with a direct-current starter motor which has a high standstill-torque to turn the engine until it fires up. The current demand is high, and this necessitates a larger battery than would be needed on a machine without a starter motor. Battery design and condition are more than ever important and the wise rider does not use the starter for long if the engine is reluctant to fire.

6   Conclusion

1   The topics referred to above amount to a general outline of the main electrical facilities of a motorcycle. The remaining chapters of this book will detail the principles and practice of all components and circuits.

2   For those needing a review of basic electrical theory Chapter 2 will cover all or most of the topics for a full understanding of what follows.

Chapter 2 Electrical Basics

Contents

1 Introduction

1   If well experienced in electrical matters readers may skip this chapter, but if they have never followed a course of instruction, or their knowledge is rusty, then time spent in reading will be an investment.

2   To read manufacturers' manuals, it is essential to have a clear understanding not only of electrical principles but also of the correct use of terminology; this is the reader's mental toolbox and is in every way as important as his or her practical toolkit.

2 The Atom – the source of electricity

1   All material consists of atoms which are, in turn, made up of protons, electrons and neutrons. The atom has a centre (or nucleus) which consists of protons and neutrons. Around the nucleus, electrons orbit at definite distances from the centre and are grouped into orbits (called shells) each at a different radius. Fig. 2.1. shows two simple atoms both of which will figure later in this book.

2   The proton carries a positive electrical charge, the electron a negative charge and the neutron has no charge. Normally an atom is electrically neutral overall, meaning that the number of (positive) protons in the nucleus is matched by the number of (negative) electrons rotating in the orbital shells. In the table below note that in each case the numbers of protons and electrons are equal.

Atom	Protons	Neutrons	Electrons
Hydrogen	1	0	1
Oxygen	8	8	8
Copper	29	34	29
Silicon	14	14	14

Neutrons and protons are strongly attracted when close together in the atomic nucleus and when they are split apart huge amounts of energy are released, a phenomenon which is exploited in the nuclear reactor and the atomic bomb.

3   Because of the relatively large mass of the nucleus it may be regarded as fixed in place in solid materials. Electrons are held less firmly in the atom and in some circumstances may leave the parent atom. It is this feature which is the basis of electronics.

4   The atom is small, requiring millions to cover the width of a hairline, yet the internal dimensions are even more remarkable. To give some idea, if the nucleus were an apple then the overall size of the atom could be thought of as that of a concert hall and the electrons as flies buzzing around!

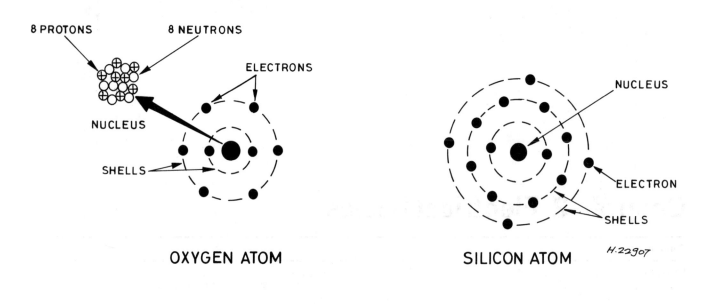

Fig. 2.1 Simple atomic systems (Sec 2)

3   Free electrons (conduction)

1   An atom is, in practice, a complicated structure; the outermost orbital electrons are sometimes held very loosely to the nucleus like a distant planet may be to the sun. Collisions may occur, which result in some electrons being driven from their normal path and drifting through the material lattice (Fig. 2.2). These are called **free electrons**. Some materials are rich in them, and others have few, or none at all. A material with many free electrons is a **conductor** and without free electrons is an **insulator**.

2   Imagine a copper wire as a mass of heavy copper atoms with swarms of free electrons in the spaces between them. These electrons are so small that there is plenty of room for them to fly about in all directions, but on the whole they do not progress very far in any one direction; their motion is random.

4   Electron flow = current

1   If a cell or a battery (a battery is merely a collection of cells) is connected to the ends of a copper wire, the free electrons drift along it, all in the same direction, just as when a pump is started, sending a current of liquid along the pipes to which it is connected.

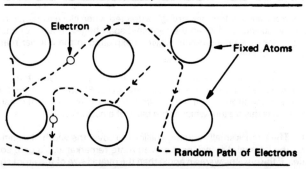

Fig. 2.2 Free electron drift (Sec 3)

2   It is important to understand that a battery does not make the electricity any more than a pump makes a liquid. The battery and the pump are merely agencies to set in motion something which already exists.

3   Carrying the analogy further, it might be said that it is not the pump which moves the fluid, but the pressure difference which the pump creates that causes the motion. This is a valuable idea because without stating the method used, it is the pressure difference alone which causes fluid flow. This also applies to electricity. Any device (eg battery, alternator, dynamo) which will set up a **potential difference** in an electric circuit can give rise to electric current flow.

4   As a pump produces a certain pressure, so a battery or alternator produces an electromotive force **(emf)** measured in **VOLTS**.

5   The idea of electron flow being the basis of electric current came long after a general convention that current flowed from the positive battery terminal, through the circuit back to the negative terminal.

Electrons, in fact, flow in the opposite direction and so care must be taken over which is used.

Conventional current flow (+ to –) is nearly always used except where stated otherwise.

5   The complete circuit

1   A circuit, as the name implies, is a complete uninterrupted path round which current may flow.

2   The battery or generator which pumps electrons round the circuit is similar in many ways to an oil pump working in a motorcycle engine. The oil flows continuously round the engine and is primarily used for lubricating bearing surfaces.

3   It is helpful to compare the oil system of Fig. 2.3 with the electrical system of Fig. 2.4.

4   The oil pump produces a pressure difference between points A and D and this causes oil to flow through the feed pipe B to the main bearing where a large pressure drop occurs. This is because of the constriction between journal and bearing and most of the pump energy is expended in forcing oil flow. Ideally, no energy is lost in the feed pipe.

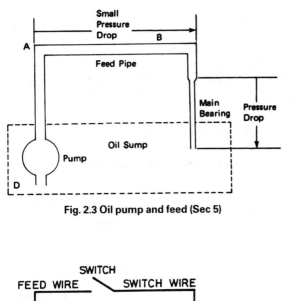

Fig. 2.3 Oil pump and feed (Sec 5)

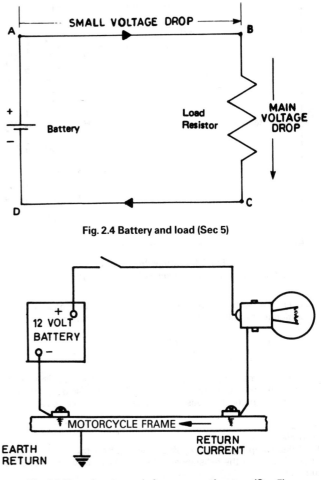

Fig. 2.4 Battery and load (Sec 5)

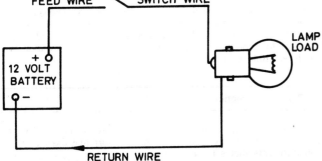

Fig. 2.5 Simple practical circuit with insulated return (Sec 5)

Fig. 2.6 Use of motorcycle frame as earth return (Sec 5)

5   In the equivalent electric circuit (Fig. 2.4), the battery produces potential difference (pd) between points A and D and this causes current to flow along the wire B to the load resistor where a large voltage drop occurs. This is because the resistor is made of high resistance wire and most of the battery energy is expended in forcing current flow. Ideally no energy is lost in the connecting wires but in practice a small loss will occur.

6   A practical realisation is shown in Fig. 2.5 with a bulb load and a switch. The motorcycle frame is used as the return wire in Fig. 2.6 and is referred to as 'earth' or 'ground'.

6   Fundamental quantities

1   The number of electrons set in motion by a battery is astronomically large, so a convenient number (how many does not matter to us!) are lumped together and called a **COULOMB**.

2   Again we are not often interested in the amount of electricity, but the speed of flow round a circuit. The number of coulombs flowing past a point each second is the **rate** of flow and 1 coulomb per second is called an **AMPERE**.

	Liquid system units	Electrical system units
Quantity	gallon	coulomb
Pressure and pressure drop	pounds per sq. inch	volt
Rate of flow	gallons per second	coulomb per second or ampere

7   Ohm's law

1   The load resistor is where the electricity will produce the desired effects. For example, an electric fire element consists of a spiral of wire with a resistance much higher than that of the connecting leads.

2   The well known effect is that heat is produced, a phenomenon which will be considered later. Equally, the headlamp bulb of a motorcycle is a load resistor and the main effect of current flow will be so much localised heat in the filament that white light is produced. Resistance is measured in **OHMS**, the name deriving from the German experimenter Georg Simon Ohm.

It is easy to visualise the value of 1 ohm, for it is such that a voltage of 1 volt would cause 1 ampere of current to flow (Fig. 2.7).

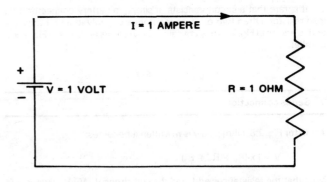

Fig. 2.7 The relationship between volts, amperes and ohms (Sec 7)

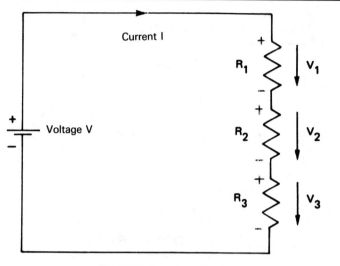

Fig. 2.8 Voltage drop (Sec 8)
Voltage drops around a circuit add up to the supply voltage

Georg Ohm is famous for his conclusion that current increases in direct proportion to the voltage applied to a constant resistance.

ie   Voltage = current x resistance
or   V   = I x R

Today this seems elementary but its statement in 1826 cost Ohm his job because it did not fit the theory of the day. Note the use of symbols V, I and R for numerical values of voltage, current and resistance in calculations.

Example
3   A headlamp bulb working off a 12 volt battery takes a current of 3 amperes. What is the resistance of the bulb filament when taking this current?

V = I x R
or   12 = 3 x R
so   R = 4 ohms

4   It pays to learn the proper abbreviations for electrical quantities to save writing the full word every time. For example, write 12 volts as 12V, 3 amps as 3A, 4 ohms as 4Ω and 36 watts as 36W.

Note that a circuit may have a VOLTAGE, but never say or write AMPERAGE – the correct term is CURRENT. Thus, a component may have a voltage of 12 volts **across** it and a current of 5 amperes **through** it.

8   Series and parallel circuits

1   It is rare that a circuit consists of simply a battery connected to a load resistor. Often two or more resistors are involved and if they are end to end as in Fig. 2.8 they are said to be in **series** and, if as in Fig. 2.9 in **parallel**.

9   Series connection

1   If, for Fig. 2.8, Ohm's Law is rewritten it becomes:

$$V = I \times (R_1 + R_2 + R_3)$$

Note that the resistances add, and the volt-drops V_1, V_2, V_3 always add up to the total supply voltage V, a point to remember when fault tracing.

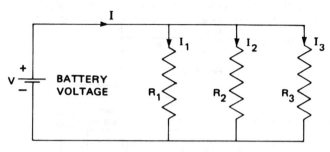

Fig. 2.9 Resistors in parallel (Sec 8)

2   **Example**
To see how this equation might be used in practice, suppose $R_1 = 3\Omega$, $R_2 = 4\Omega$, and $R_3 = 5\Omega$.
What current would be drawn from the battery if V = 12 volts?

12 = I x (3 + 4 + 5)
or 12 = I x 12
so I = 1 ampere

3   In practice, the internal resistance of the battery may be significant (especially if it is wearing out) and there may be unwanted resistance in the cables and connections. These undesired resistances would have to be taken into account for some purposes by using Ohm's Law as above. See the example given later.

10   Parallel connection

1   Referring to Fig. 2.9 it is clear that the battery must supply the current to all three branches and that the total current is the sum of the branch currents: that is, $I = I_1 + I_2 + I_3$

2   Each branch has the full voltage V applied to it, so in this case the separate currents may be calculated and added.

3   Note that this is the most frequent arrangement to be met in a motorcycle electrical system – for instance R_1 could be the lighting load, R_2 the horn, R_3 the ignition, and the current demand on the battery would be the sum of the separate currents.

4   **Example**
Suppose again the supply voltage to be 12 volts and the load resistors were $R_1 = 6\Omega$, $R_2 = 3\Omega$, and $R_3 = 4\Omega$, as in Fig. 2.10.

$$I_1 = \frac{V}{R_1} = \frac{12}{6} = 2A$$

$$I_2 = \frac{V}{R_2} = \frac{12}{3} = 4A$$

$$I_3 = \frac{V}{R_3} = \frac{12}{4} = 3A$$

The total current drain from the battery is therefore I = 9A.

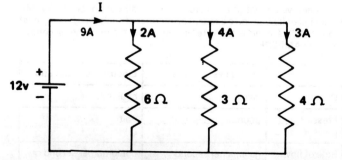

Fig. 2.10 An example of current drain by resistors in parallel (Sec 10)

By using Ohm's Law again, it will be seen that if the equivalent resistance of the 3 branches in parallel, R, is worked out it is given by:

$$V = I \times R$$

$$12 = 9 \times R$$

$$R = \frac{12}{9} = 1\tfrac{1}{3} \ \Omega$$

The general case for resistors in parallel is:

$$\frac{1}{R} = \frac{1}{R_1} + \frac{1}{R_2} + \frac{1}{R_3}$$

Where R is the effective resistance of $R_1 R_2 R_3$ etc., connected in parallel.

11 Energy and power

1 **Energy** (or work, as it is sometimes called) is measured in **JOULES** where 1 joule is the energy expended when a pressure of 1 volt drives a current of 1 ampere through a load for 1 second.

So   joules = volts x amperes x seconds

or, in symbols   J = VIt

Example
If a 12 volt battery delivers 3 amperes of current to a headlamp bulb for 20 minutes, how much energy is used?

$$\text{Energy} = V \times I \times t$$
$$= 12 \times 3 \times 20 \times 60$$
$$= 43,200 \text{ joules}$$

The joule is not used very much in routine electrical work, but it is of interest to note that it is also the unit of energy in mechanical engineering, if SI (metric) units are used. It is the energy expended by a force of 1 Newton moving through a distance of 1 metre in the direction of the force, ie 1 metre-Newton = 1 Joule.

2 **Power** is closely related to energy, for it is simply the rate of utilising energy. The unit of power is the **WATT**.

$$\text{Watts} = \text{joules per second ie } \frac{\text{joules}}{\text{seconds}}$$

Remembering that joules = volts x amperes x seconds we have:

$$\text{Watts} = \frac{\text{joules}}{\text{seconds}} = \text{volts x amperes}$$

so $\underline{\text{Watts} = \text{volts x amperes}}$ for a direct current circuit

In the example described, the battery delivering 3A at 12V is giving a power of $W = V \times I = 12 \times 3 = 36$ watts

12 Wiring volt-drop

1 Examination of motorcycle wiring will show that the wires and

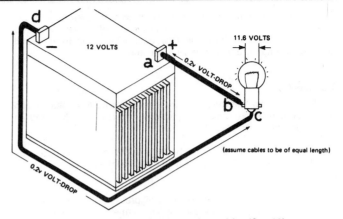

Fig. 2.11 Volt-drop in connecting cables (Sec 12)

cables are of different thicknesses, and that often the wire is not one solid strand, but made up of several strands twisted together.

The designer chooses a cable so that the current flowing from the source to the load does not produce an undue waste of energy in the wires carrying it.

It is important to remember that although the wires are made of copper, which is a good conductor, nevertheless there is some finite resistance in which heating loss and volt-drop will occur. This means less power to the load, and inefficiency.

The battery shown connected to the bulb in Fig. 2.11 has a terminal pressure of 12 volts and ideally all this voltage should appear across the bulb; however, here the connecting wires have a resistance which gives a loss of 0.2 volt for both go and return, leaving only 11.6 volts to light the bulb filament.

2 The result in this case is poor illumination due to the waste of power in the wires. Better results would be obtained by using thicker cables, but the limits to increasing diameter are determined by the cost of copper and undesirable stiffness of thick wires.

13 Electrical testmeters

1 The quantities most often met in electrical work are amperes, volts and ohms. Not surprisingly the meters (sometimes called instruments) used to measure them are ammeters, voltmeters and ohmmeters. There are a few basic rules on their use which must always be remembered, because if a meter is misused it can be a very expensive mistake.

Ammeter

2 The ammeter measures current **through** a circuit; it is connected so that this current flows through the ammeter (in **series** with the lamp load as shown in Fig. 2.12). The instrument designer keeps the internal resistance of the ammeter as low as possible so as not to interfere with the measured circuit.

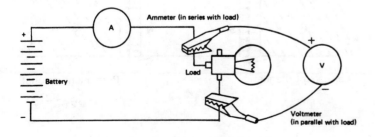

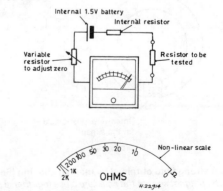

Fig. 2.12 The use of ammeter, voltmeter and ohmmeter (Sec 13)

If by accident the ammeter were connected across the load instead of in series with it, this would be disastrous. Because of the low ammeter resistance a heavy current would flow, destroying the instrument and possibly melting the connecting wire insulation.

Voltmeter

3   The voltmeter measures electrical pressure (called voltage) and should be connected across the part of a circuit to be measured (in parallel across the lamp as in Fig. 2.12).

For the circuit not to be disturbed by the presence of the voltmeter, the internal resistance of the meter is high – ideally infinite, but never so in practice.

An hydraulic pressure gauge measures oil pressure but no oil actually passes through it, and in the case of the voltmeter no current should ideally go through it.

Ohmmeter

4   An internal battery in series with the meter movement and a variable zero-setting resistor are the main components of the ohmmeter.

With the test prods shorted together the zero knob adjusts the internal resistor until the pointer reads full scale. Under the pointer the scale is marked 'zero' on the ohms scale. The prods may then be applied to the component to be tested and the pointer will read downscale due to the added resistance of the component.

The scale is calibrated against known standard resistors and is seen from Fig. 2.12 to be cramped at one end and is a non-linear scale.

There is one rule in using an ohmmeter – never apply the test prods to a live circuit. At the very least, the reading will be in error if the test circuit is live and probably the ohmmeter will be destroyed. *Always disconnect the motorcycle battery if you are testing a component in-situ on the bike.*

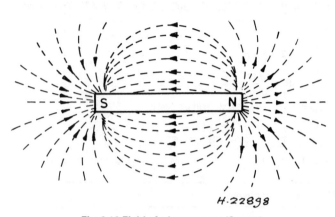

Fig. 2.13 Field of a bar magnet (Sec 14)
Direction of arrowheads is agreed convention

Further information

5   All meters are available in analogue form (with a pointer) or digital form, and may be combined into multi-purpose meters. See Chapter 16 for further details.

14   Permanent magnets

1   A bar magnet free to pivot about its centre point will take up a position so that one end will point to the earth's north pole. That end of the magnet is referred to as its north pole and the opposite end the south pole.

2   Around the magnet is a region to which iron will be attracted and this region is said to have a magnetic field; it is most concentrated at the N and S poles. The pattern of the **magnetic flux** of this region may be

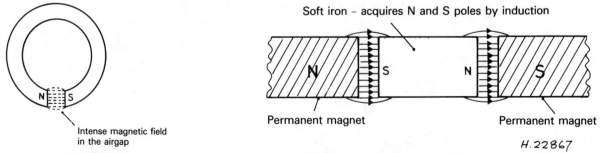

Fig. 2.14 Forces between magnetic poles (Sec 14)

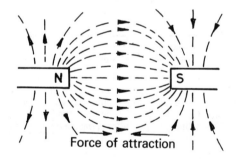

Fig. 2.15 A strong field obtained by magnet shaping (Sec 14)
By shaping the magnet so that the poles are close together, a stronger and more useful field is obtained

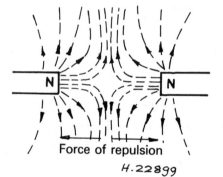

Fig. 2.16 Magnetic induction (Sec 14)

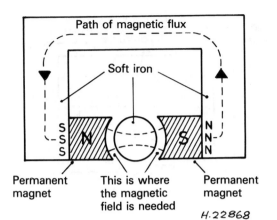

Fig. 2.17 Example of magnetic induction – soft iron used to carry magnetic flux around an iron circuit (Sec 14)

visualised by laying a piece of cardboard over the magnet and sprinkling iron filings on to the cardboard.

These take up a pattern and it helps visualisation if we think of magnetic lines of force going from N to S (Fig. 2.13). In reality, there are no individual lines but a magnetic flux which permeates the whole of the space involved.

3   Magnetic flux is measured in WEBERS but rather more important is how concentrated is this flux in a given area through which the magnetic field is imagined to pass. The number of Webers passing through an area of 1 square metre (1 m^2) is the MAGNETIC FLUX DENSITY (symbol B) and the unit of flux density is the TESLA.

4   It is found that if the N pole of one magnet is brought close to the S pole of another, a significant force of attraction from one to the other will be felt. Similarly, if two N (or two S) poles are brought close to each other then there is force of repulsion (Fig. 2.14).

Magnetic lines of force may be imagined as elastic threads which seek to shorten yet repel each other sideways, giving rise to patterns which help an understanding of magnetic attraction and repulsion.

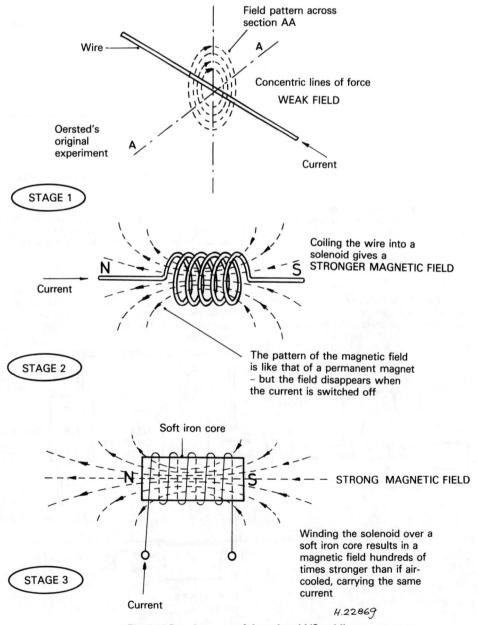

Fig. 2.18 Development of the solenoid (Sec 14)

5   Electrical machines and some instruments which use permanent magnets need strong magnetic fields. The straight bar magnet gives a weak field but a much better density of field is obtained if the bar is bent so that the N and S poles are close (Fig. 2.15).

Magnet steel is expensive and is often made in rectangular blocks. Making a complex shape such as a horseshoe or a square out of magnet steel is not a good design because of cost. The solution is to use cheaper iron to make up part of the path for magnetic lines of force thanks to the phenomenon of magnetic induction.

6   Magnetic induction is an important effect. If a block of iron is brought into a magnetic field if will temporarily acquire N and S poles and behave like a magnet so long as the external magnetic field is present. Such iron is referred to as soft iron because it loses virtually all of its magnetism when removed from the magnetic field (Fig. 2.16). If soft iron is used to make up a **magnetic circuit** it in effect carries the magnetic field to where it will be used and butts up to the permanent magnet steel, the N and S poles of which are transferred to the ends of the soft iron (Fig. 2.17).

7   There is a relationship between current and magnetism, discovered in 1820 by the Danish experimenter Oersted, and this lies behind much of modern electrical equipment. He found that a wire carrying a current produced a surrounding magnetic field. Further, this field disappeared when the current was switched off.

By winding the wire into coils (ie a SOLENOID), the intensity of the magnetic field was raised considerably and moreover the field had a pattern similar to that of a permanent bar magnet (Fig. 2.18). It was found also that if the coils were wound over a core of soft iron the magnetic field intensity was much greater again. This was the invention of the electromagnet.

15   Electromagnets

1   A limitation to the amount of power generated in permanent magnet dynamos and other electrical equipment is due to the relatively weak magnetic field strength of the permanent magnet and lack of control of this field strength. The solution lies in the use of the electromagnet (or solenoid), which consists of an iron core over which a coil is wound.

2   Passing direct current through the coil will induce a magnetic field in the iron, which may then bear a strong resemblance to an ordinary permanent magnet with the differences that:

  (a)   The strength of the magnetic field can be controlled (within limits) by varying the current in the coil.
  (b)   The magnetic field virtually disappears when the current is switched off.

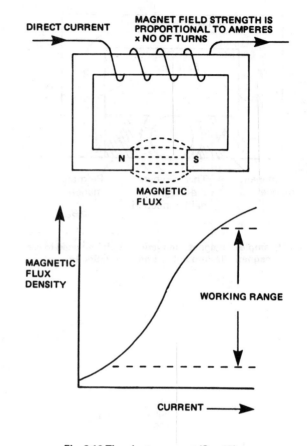

Fig. 2.19 The electromagnet (Sec 15)

3   The arrangement of the electromagnet is shown in Fig. 2.19, together with a graph showing the way in which field strength varies with coil current. Note that beyond a certain current the magnetic flux density flattens off – the iron is then said to be saturated.

4   The electromagnet finds many uses in electrical equipment for motorcycles; instead of a permanent magnet in a dynamo or alternator it is possible to use electromagnets, with the advantage that the electrical output can be regulated by varying the current in the electromagnet windings. In motor and generator practice, the electromagnets producing magnetic flux are called field poles and the coils are field windings.

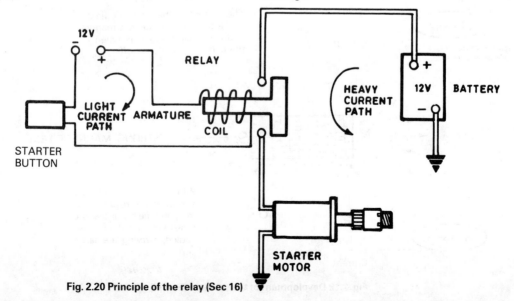

Fig. 2.20 Principle of the relay (Sec 16)

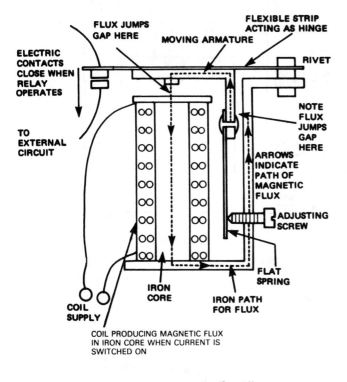

Fig. 2.21 Magnetic relay (Sec 16)

16   Electromagnetic relays and solenoids

1   The relay is used to switch heavy current on, or off, by means of a much smaller control current (Fig. 2.20). A typical example is the starter motor, where the current may rise to more than a hundred amperes. In this particular instance, the heavy cable needed to carry this current from the battery must be short to avoid voltage loss, and could not conveniently be brought to a handlebar switch anyway because of the cable stiffness and bulk. The relay overcomes this problem since it is located in the short path between battery and starter and only a thin control cable need go to the starter button.

2   It is well known that magnetic poles will exert a pull on nearby iron or steel. This effect is used in the relay in which a strip of iron is pulled by the magnetic field created when current is switched on. The movement of the iron strip or **armature** can be made to open or close electrical contacts, which may act as a switch for a variety of uses, some of which will be described later in this book.

3   A simple relay is shown in Fig. 2.21 in which the armature is held in one position by the flat spring until the coil current is switched on. Then the magnetic flux set up by the coil causes the armature to be attracted to the central iron core and so closes the contacts. When the current is switched off the magnetic field disappears and the armature returns to the rest position, the contacts opening. This type of relay is widely used in motorcycle and automobile engineering.

4   See Fig. 2.22 for a schematic of an actual starter solenoid. This relies on the fact that an iron core is attracted towards the mid point of a coil carrying current. The pull exerted on the iron armature can be so great that in the case of the pre-engaged starter motor (more often used on automobiles than motorcycles) its movement may be powerful enough to engage the starter pinion gear into a flywheel gear ring and also switch on the heavy current of the starter motor. It will be seen that this is a relay in a different form.

17   Magnetic field strength

1   It is found that the magnetic field in an iron circuit depends upon several factors over which the designer has control:

   (a)   The number of turns of wire on the coil.
   (b)   The current flowing (amperes).
   (c)   The iron path details.

2   In general, magnetic flux will pass more readily through iron than air and so if a strong field is required, then an iron path of large cross-sectional area is necessary, together with a coil designed to make the product of amperes x turns as large as possible (Fig. 2.23).

18   Motors and generators

1   Millions of motors, dynamos and alternators are in use in motorcycles and other vehicles, representing the greatest use of electrical machines in any branch of industry. It is a credit to designers that relatively few failures occur, for these machines are subject to heavy utilisation, need very little maintenance and work in a hostile environment, having to cope with wide temperature ranges, dust, damp and, in the case of generators, speed variations from a few hundred to thousands of revolutions per minute with high acceleration forces.

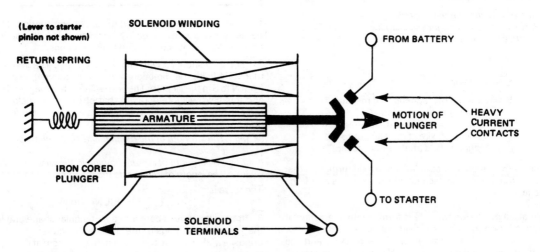

Fig. 2.22 Diagrammatic representation of a starter solenoid (Sec 16)

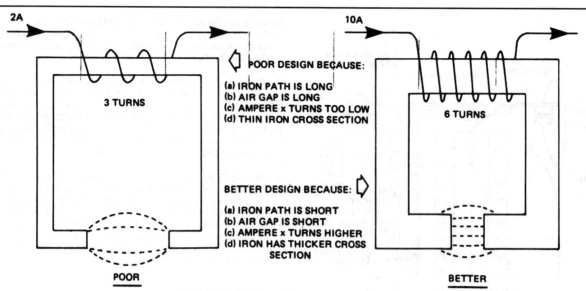

Fig. 2.23 Design factors for iron circuits (Sec 17)

2 The motor and generator (included here are dynamos and alternators) are not really separate for it is only a question of energy flow. Thus in the case of the direct-current motor, electrical energy is put in and mechanical energy emerges at the shaft. The same machine could be driven by an external prime mover and electrical energy would be available at the terminals. The dc motor and the dc generator are, then, essentially the same device. A similar picture may be stated for the alternator which could be driven as a motor by connecting it correctly to an alternating current supply. The relationship between the dc motor and generator is particularly important here.

3 Most electrical pointer instruments are really a highly specialised form of direct-current electric motor operating over a limited angular range of 90° to 120° only. Designers use the same form of calculations in designing both moving-coil instruments and dc motors.

4 The details of dc generators, alternators and motors will be dealt with in the later chapters of this book. Here the two important principles of motor and generator action are stated, and armed with this information, the way in which machines and instruments work will be readily understood.

19 The generator rule

1 If a wire moves across a magnetic field it is found that a voltage is generated in it for so long as there is motion (see Fig. 2.24). The voltage obtained is found to depend upon:

(a) The length of wire in the magnetic field.
(b) The velocity of the wire at right angles to the magnetic field.
(c) The strength of the magnetic field.

The actual value in volts is:

$$E = BLV \text{ volts}$$

where:

B = strength of magnetic field measured in webers per square metre (or Tesla)
L = length of wire (metres)
V = velocity of wire at right angles to the magnetic field (metres per second)

No need to be concerned about any calculations to read further: all that is important is to remember the factors which fix the size of the generated voltage.

2 In order to make a generator, the wire is formed into a rectangular coil and spun round inside the magnetic field. All the rest is detail, but upon this basic rule depends the operation of the dynamo and the alternator. This theme occurs in the book several times – it is well worth remembering.

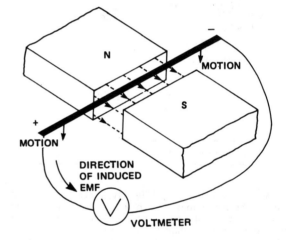

Fig. 2.24 Induced emf in moving conductor (Sec 19)

20 The motor rule

1 This is the converse of the generator situation. Electric current passed down a wire located in a magnetic field will experience a force at right angles to both current and field directions.

2 Fig. 2.25 shows a wire carrying a current. The wire is situated in a magnetic field, the direction of which is conventionally agreed to be from N to S in the air path. The wire will create a magnetic field of its own and this field will interact with that of the motor field giving rise to a force acting downwards. The numerical value of the force will depend upon:

(a) The strength of the magnetic field, B webers per sq. metre (Tesla).
(b) The amount of current flowing in the wire, I amperes.
(c) The length of wire inside the magnetic field, L metres.

The force is:

$$F = BIL \text{ Newtons}$$

3 If now the wire is bent into a rectangular shape and located within the magnetic field again, the direction of current in the two sides is opposite and so will be the forces acting on them. It now remains only to pivot the rectangular coil on bearings for it to become a simple electric motor, for the two forces will give rise to rotation (Fig. 2.26).

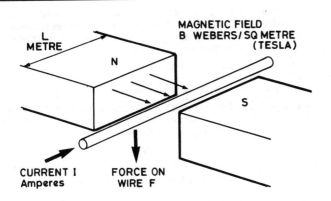

FORCE ON WIRE F = BIL NEWTONS

(For those who think in Imperial Units
1 Newton is approx.¼ lb force)

Fig. 2.25 Force on a wire carrying a current (Sec 20)

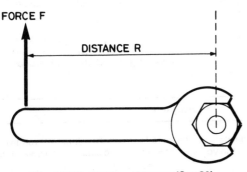

Fig. 2.27 Illustration of torque (Sec 20)

Torque = F x R
In the Metric system torque is measured in Newton-metres (Nm), or less correctly as kilogramme-metres (kgf m). In the Imperial system torque is measured in pounds-feet (lbf ft).

This idea of motor operation will be particularly useful when reading Chapter 15 on starter motors, where the subject will be developed further.

4   Torque is an important concept in engineering. In Fig. 2.27 torque is applied to a nut by means of a spanner and is a measure of turning capability. It is simply the force and distance multiplied, but on the condition that the direction of force is at right angles to the direction to the nut centre.

5   Looking again at the simple motor of Fig. 2.26, the coil radius is R, and there are two operating sides each giving a force F, so:

Motor torque = 2 x F x R   Newton-metres
                               (or pounds-feet in Imperial units)

21 Resistance

1   The resistance of a wire will depend on the length (L), cross sectional area (A) and the specific resistance (ρ) which is the characteristic of the wire material.

Specific resistance ρ is that resistance measured between opposite faces of a cube of size 1 metre, made of the wire material (Fig. 2.28). This material is usually copper for most wiring purposes on a motorcycle. The value of ρ for copper is 1.72×10^{-8} ohm-metres (Ω–m).

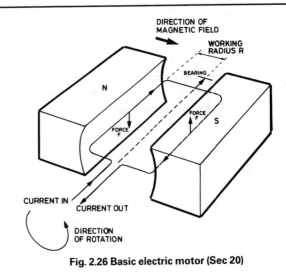

Fig. 2.26 Basic electric motor (Sec 20)

If we wish to calculate the resistance R of a coil of copper wire, length L metre and wire cross sectional area A sq. metres, then:

$$R = \frac{\rho L}{A} \text{ ohms}$$

Example: A solenoid wound in copper wire of 0.657 sq. mm cross sectional area uses 70 metres of wire. Calculate the resistance of the finished solenoid winding using the following formula.

$$R = \frac{\rho L}{A} = \frac{1.72 \times 10^{-8} \times 70}{0.657 \times 10^{-6}}$$

R = 1.83 ohms

Now try working out the resistance of a copper wire coil using 120 metres of wire 0.7112 mm in diameter, remembering that cross sectional area (CSA) is given by:

$$CSA = \frac{\pi d^2}{4}$$

Ans.   R = 5.196 ohms

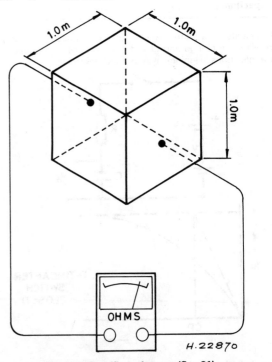

Fig. 2.28 Specific resistance (Sec 21)
The resistance between opposite faces of a 1 metre cube is the Specific Resistance of the metal

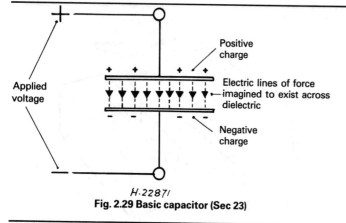

H.2287I

Fig. 2.29 Basic capacitor (Sec 23)

22   Temperature Coefficient of Resistance

1   Most metals increase in resistance as temperature rises and semiconductors fall in resistance with an increase in temperature. Both effects are important and will be met again further into this book.

Temperature coefficient α is defined as the change of resistance per ohm per degree Celsius. The value of the coefficient is usually given at 20°C and for copper is + 0.0043.

Example: If the solenoid in paragraph 1 of the previous section were heated to 50°C in use, what would be the resistance assuming the resistance at 20°C to be 1.83 ohms?

Resistance at 50°C   =   Resistance at 20°C + increase due to heating

Increase due to heating   = R_{20} x 0.0043 x (50 – 20)
                 =   0.129 R_{20}

Resistance at 50°C   = R_{20} + 0.129 R_{20}
           R_{50} =   1.83 + (0.129 x 1.83)
           R_{50} =   2.07 ohms

23   Capacitance

1   A capacitor (sometimes known as a condenser) is a component which will store charge and give it out again when required. It finds many applications in ignition systems and electronics.

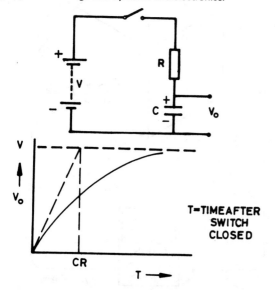

Fig. 2.30 Charging capacitor C through resistance R (Sec 24)
Voltage across C reaches 63% of V in CR seconds
CR = Time constant

2   The most basic capacitor consists of two parallel metal plates as shown in Fig. 2.29; applying a voltage V between the plates will result in a surge of current to charge the plates. The amount of charge (q coulombs) stored depends on:

The area and spacing of the plates.
The applied voltage.
The type of insulator between the plates.

The charge q stored by applying 1 volt is called the CAPACITANCE, the symbol for which is C. Capacitance is measured in Farads and the relationship between voltage, capacitance and charge is:

$$q = CV$$

3   In practice the farad is too large a unit for practical purposes and the microfarad (μF) is used, being one millionth of a farad.

In order to make the physical size of a capacitor smaller, the 'plates' may consist of two long rectangular aluminium foils separated by a slightly wider strip of impregnated paper and rolled up like a Swiss roll. Wires are attached to the two foils and the whole assembly is encapsulated in some form of plastic or metal container. The metal container is often connected internally to one of the foils and the case bolted down to earth (ie the motorcycle engine). This is the most usual case for contact breaker coil ignition systems.

Capacitor design is highly developed and several other means of making a capacitor exist, but the basic idea of two separated plates is good for all types.

4   Leakage may take place through the insulator (known as the dielectric) resulting in a fall of voltage between the plates. Serious leakage can cause malfunction of ignition with misfiring, poor starting or total failure as a result.

24   CR charge and discharge

1   If a capacitor C is connected to a supply voltage V through a resistor R (Fig. 2.30) the voltage rise V_o across the capacitor follows a curve.

The time taken for the voltage to rise to 63% of the supply voltage V is the **time constant** of the circuit and equals CR seconds.

2   Similarly the time taken to discharge a capacitor C through resistance R is CR seconds where discharge is meant that the voltage falls to 37% of the initial voltage (Fig. 2.31).

Both CR charge and discharge are widely used in electronic timing circuits.

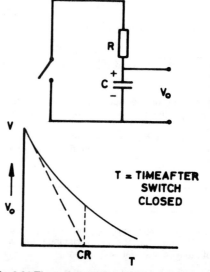

Fig. 2.31 Time of discharge of CR circuit (Sec 24)
Capacitor C initially charged to V volts
Voltage across C falls to 37% of V in CR seconds
CR = Time constant

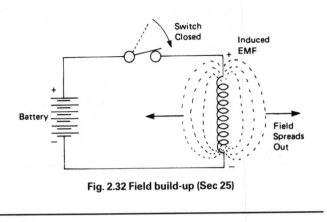

Fig. 2.32 Field build-up (Sec 25)

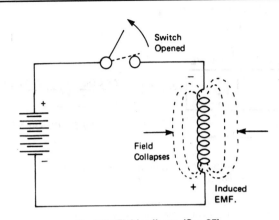

Fig. 2.33 Field collapse (Sec 25)

25 Inductance

1 Already we have seen that a coil carrying a direct current will set up a magnetic field around it. This is the steady state condition but of great importance is what happens when we attempt to **change** the current. Suppose a coil is switched on to a battery supply and the current begins to flow (Fig. 2.32). Magnetic lines of force spread out from the centre of the coil and in doing so pass through the coils of wire and generate an electromotive force, ie a voltage. This emf always acts so as to oppose the change of current (Lenz' Law) and the voltage depends on:

(a) The rate of change of current.
(b) The coil design. This factor is the inductance of the coil and is measured in henrys.

DEFINITION: A coil has an inductance of 1 henry when a current change of 1 ampere per second in it results in an induced emf of 1 volt.

2 Opening a switch carrying current through an inductive coil will cause the current to fall very rapidly (Fig. 2.33). This results in the collapse of the surrounding magnetic field towards the coil centre and an induced emf will appear as shown. This can be a sharp pulse voltage and may be much higher than the voltage supplying the coil current.

A sudden break of coil current is the foundation of ignition coil operation and will be met again later. Note that the direction of the emf is to try to maintain the current – Lenz' Law again!

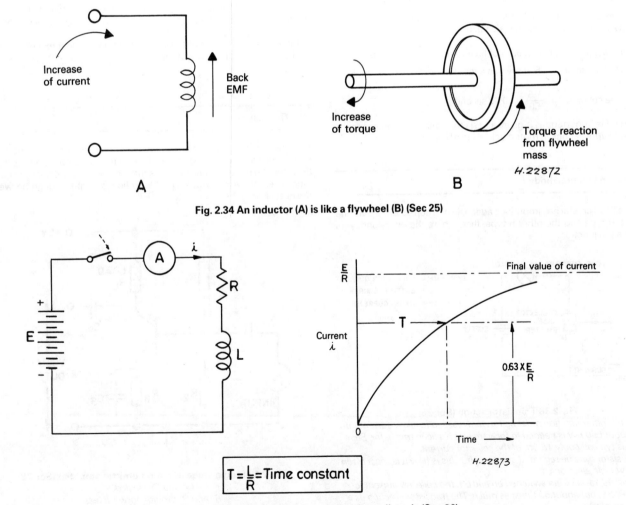

Fig. 2.34 An inductor (A) is like a flywheel (B) (Sec 25)

$$T = \frac{L}{R} = \text{Time constant}$$

Fig. 2.35 Current growth in an inductive coil on dc (Sec 26)

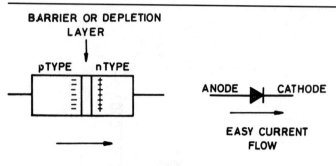

Fig. 2.36 A p-n junction diode (Sec 27)
Current flows easily if external polarity is + to p type

3   A close analogy may be drawn between the inductor (ie a coil having the property of inductance) and the flywheel (Fig. 2.34). A sudden switch-on of current will produce a back – emf so that for an instant, no current will flow and then rise; a sudden application of torque to a flywheel does not produce immediate rotation but a gradual rise of rotational speed.

26   Inductance in a dc circuit

1   Consider what happens when an inductive coil of L henry and a winding resistance of R ohms is switched on to a dc supply of E volts (Fig. 2.35). At the instant of switching on, current rises gradually and reaches a final value given by Ohms Law of E/R amperes. Theoretically the rising curve never actually reaches this value but for all practical purposes does so in a short time.

A measure of how long it takes for the current to rise is defined in the TIME CONSTANT for the circuit such that:

Time for current to rise to 63% of final value is $\frac{L}{R}$ seconds

A coil of inductance 1.5 henry and a resistance of 50 ohms would have:

$$\text{time constant} = \frac{1.5}{50} = 0.03 \text{ seconds}$$

This circuit is important as it gives a basis for timing and delay circuits which find applications in motorcycle electronics.

27   The p-n junction diode

1   If a silicon crystal has impurities added, ie it is doped, such that one region is p-type and the other n-type, then where the diffusion layers meet is a p-n junction.

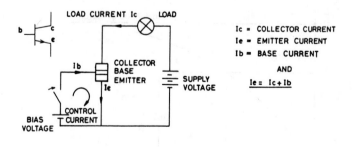

Fig. 2.38 Transistor action (Sec 28)
The base-emitter junction must be forward biassed to allow current into base. About 650 mV is needed to forward bias a silicon transistor. Base current is typically only 1/50th of the collector current.
The transistor may be regarded as a switch – this is how it is most often used in vehicle electronics.
If Ib is varied, rather than switched on and off, the collector current Ic will also vary, but about 50 times as much. The transistor is acting as a current amplifier.

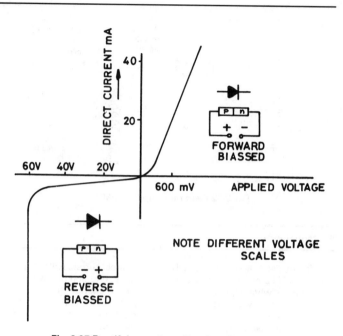

Fig. 2.37 Rectifying action of juction diode (Sec 27)

P and n-types both mean silicon with impurities added, one of which gives an excess of electrons in the material and the other a deficiency of electrons, known as holes.

2   The effect at the meeting layer is that of a barrier potential rather as though a battery had been connected across the junction (Fig. 2.36).

External current may flow across the junction in one direction but not in the other. In other words, the p-n junction is a rectifier or diode (Fig. 2.37).

28   The transistor

1   The junction transistor is a sandwich of p-n-p or n-p-n material, rather like two diodes back to back. If a current can be made to flow between the middle section of the sandwich and one outer layer, then a much greater current would be able to flow straight through between the outer layers.

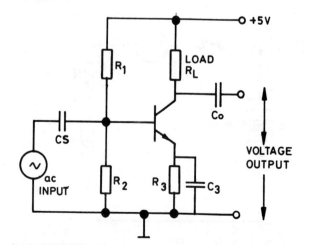

Fig. 2.39 Single stage common-emitter amplifier (Sec 28)
Co and Cs block dc
R_1 and R_2 provide forward bias
R_3 acts as temperature compensator

	MODE	CURRENT GAIN	VOLTAGE GAIN	INPUT RESISTANCE
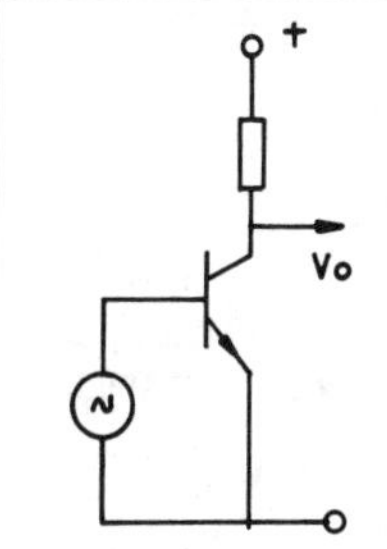	COMMON EMITTER	LARGE 50~500	HIGH	MEDIUM ABOUT 2kΩ
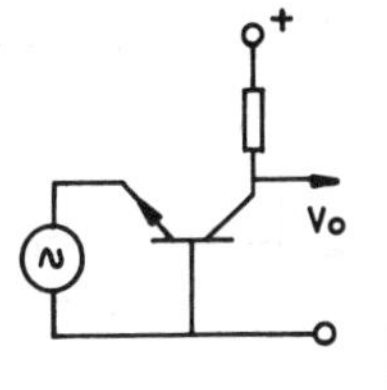	COMMON BASE	LESS THAN 1.0 ABOUT 0·99	HIGH	LOW ABOUT 50 Ω
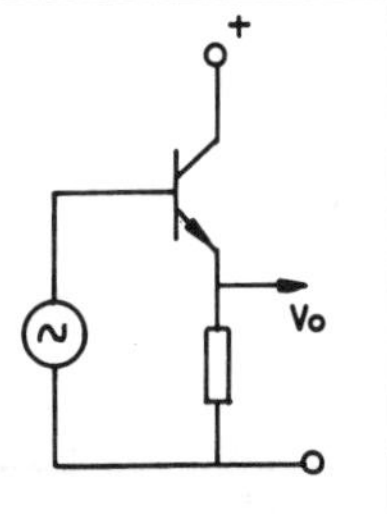	COMMON COLLECTOR	LARGE	LESS THAN 1.0	VERY HIGH ABOUT 1MΩ

Fig. 2.40 Transistor operation modes (Sec 28)
Biassing not shown

Fig. 2.38 shows the action. Current into the base I_b will permit a current flow between collector and emitter. The current flow from collector is much larger than the base current and is controlled by it. Switching I_b on or off simultaneously switches on or off the main collector current flow. Regarded this way the transistor is a **switch.**

2   If on the other hand the base current I_b is varied, say, in a sine wave fashion, the collector current will also vary in a sine wave shape but with about (typically) 50 times the amplitude. Used this way the transistor is a **current amplifier.**

3   To obtain voltage amplification (or gain) a load resistor R_L in the collector circuit may be used. Current variations through R_L produce voltage variation across it (Fig. 2.39).

Bias is obtained by resistors R_1 and R_2 to avoid the use of a bias battery. R_3 compensates for temperature effects; as temperature rises the emitter current will rise, but the extra volt-drop this causes in passing through R_3 is sensed by the base as a bias tending to reduce emitter

current. Capacitor C_3 passes an alternating component to earth preventing ac feedback to the base.

4   The junction transistor can be operated in three different ways which are named according to which terminal is common to both the input and output. They are common-emitter (CE), common-base (CB), and common-collector (CC). Their characteristics are shown in Fig. 2.40.

29 The field-effect transistor (FET)

1   While the junction transistor is essentially a current operated device, the field-effect transistor has a much higher input resistance and is voltage-controlled.

2   The junction field-effect transistor JFET is shown in Fig. 2.41. A p-type region (the gate) is let into two sides of an n-type silicon base, forming a channel. Current will flow from one side of the n-silicon to the

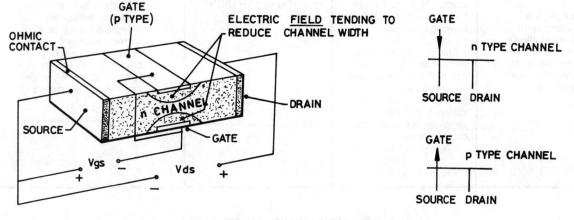

Fig. 2.41 Junction Field Effect Transistor (JFET) (Sec 29)

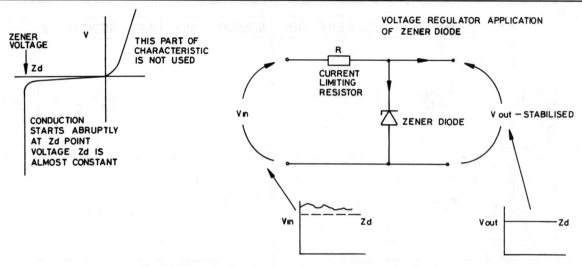

Fig. 2.42 Zener diode – characteristic and one application (Sec 30)
The Zener diode conducts by reverse current

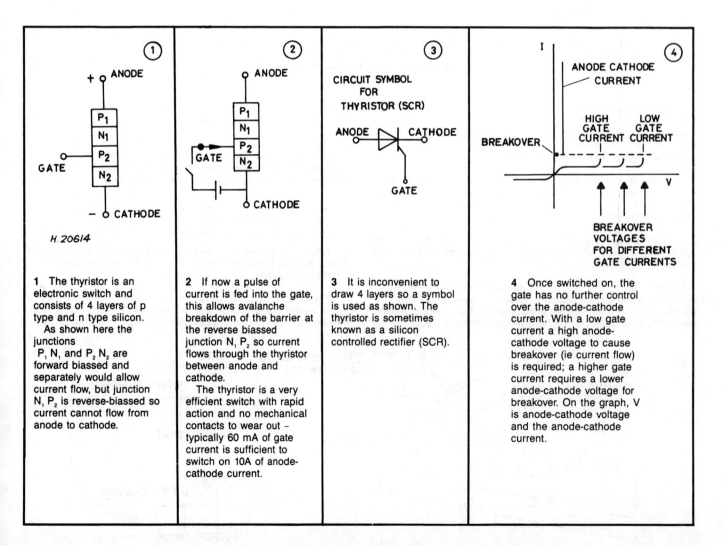

1 The thyristor is an electronic switch and consists of 4 layers of p type and n type silicon.
   As shown here the junctions $P_1 N_1$ and $P_2 N_2$ are forward biassed and separately would allow current flow, but junction $N_1 P_2$ is reverse-biassed so current cannot flow from anode to cathode.

2 If now a pulse of current is fed into the gate, this allows avalanche breakdown of the barrier at the reverse biassed junction $N_1 P_2$ so current flows through the thyristor between anode and cathode.
   The thyristor is a very efficient switch with rapid action and no mechanical contacts to wear out – typically 60 mA of gate current is sufficient to switch on 10A of anode-cathode current.

3 It is inconvenient to draw 4 layers so a symbol is used as shown. The thyristor is sometimes known as a silicon controlled rectifier (SCR).

4 Once switched on, the gate has no further control over the anode-cathode current. With a low gate current a high anode-cathode voltage to cause breakover (ie current flow) is required; a higher gate current requires a lower anode-cathode voltage for breakover. On the graph, V is anode-cathode voltage and the anode-cathode current.

Fig. 2.43 The Thyristor (Sec 31)

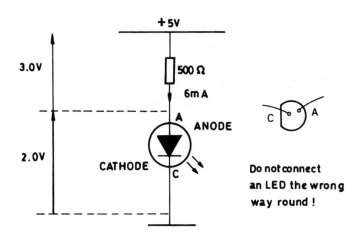

Fig. 2.44 LED and typical operation conditions (Sec 32)

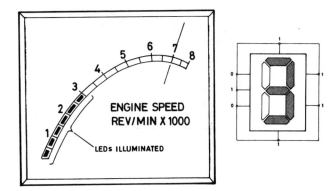

Fig. 2.45 Light emitting diode applications (Sec 32)
LEDs are set in separate compartments on a printed circuit board (PCB)
Each LED has a silvered reflector on the curved compartment wall

other, ie from source to drain, and is controlled by the voltage applied between the gate and source. Eventually the gate field effect pinches off the source-drain current. P-channel devices work the same way but with supply polarities reversed.

3 An even higher input resistance (greater than 10^{12} ohm) has been achieved by a further FET development, the metal-oxide field-effect transistor MOS, in which the gate is electrically insulated from the n or p channel.

30 Zener diode

1 This diode is used as a voltage limiter, applications being in voltage stabilisers or peak voltage clipping.

Below its operating voltage the Zener diode behaves (almost) as an open circuit, but when a certain voltage is reached reverse current flows, the voltage across the Zener remaining almost constant (Fig. 2.42).

2 Connected across the dc output from the alternator rectifier, the Zener diode drains off excess current once the desired voltage is attained. They were used in this form on later Lucas charging systems and now are employed in most sophisticated circuits – see Chapter 6.

31 The thyristor (SCR)

1 This is a 4 layer pnpn device which has the property of rapid current switching. Like a mechanical switch, it is either fully on or fully off but has no moving parts and is switched from the OFF to the ON state by a small current fed into the gate terminal.

2 When the gate current triggers the thyristor, current flows from anode to cathode and from this point the gate has no further effect. Only by reducing the anode-cathode voltage to (near) zero can the device be switched off. This characteristic is ideally suited for capacitor discharge ignition (CDI) – see Chapter 3 – and also for several other electronic applications.

3 Referring to Fig. 2.43, if the anode is positive relative to the cathode, a triggering pulse of current at the gate switches on the device in a few microseconds.

It will then have an almost constant voltage drop of about 1 volt independent of the amount of current flowing from anode to cathode. A thyristor switching a 10A current might typically require a gate triggering current of 60mA at 3 volts.

The thyristor is alternatively known as a Silicon Controlled Rectifier (SCR).

32 Light emitting diodes (LED)

1 A forward-biassed p-n junction diode will emit light when carrying current, the colour depending upon the proportions of phosphorous and arsenic in the alloy used for the semiconductor (Fig. 2.44). Colours may be red, yellow or green, but maximum optical efficiency is obtained using red light.

A current limiting resistor must be used to set the current within the range 2mA to 25mA, the voltage drop across red diodes being 2.0V. LED life is very long; it is rugged and consumes very low power.

Bar charts are formed by using a series of LEDs or an alpha-numerical (letters and numbers) display may be utilised (Fig. 2.45).

33 Photodiodes and phototransistors

1 A pn junction fabricated from silicon with a high impurity layer is found to be sensitive to light. Electronic action at the junction under light stimulus will generate a voltage and will give current into a load circuit, the energy coming from the light falling on the photo sensitive junction. About 600 millivolts is a typical output voltage.

2 If light falls on the base-collector junction of a transistor with similar impurity doping, then amplification will take place. The device is then a phototransistor and gives a larger output voltage than a diode. Both the diode and the phototransistor have transparent cases to allow light to reach the sensitive junctions.

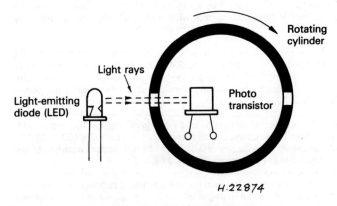

Fig. 2.46 Opto-electric trigger (Sec 33)

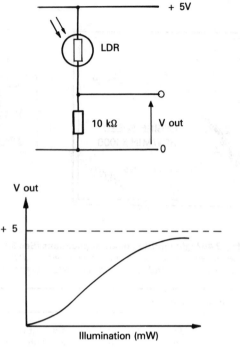

Fig. 2.47 LDR and light response curve (Sec 34)

3   Such an opto-electronic transistor can be obtained to suit different light frequency bands. An example is the phototransistor used with a light emitting diode (LED) as a trigger in an optoelectronic ignition circuit (Fig. 2.46).

34   Light-dependent resistors (LDR)

1   This is a resistor having a resistance which varies according to the amount of light falling upon it (Fig. 2.47). The dark resistance is very high (a few megohms) and falls to a low value (about 100 ohms) in sunlight.

2   Response time is slow, of the order of 100 milliseconds, but the LDR is much more rugged than the photodiode or the phototransistor.

35   The Darlington Pair

1   There are many circuit design arrangements of transistors but one in particular is worthy of note here. Transistors may be used for low level voltage or current amplification, in which case they are physically small and use low currents, or they may be required to deliver power to some form of load such as an ignition coil or an actuator. Then the transistor is designed to deal with larger currents and is physically bigger.

2   The two may be combined in one device in which transistor T1 amplifies the input signal V1 (Fig. 2.48). Direct connection of the emitter of T1 to the base of T2 provides the base current for T2 and this in turn controls a much larger current from collector to emitter of the power transistor T2.

3   The current amplification of T1 (the gain) may be 100 and also for transistor T2. Thus the overall current gain will be 100 x 100 = 10 000. An assumed input current of 0.01 mA to T1 will produce a current of 100 mA in the load of transistor T2 (Fig. 2.48).

4   With the Darlington pair, the voltage gain is approximately unity; ie the input and output voltages will be nearly equal. From this it follows that the power gain will also be 10 000.

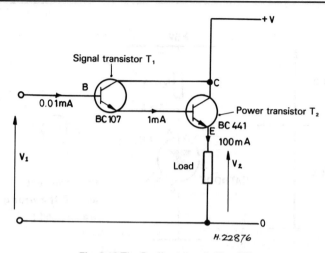

Fig. 2.48 The Darlington pair (Sec 35)
T₁ and T₂ are housed in one package with three leads E, B, C

5   Darlington pairs are provided in one package and come with just three connector wires: emitter, base and collector, just as though it were one transistor. The circuit is to be found in advanced ignition systems and has many other applications where a power drive is required.

36   Integrated circuits

1   The integrated circuit (IC) is probably the most important single advance ever made in electronics. It consists of complete circuits comprising **passive** components, ie resistors, inductors and capacitors together with **active** components, ie transistors and diodes. Without the integrated circuit, there would be no electronic digital watches, personal computers or the great achievements in space research, automation or in communication systems.

2   Two types of IC are used, the hybrid and the monolithic.

In one type of hybrid IC, the components are produced by deposition of a thin film (in vacuum) on a base of alumina. The active devices are added afterwards by bonding transistors and diodes on to the circuit by ultrasonic techniques. Thick film technology is based on printing thick films (about 25μm thick) on to an alumina substrate. The film makes up the passive circuit components using similar techniques to silk screen printing. The transistors (known as 'flip-chip' transistors) are added later and are transistor chips without the casing, being bonded into the circuit by welding.

3   Most important is the monolithic IC, so called because the entire circuit is fabricated within a single block of silicon crystal. Complete circuits including the transistors, cover clocks, timers, logic systems, etc., and can be bought in a single package. These packages are

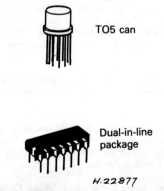

Fig. 2.49 Integrated circuit packaging (Sec 36)

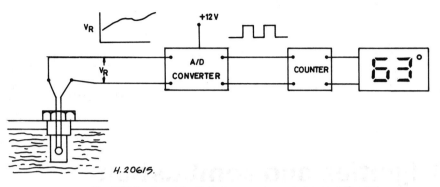

Fig. 2.50 Analogue to digital conversion requirement (Sec 37)

containers either in the form of a small can (the TO5) or the dual-in-line (DIL) type (Fig. 2.49).

4   DIL ICs consist of a plastic base into which the integrated circuits are embedded. Fourteen or sixteen leads are brought out along the two sides of the bar which is typically 20 mm long by 5 mm wide and 2.5 mm deep. Larger units with more output leads are common for circuits of greater complexity such as clocks and calculator chips.

37 Analogue and digital signals

1   Analogue quantities are those which are continuously present, the most common example being the reading of a pointer on an instrument. The difficulty with analogue measurement is low accuracy, where for example, the pointer reading at the low end of a scale could be comparable with the pointer thickness and so liable to be misread.

2   Digital quantities are expressed in numbers and moreover only two numbers (0 and 1) are used. Any number in the conventional **denary** scale (ie to base 10) can be converted into **digital binary** form (ie to base 2) and vice versa.

Examples where analogue/digital conversions are used will be found later in this book, particularly in relation to ignition and fuel injection systems. An instrument example is shown in Fig. 2.50 where temperature of an engine coolant is sensed by a temperature-dependent resistor (schematic only). The variation of resistance with temperature will be an analogue quantity and before it is useable in a computing device it will need to be converted into digital form.

3   The principle of AD conversion is to convert the analogue quantity into a voltage of ramp form (ie a straight line rise against time). As the voltage rises, a square wave pulse generator (called a clock) operates and the number of pulses is counted. This is a digital measure of an analogue quantity.

38 Sensors and Actuating devices

1   Measurements of quantities such as speed, temperature, pressure, airflow, etc., is by a range of **sensor** devices.

When the sensors have passed signals for processing, the desired result is often some form of movement. This is performed by **actuators**. Sensors and actuators are described in the text as they occur.

39 Further reading

1   Only a simple survey of electrical principles has been possible in this chapter, but all topics are directly relevant to the motorcycle.

2   Readers who wish to read further are referred to **Electronics** by G H Olsen, 2nd edition, published by Butterworth-Heinemann.

Chapter 3 Ignition and combustion

Contents

1 Spark requirements for combustion

1   Petrol (gasoline) engines require an electric spark at the spark plug electrodes in order to ignite the compressed air-fuel vapour. This spark must occur at a precise point in the cycle of engine operation so that maximum downward pressure on the piston occurs shortly after top dead centre.

The plug voltage requirements may be anywhere within the range 5000 to 30,000 volts and depend upon several factors, including the mixture strength, the shape of the combustion chamber, the compression rate, the temperature, and the condition of the plug and its gap dimension.

2   Once the fuel vapour breaks down under the electric stress of the plug voltage, a high intensity spark travels from the negative centre electrode to the positive earth (ground) electrode. The spark temperature of several thousand degrees centigrade is sufficient to ignite the fuel vapour in the vicinity which then continues to burn by itself by the process of a travelling flame wave.

3   In normal conditions, the spark will occur before the piston has reached TDC. Emanating from the spark region a flame front will travel across the vapour-filled space and, although combustion is completed in a fraction of a second, the gas pressure increases steadily, rises to a maximum and then falls away (Figs. 3.1 and 3.2). The time from the point of ignition to the completion of combustion is about 2 milliseconds, so the spark will be timed to occur to allow for the delay in pressure build-up. At cruising speeds a typical angle of advance (ie before TDC) is 30 to 40°, but it will be seen that a particular angle of advance suits one speed only and it is essential to incorporate a form of control to vary the ignition advance angle with speed.

4   Manufacturers' tests will determine the optimum ignition advance angle for all speeds and loads. The factors which have to be considered are:

(a)   *Pollution levels of exhaust*
(b)   *Absence of engine knock or detonation*
(c)   *Good fuel economy*
(d)   *Maximum engine power output*

5   The energy contained in the spark discharge must be sufficient to ignite the air:fuel mixture and for an air:fuel ratio of 14.7:1 the minimum

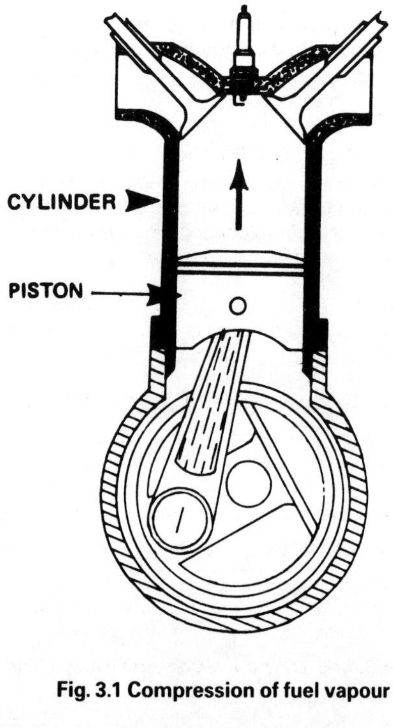

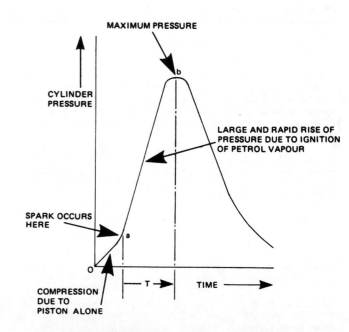

Fig. 3.1 Compression of fuel vapour

Fig. 3.2 Pressure rise and fall in the cylinder

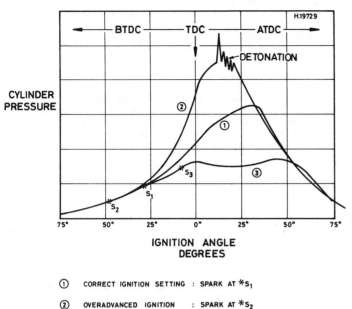

① CORRECT IGNITION SETTING : SPARK AT *s_1

② OVERADVANCED IGNITION : SPARK AT *s_2

③ OVERRETARDED IGNITION : SPARK AT *s_3

Fig. 3.3 Effects of ignition angle

energy requirement is 0.2 millijoule (for a definition of the joule see Chapter 2).

This figure rises to 3 mJ or more if the mixture is weaker or richer and, allowing for adverse conditions, a practical energy level of each spark must be about 30 mJ for reliable operation. If an ignition system cannot supply this level of energy to the spark plugs whether by design shortcomings or by electrical losses, then misfiring will occur.

2 Combustion factors

1   The air:fuel ratio (λ) required in theory for complete combustion is 14.7:1. At this ratio, $\lambda = 1.0$.

In practice an air deficiency of about 10% ($\lambda = 0.9$) gives maximum engine power and corresponds to fastest flame travel across the cylinder head space, but unfortunately unacceptable pollution by hydrocarbons and carbon monoxide is the result. Where excess air is supplied, that is, a weaker mixture, power falls off due to a slower flame speed.

The optimum ratio for producing the cleanest exhaust is when $\lambda = 1.1$ approximately. Pollution is a subject of major interest due to regulations by governments world-wide and will be discussed at various points within this book.

2   Power and economy are linked to the speed of the flame in the cylinder after ignition. The flame speed in turn depends upon many factors including:

Cylinder design. If the compression ratio is high then, because of the greater density of the inhaled fuel charge, the flame speed is high.

The location of the spark plug and the length of the spark gap come under the cylinder design. In general, the better the exposure of the cloud of fuel vapour to the igniting spark, the better the combustion performance.

Ignition timing. Spark timing is crucial and must be such that gas pressure reaches a maximum to give downward piston thrust at about 12° ATDC (after top dead centre). If the spark is made to occur too early (over advanced) flame speed is so high that the charge is virtually exploded, an effect known as detonation (see later). This will damage the engine and must be avoided.

Conversely, if the spark occurs too late (retarded), burning is slow and the gas pressure maximises too late. Low power and poor fuel consumption are the results (Fig. 3.3).

Fuel charge turbulence. In practice, the vapour cloud is not stationary when the spark occurs but is a swirling mass. Flame propagation is helped by such turbulence and cylinder heads are designed to give good fuel charge turbulence.

Exhaust gas presence. Any exhaust gas that remains in the cylinder and mixes with the incoming fresh charge will lower the flame speed and result in reducing the maximum temperature reached. From the pollution standpoint this is advantageous since the generation of undesirable oxides of nitrogen rises very rapidly with an increase in maximum combustion temperature.

In fact, in some engines it is practice to pass back to the cylinder a proportion of the exhaust gases, a process that is known as Exhaust Gas Recirculation (EGR). There are limits to the amount which may be fed back, however, beyond which fuel consumption rises rapidly.

Detonation

3   From the previous paragraphs it would appear that the highest possible flame front speed should be obtained in order to achieve best engine power. There is a limit, however; reached when the flame speed becomes supersonic. Under these conditions the flame does not travel across the cylinder head space steadily but the fuel charge explodes.

This is known as **detonation** and can cause serious engine damage. Detonation occurs at a particular pressure level, this being determined by fuel grade, design of cylinder head and other factors.

Knock

4   Before the onset of detonation another form of fuel ignition malfunction may occur. Remote from the point where the flame starts, namely at the spark plug electrodes, a volume of gas (the end gas) will be heating due to the approaching flame front. The combination of compression due to the upward piston motion and flame front heating can cause spontaneous ignition and a rapid increase in pressure. This is called **knock** and is often regarded as a combined effect with detonation but in fact the two effects are different although similar in results.

Effects of Knock and Detonation

5   At the onset of these phenomena, a light rattling noise known as pinking occurs and is often first noticed when the engine is heavily loaded. Because energy is expended in unwanted noise and heat, reduced power to the road wheel will occur.

In serious cases and where the effect has been present for some time, the power will be markedly reduced and blue exhaust smoke given off. Eventually the piston crown may actually melt.

Factors which may contribute to knock and detonation include:

(a)   **Poor cylinder head design.** *Modern designs allow for efficient cooling of the cylinder head, particularly the region remote from the plug where the 'end gas' is located. Attention is given to the desirable turbulence of the induced fuel vapour charge.*

(b)   **Air:fuel ratio.** *A weak mixture is more likely to detonate.*

(c)   **Fuel grade.** *Compression ratio and grade of fuel are related – a low compression ratio engine can use a fuel with a lower octane number.*

(d)   **Ignition timing.** *Over-advanced timing may result in detonation.*

Knock Sensing

6   For best efficiency an engine should be tuned to run up to the limit where knock occurs. This may be achieved with the aid of electronic controls found in an increasing number of modern engine designs.

At the onset of knock, high frequency vibrations are set up in the end-gas region. It is possible to pick up these structure-borne vibrations by a sensor which gives an electrical signal voltage proportional to the knock level. Many other vibrations are also present in a running engine but these can be filtered out, leaving the sensor knock voltage alone to be sent on to an on-board electronic control unit (ECU).

When knock signals occur, the ECU retards the ignition to reduce the knock level. Such arrangements are often part of a more comprehensive system of engine management, at present restricted to only a few advanced motorcycle engine designs.

Pre-ignition

7   A local hot point within the cylinder head volume may give rise to spontaneous fuel combustion, producing a pinking sound and a substantial loss of power. This is known as **pre-ignition**.

The cause is frequently a deposit of carbon which heats to the incandescent point and causes the fuel to ignite before the spark occurs at the plug. Older engines needed frequent decarbonising to remove such unwanted carbon residues but modern engines and fuels have reduced the need considerably.

A linked effect is that of 'running on' in which the engine continues to run after the ignition has been switched off. This is due to the hot carbon spot firing the incoming fuel charge spontaneously.

Modern anti-pollution requirements have resulted in 'lean burn' engine design in which the air:fuel ratio is high (ie the mixture is weak). Weak mixture gives hotter combustion chamber temperatures than in earlier designs so measures are taken to shut off fuel supply when the ignition is switched off. This is achieved either by switching the incoming air into the manifold (and not going through the carburettor) or to block off the slow running jet in the carburettor.

Combustion and Pollutants

8   When air and fuel are mixed into a vapour and ignited inside the engine cylinder, combustion drives the engine and produces power at the rear wheel. There are, in addition, products of combustion which are passed out via the exhaust system.

If the proportions of air and fuel are correct at about 14.7:1 by mass (the Stoichiometric ratio) then the exhaust produces carbon dioxide, water and nitrogen, all being harmless. In practice, because perfect mixing cannot be achieved, there will also be carbon monoxide (CO) and oxygen present.

Perfect combustion is never achieved and some of the products from incomplete burning are harmful and pollute the atmosphere. About 1% of the exhaust gas is harmful, this proportion being made up of carbon monoxide (CO), oxides of nitrogen (NOx) and hydrocarbons (HC). All three are dependent upon the air-to-fuel ratio; the problem being that if the proportion of CO and HC increases that of NOx decreases and *vice versa*.

Oxides and nitrogen (NOx) have no smell and are tasteless but as they emerge and mix with atmospheric oxygen they produce red-brown nitrogen dioxide (NO_2) which, if breathed in, causes irritation of the lungs. Oxides of nitrogen combine with water to produce nitric acid which precipitates as acid rain. The gas components of nitrogen oxide (NO) and nitrogen dioxide (NO_2) are classified together as NOx.

Hydrocarbons (HC). Exhaust gas hydrocarbons are present in various forms and all are dangerous. They emerge from parts of the cylinder volume where full combustion has not taken place and also blow-by past the piston and into the crankcase, where they are ventilated back to the air filter for recombustion. It has also been found that hydrocarbon emissions take place by evaporation from the fuel tank and the carburettor. Some US models have sealed tanks and an evaporative emission control system which ensures no leakage of fumes.

Carbon monoxide (CO) prevents the body from absorbing oxygen into the blood stream and is highly dangerous, especially as it has no smell. It is known that as little as 0.3% of carbon monoxide in the air can cause death within 30 minutes.

Lead. Lead compounds deposited by motorcycles as a result of combustion act as cellular poisons in blood, bone marrow and the nervous system. Lead is not a naturally occurring component of the fuel but an additive to prevent engine knock. About 75% of added lead is blown out of the exhaust and the remainder is absorbed in the engine oil.

It is estimated that at present traffic densities, some 3000 tonnes of lead per year are deposited by exhaust over the United Kingdom.

The Catalytic converter

9   The toxic components of exhaust gas can be reduced substantially by the use of a catalytic converter built into the exhaust system. At the time of writing catalytic converters have not been widely used on motorcycles, but are featured on certain BMW K-series models, the Yamaha GTS1000 and Yamaha TDR125 2-stroke.

Several designs have been evolved, but the type which is now mostly used is the three-way catalytic converter since it will degrade CO, HC and NOx simultaneously.

The two characteristics of the converter are:

   (a)   *The after burning of CO and HC is promoted reducing them to carbon dioxide (CO_2) and water (H_2O) both of which are harmless.*

   (b)   *The converter converts the nitrogen oxides (NOx) into neutral nitrogen (N) which is a harmless constituent of air.*

The catalytic converter will reduce more than 90% of the exhaust gas toxic substances to harmless alternative substances but in order to achieve this, two conditions apply:

   (a)   *Unleaded petrol must be used exclusively because lead would destroy the catalytic properties of the noble metals used in the converter.*

   (b)   *The air:fuel ratio must be held at the Stoichiometric Ratio 14.7:1 precisely (Lambda $\lambda = 1.0$) and this implies the use of a Lambda closed-loop control system (Fig. 3.4)*

Note that in Fig. 3.4 the term single-bed here means only one box in the exhaust system. Early versions used more than one.

The use of converters without a Lambda closed-loop control system is possible, but the best result in elimination of toxic products will not normally exceed 50%.

The converter has to be located at a point in the exhaust system so that the temperature range will be within 400°C to 800°C (750 to 1470°F). Useful conversion takes place only above 250°C (480°F). Above 800°C (1470°F) thermal ageing of the substrate and the sintering of the noble

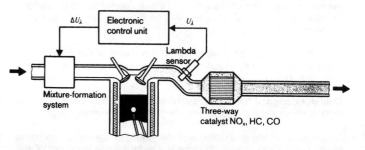

Fig. 3.4 Single-bed three-way catalyst

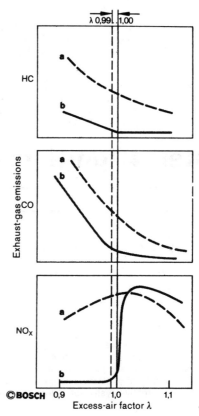

Fig. 3.5 The location of the catalyst box is important

metals used to coat the substrate will occur. Improvements in the usable temperature range are likely so that the converter positioning will not be so critical.

A typical converter is shown in Fig. 3.5. It consists of one or more ceramic blocks made of magnesium-aluminium silicate, perforated by several thousand small through-holes which carry the exhaust gases.

The ceramic is, in manufacture, first washed with a coating of aluminium oxide, effectively increasing the surface area of the catalyst by several thousand times. This coating then has a surface layer deposit of the precious (noble) metals rhodium and platinum.

Platinum and palladium cause oxidisation of the hydrocarbons (HC) and carbon monoxide (CO) and rhodium the reduction of oxides of nitrogen (NOx). The total weight of precious metals used in a converter is of the order of 3 grammes.

Results achievable by a 3-way converter are shown graphically in Fig. 3.6 where the need for keeping the air:fuel ratio at $\lambda = 1.0$ is seen to be vital. A small rise in λ towards a weaker mixture will produce a substantial rise in the oxides of nitrogen (NOx).

Fig. 3.6 Results achievable by a three-way converter

CH	Hydrocarbons	a	Without aftertreatment
CO	Carbon monoxide	b	With aftertreatment
NOx	Oxides of nitrogen		

The exhaust gas emissions are influenced by the air/fuel mixture and by the aftertreatment. The absolute necessity for a high degree of control accuracy is shown by the pronounced increase of the noxious carbon monoxide (CO) just below the $\lambda = 1.0$ point, as well as by the sudden jump in the noxious oxides of nitrogen (NOx) just above the $\lambda = 1.0$ point

Chapter 4 Ignition: Coil and battery

Contents

1 Coil ignition

1   For the first 20 years of the present century petrol-driven (gasoline-driven) vehicles usually employed the magneto for spark production. This was a high voltage generator driven by the engine which required no battery, but as the advent of electric lighting involved the use of a storage battery, the alternative system of coil-ignition took over. This

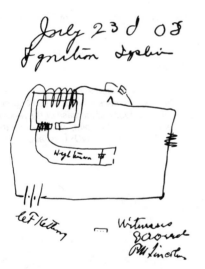

Fig. 4.1 Coil and battery ignition system – patent sketch 1908 (Sec 1)

had been patented as early as 1908 by C F Kettering of the Dayton Engineering Laboratories Company (DELCO) and his sketch (Fig. 4.1) compared to that in Fig. 4.2 shows that the method has changed little in 80 + years.

2   The development in electronics has brought about the end of the Kettering coil and battery ignition monopoly and in the last three decades more changes have been introduced in the design of ignition systems than in the previous 80 years.

3   The coil and battery system is still to be found on motorcycles and a knowledge of its operation is essential, but it now forms part of a group of other systems shown diagrammatically in Fig. 4.3. For all the advances in design, the ignition coil remains. It is how it is supplied with ignition energy that has changed.

2 The Ignition coil

1   Ignition coils depend upon electromagnetic induction for their operation and are today efficient and reliable because of long development and lack of moving parts. When current is switched on through a coil of wire, a magnetic field is developed and appears to come from the coil centre.

Clearly, as the current increases (see Fig. 2.32), the magnetic field spreads out and the individual turns are cut by the field. Similarly, if the

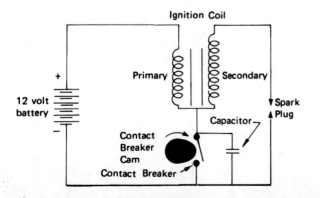

Fig. 4.2 Present day form of coil and battery system (Sec 1)

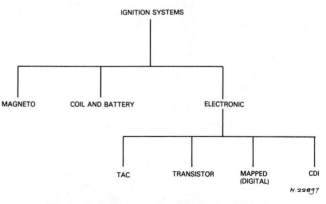

Fig. 4.3 Classification of ignition systems (Sec 1)

TAC   Transistor-controlled contacts (obsolete)
CDI   Capacitor discharge ignition

current is switched off (see Fig. 2.33), the magnetic field collapses in towards the centre and again the turns of wire are cut by the field.

It is important to note that once the coil current settles down to its final value, determined only by the wire resistance, the surrounding fields become stationary.

2   In Chapter 2 it is explained that a voltage is induced in a wire passing through a magnetic field. It is of no importance whether the field or the wire is moving, so long as there is relative movement, and in the case described, the field is passing through the wires simply by increasing and decreasing the strength of the field. So, when the current in the coils is switched on or off there will be an induced emf, but since the voltage depends on the **rate** at which the current is changed, it is usual to **break** the current rather than **make** it, the exception to this being the energy transfer system described in Chapter 5.

3   During the very short period of time over which the magnetic field reduces to zero, the induced voltage which may be measured across the coil reaches up to 300 volts. Note that this induced emf is not directly related to the 12 volt supply; the battery has simply been a means of creating the magnetic field. The switch is the means of rapidly altering the magnetic field so the coils are cut by magnetic force lines as the field either builds up or collapses.

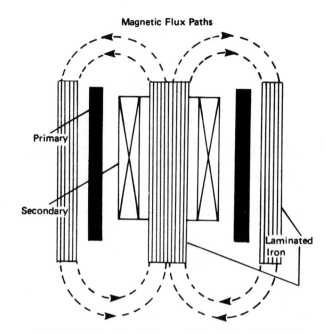

Fig. 4.4 Ignition coil windings and magnetic paths (Sec 3)

3 Primary and secondary windings

1   The voltage required to produce a spark across the plug electrodes cannot be obtained from the simple coil shown in Figs. 2.32 and 2.33, because increasing the number of turns of wire would raise the resistance so high that the battery could not force through the necessary current.

2   One solution is to use two coils wound concentrically, the primary with about 300 turns through which the battery current flows, and a secondary which has a large number of turns, perhaps 20,000. When the current is broken (or closed) by a contact breaker, the change of magnetic flux affects each turn of wire **in both primary and secondary windings**. The secondary voltage is high enough to produce the required spark.

3   Wound on a laminated iron core to increase the flux density, and enclosed in a metal case or by resin encapsulation, the device is called an ignition coil, a specialised example of a transformer used in several branches of electrical engineering (Figs. 4.4 and 4.5). Most common on motorcycles is the moulded open magnetic circuit ignition coil, especially because of its resistance to vibration. The windings and iron core are completely encapsulated in a synthetic resin. The centre core does not have such a complete magnetic path and consists of a bar of straight laminations, and is the earth (ground) connection.

4   The secondary is wound on top of the primary winding in this type, to give maximum insulation from the steel core. Among the varieties of moulded ignition coils will sometimes be found a type with a closed iron path which shows outside the windings. The operation and winding construction are, however, the same as the centre core types.

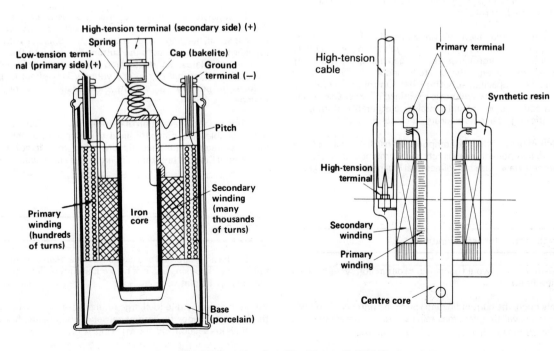

Fig. 4.5 Construction of ignition coils (Sec 3)

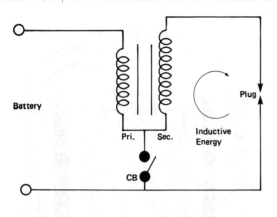

Fig. 4.6 Inductive energy discharge (Sec 4)

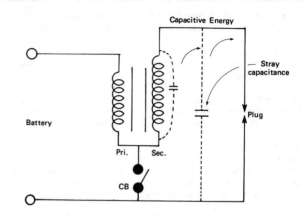

Fig. 4.7 Capacitive energy discharge (Sec 4)

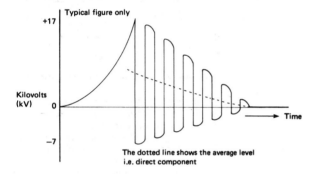

Fig. 4.8 Waveform of spark discharge at the plug (Sec 4)

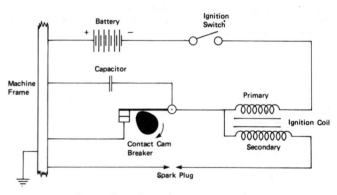

Fig. 4.9 The effect of the capacitor (Sec 5)

4   Spark energies

1   When the contact breaker opens, the collapse of the magnetic field results in inductive energy passing round the secondary circuit as a component of the spark (Fig. 4.6).

2   The coil and external high-tension wires also have a certain capacitance which is charged by the generated voltage in the secondary coil and which must discharge across the plug gap during the spark (Fig. 4.7). Of the two forms of energy, that due to the inductive effect is much larger than that due to capacitance, but both have an important effect on the voltage waveform. This waveform is examined by mechanics using electronic diagnostic equipment and contains considerable information on the state of the engine and its auxiliary electrical circuits.

3   The waveform of the inductive component is oscillatory, whilst that of the capacitive component is unidirectional. Combined, they give an oscillatory damped wave with a unidirectional (dc) property (Fig. 4.8).

5   How does the capacitor assist ignition?

1   It is helpful to see what would happen in a coil ignition system which has no capacitor fitted.

As the contacts open, the current flowing round the primary circuit will tend to continue and will therefore maintain the circuit momentarily as a spark across the contact points.

2   The voltage induced in the secondary winding depends on the **rate**

at which the primary current is reduced. A lingering spark across the points is therefore undesirable, since the current is obviously being cut off **slower** than if no spark occurred. Additionally, the mating surfaces of the two contacts would become rough and pitted due to metallic transfer via the spark, thus creating increased contact resistance.

3   If a capacitor of about 0.2 μF (microfarads) were connected across the contacts, then at the point of opening, the current would flow into the capacitor, leaving none to establish a spark across the contact breaker points. In addition, the current flowing into the capacitor will charge the plates, so developing a capacitor terminal voltage in opposition to the battery supply voltage. This effect helps to rapidly reduce the primary coil current and boosts the secondary induced voltage (Fig. 4.9).

4   Thus the rapid reduction of current flow during the points' opening phase enables the magnetic field to collapse suddenly, producing a higher voltage in the secondary winding than if no capacitor were connected. Contact breaker point erosion is also substantially reduced.

6   The Capacitor

1   The basic properties of a capacitor have been covered in Chapter 2, but it is worth looking again at how initial current flow into the capacitor charges up the plates.

When the voltage due to charge on the plates is equal and opposite to the supply voltage, the current ceases. This is the feature explained in the previous section and shown in Fig. 4.10.

2   Capacitors are made in a variety of forms. The type shown in

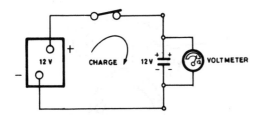

WITH SWITCH CLOSED, BATTERY CHARGES CAPACITOR LIKE A PUMP. CAPACITOR VOLTAGE BUILDS UP UNTIL, WHEN EQUAL TO BATTERY VOLTAGE, NO FURTHER CHARGE WILL FLOW.

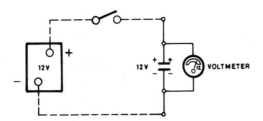

WHEN BATTERY IS DISCONNECTED BY OPENING SWITCH CHARGE and VOLTAGE are RETAINED.

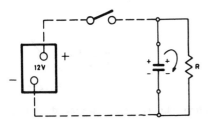

IF A RESISTOR IS CONNECTED ACROSS CAPACITOR, THE CHARGE DRAINS AWAY AND VOLTAGE FALLS. IF RESISTANCE IS HIGH, VOLTAGE FALLS SLOWLY AND VICE VERSA.

Fig. 4.10 Charge and voltage retention of a capacitor (Sec 6)

Fig. 4.11 being typical of an ignition capacitor with one terminal internally connected to an enclosing metal can which is earthed (grounded) to the motorcycle engine/frame.

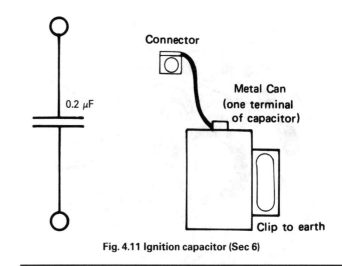

Fig. 4.11 Ignition capacitor (Sec 6)

7 Faulty capacitor symptoms

1   If the internal connections of the capacitor break it is said to be open-circuit (OC) although this is not a very frequent fault. The effects would be severe sparking and burning of the contact breaker points, difficult starting and poor running.

2   Another possible failure is short circuiting (SC) internally, having the effect of permanently bridging the contacts. Under these circumstances, there is no primary current interruption and no spark at the plug.

3   The third possible fault is a condition between OC and SC, where the insulation resistance between the capacitor lead and its case falls to a low value, say much less than 1 megohm. Starting and slow running may be acceptable but the performance falls off at high speeds.

8 The Contact breaker

1   The purpose of the contact breaker is to interrupt primary current flow to the ignition coil; it is essentially an engine driven switch. It is located often on the end of the crankshaft and is operated by a rotating cam and a heel which follows the cam contour under light pressure from a flat spring (Fig. 4.12).

When the heel touches the cam over the low radius sector, the contacts are closed; the heel is forced outwards as the cam lobe comes under it

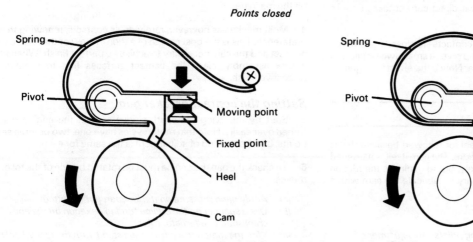

Fig. 4.12 Contact breaker operation (Sec 8)

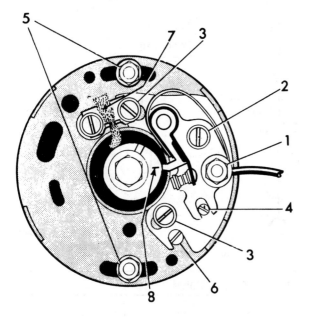

Fig. 4.13 Contact breaker assembly (Sec 8)

1	Lead terminal
2	Points gap adjuster screw
3	Baseplate securing screw
4	Eccentric gap adjuster screw
5	Timing plate securing screw
6	Baseplate eccentric adjuster screw
7	Lubrication wiper
8	Cam lobe peak

and the contacts are opened. In Fig. 4.13 only one cam lobe and contact set are shown but it is common practice to use two sets of contacts with one cam lobe for twin cylinder machines. In some cases, more than one cam lobe will be found.

The contact breaker assembly shown in Fig. 4.13 shows the baseplate on which the contact breaker set is mounted together with the cam heel, spring and adjustment screws.

2   When the cam opens the contacts, current is interrupted in the ignition coil and a spark is generated at the plug. The important requirements are as follows.

   (a)   The contacts must open at the correct point of piston travel.
   (b)   The gap between the contacts when fully open should correspond with the manufacturer's specification.

3   If the gap is incorrect, the angle through which the points will be closed will be incorrect with the possible result of reduced ignition performance and misfiring. The correct gap setting ensures that the duration of contact closure is sufficient for primary current to build up; remember Chapter 2 which showed that direct current takes time to build up in an inductive coil.

4   The angle of cam rotation when the contacts are closed is the **dwell angle**. Fig. 4.14 shows that too wide a gap gives a small dwell angle and too small a gap gives a large dwell angle. Notice the effects on ignition timing.

9   Contact breaker service

1   Wear will take place on the cam heel (or follower) because this is usually made of nylon or some form of fibre. The cam itself is hardened and so should retain its profile indefinitely, but to minimise the friction between the cam and heel, it is necessary to lubricate the cam with a smear of grease.

2   Items to check include.

   (a)   Cam follower wear, necessitating points gap adjustment.
   (b)   Poor condition of contact surfaces (see Fig. 4.15).

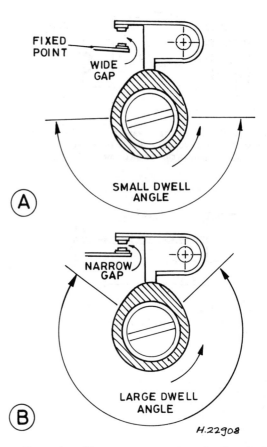

Fig. 4.14 Illustration of how contact gap alters dwell angle (Sec 8)

A   A wide gap gives later closing and earlier opening of points. Results in a reduction of dwell angle and advancing of ignition timing
B   A narrow gap gives earlier closing and later opening of points. Results in an increase of dwell angle and retardation of ignition timing

   (c)   Corrosion on any part of the assembly.
   (d)   Insulation of the moving arm from earth (ground).
   (e)   Oil or dirt on the contact breaker points.

3   Dressing of the contact surfaces may be carried out with a strip of fine (400 grit) sandpaper. Clean the contact surfaces with a suitable solvent or a proprietary fluid approved for use in electrical circuits. Some mechanics keep a special dressing stone for trimming contacts but the work cannot of course, be carried out with the breaker assembly in place on the machine.

4   Most mechanics however, rarely dress contacts, renewing them in preference. This is the best course of action in view of the low cost of a new set and the care necessary to achieve a perfect finish. When fitting a new assembly, clean the contact surfaces first to remove any protective finish.

Setting the contact breaker gap

5   Start by removing the spark plug(s) so that the engine may be turned over easily. Note that motorcycles have one, two or three sets of points, but the method of adjustment is the same for each.

6   To check the gap the engine must be rotated by one of the following means.

   (a)   Apply hand pressure on the kickstart (where fitted).
   (b)   Use a spanner on the engine turning hexagon on the end of the crankshaft or alternator rotor.
   (c)   With the motorcycle on its main stand, turn the rear wheel by hand with the engine in a high gear.

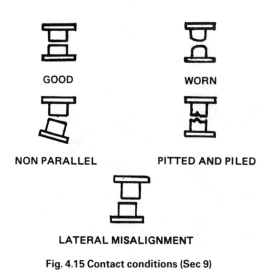

Fig. 4.15 Contact conditions (Sec 9)

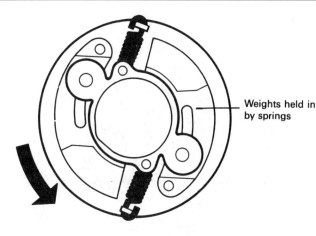

Unit at low speed (not operating)

7   Turn the engine until the contacts open to the maximum and insert a feeler gauge which corresponds to the recommended gap between them. If no information is available, try 0.3 – 0.4 mm (0.012 – 0.016 in). The feeler gauge should just slide through the gap between the contacts with a slight drag.

If too tight or too loose, slacken the baseplate screw so that the fixed contact may be moved to give the correct gap. This is done with either a flat-bladed screwdriver twist in a slot or by turning an eccentric screw. When the gap is correct tighten the baseplate screw.

8   If the engine has more than one set of contacts, repeat the process. It is worth rechecking the gaps after the engine has been turned by hand a few times.

9   Setting the gap by feeler gauge can give satisfactory results if done carefully, but accurate setting is vital, particularly on high performance engines. A better method is to use a dwell meter.

Using a dwell meter

10   As stated above, the real purpose of setting the gap correctly is to ensure that the contacts are closed long enough during an engine cycle for current to build up in the ignition coil primary winding.

11   With the engine running a dwell meter connected to the contacts will read the angle of rotation during which the contacts are closed and give the reading in degrees or percentage dwell. The correct figure can be found in the workshop manual.

12   The gap should be adjusted until the correct dwell angle is registered on the meter. This usually means stopping the engine to carry out the adjustment although experienced mechanics have been known to do it with the engine running!

13   Having set the contact breaker gap(s), the next step is to set the ignition timing.

---

10 Ignition timing

Ignition advance control

1   Air-cooled motorcycle engines have no temperature control and are therefore more susceptible than liquid-cooled engines to maladjustments of ignition and carburation, which can lead to overheating. Whether air or liquid-cooled, accurate ignition timing is of high importance and the instructions stated by the manufacturer must be adhered to exactly.

2   While some small 2-strokes have fixed ignition advance, the

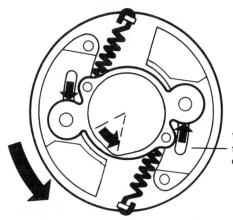

Unit fully advanced (high speed)

Fig. 4.16 ATU operation (Sec 10)

4-stroke engine requires some means of increasing ignition advance as the engine speed rises. In the early days of motorcycling, a handlebar control was fitted to permit the rider to advance the timing as the speed rose, but this was a poor compromise (see Chapter 5 on Magnetos).

3   Automatic advance has been achieved by mechanical means until the arrival of electronic ignition systems. The mechanical automatic advance unit, sometimes known as the automatic timing unit (ATU) is attached to the contact breaker assembly and causes the contacts to open earlier as the engine speed increases. At rest and low speeds the ATU has no effect, but above a certain speed increases the ignition advance progressively up to a maximum amount (fixed by the designer) beyond which it has no further effect.

4   Operation of the ATU depends on centrifugal force acting on a pair of bob weights, the principle being shown in Fig. 4.16. Instead of fixing the contact breaker cam directly to its driveshaft, it is combined with the ATU. The ATU comprises a baseplate with a central support pin which carries the cam. The cam can turn on the pin but its movement is controlled by two spring-loaded bob weights. At rest and at low speeds, the springs hold the cam in the retarded position but as engine speed rises, the weights are flung outwards, turning the cam relative to the baseplate and thus advancing the ignition point. A twin set complete with contact points and capacitors is shown in Fig. 4.17.

5   The correct operation of the ATU can be checked using a stroboscope (timing light) as described under the dynamic timing check heading below. Failure is often due to broken or weak springs, or the weights sticking on the pivots due to rust. The unit requires no regular maintenance other than to see if it has free movement; if necessary apply lubricant to the weight pivots.

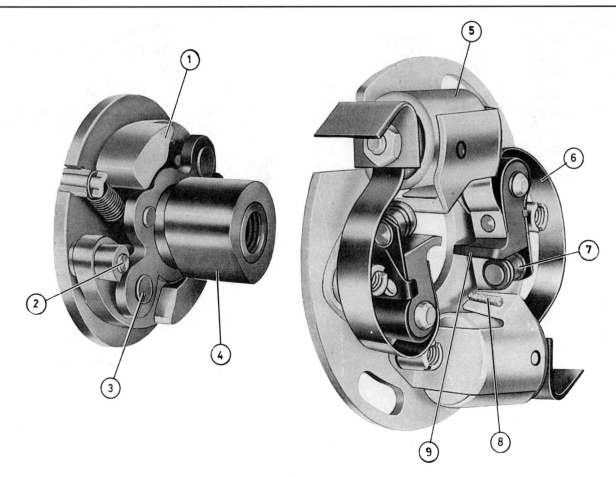

Fig. 4.17 ATU with twin contact breaker unit (Sec 10)

1	Centrifugal weights	4	Cam	6	Contact leaf spring	8	Cam lubrication pad
2	Centrifugal weight pivot	5	Capacitor	7	Contacts	9	Cam follower (or heel)
3	Cam pivot						

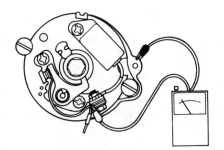

Fig. 4.18 Multimeter/buzzer shown connected across points (Sec 10)

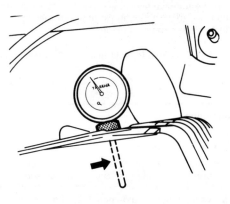

Fig. 4.19 Dial gauge and adaptor (arrowed) shown in position (Sec 10)

Ignition timing check

6 The ignition timing is set so that the contacts open at a particular point of the crankshaft revolution. The workshop manual will state whether the timing must be carried out with the automatic advance unit fully advanced or fully retarded. For those tests where the timing is to be set at fully advanced, the cam must be locked in the full advance position by any one of various methods, from jamming the weights with a matchstick to fixing a special washer to lock the cam solid.

7 The equipment required to check the timing will depend on the form in which the motorcycle manufacturer has expressed the timing specification. There is also a choice of whether the timing is checked statically (engine stopped) or dynamically (engine running), the latter is necessary for checking the operation of the ATU.

8 For all the static methods of checking the timing, some means will be necessary for determining the exact point at which the contact breaker points separate - it is not sufficient to do this visually. Methods include connecting a bulb across the contacts or a multimeter on the VOLTS range, or best of all, a buzzer.

9 When the contacts are closed the voltage across them will be zero (or very low) but when they open full battery voltage will appear. At this point the bulb will light, the meter will read or the buzzer will sound, according to the method chosen (Fig. 4.18). It follows that for all the methods given, the ignition must be switched on.

10 On multi-cylinder engines, ensure that the correct set of contacts is checked for a particular cylinder; ie contacts might be marked 1.4 to correspond with F 1.4 on the ATU of a four cylinder engine. Timing marks are sometimes used for ignition timing as described below and on almost all machines are found on the flywheel or alternator rotor periphery.

Before commencing a check of the timing, the points gap(s) must first be checked and if necessary adjusted.

Static – dial gauge method

11 A static check is made where the timing is expressed in terms of

piston position (eg 1.87 mm before top dead centre – BTDC). This will require the use of a dial gauge with a spark plug hole adaptor (Fig. 4.19). The foot of the gauge touches the piston crown and registers any up or down movement. When it reaches the maximum point as the engine is slowly turned this is TDC. The dial is set to read zero at this point and then the engine is turned until the specified distance BTDC is reached.

12 At this point, the contact breaker should just be on the verge of separation. Note that it is possible to be on the wrong part of a 4-stroke cycle – the piston must be on the compression stroke – the best way of ensuring this is to check that the inlet valve has just closed as the piston begins to rise in the cylinder.

Static – degree disc method

13 If the timing setting is expressed in terms of crankshaft position (eg 20° BTDC) a degree disc will be required and a means will have to be found of attaching it to the crankshaft end (or camshaft end on older machines – Fig. 4.20). A pointer will also need to be attached to the casing so that the disc can be read accurately. Clamp the disc so that it reads zero at TDC and then turn the engine slowly until the specified number of degrees before TDC is reached. At this point the points should just be on the verge of separation.

14 TDC can be found by using a dial gauge in the spark plug hole. Another method is to use a short rod glued to an old spark plug centre. This is laid in the spark plug hole and the degree disc reading noted when the piston just touches the rod. Turn the engine backwards until the piston touches the rod again; TDC is midway between the degree disc readings.

Static – flywheel or ATU reference mark alignment method

15 If the flywheel or ATU has suitable marks (a scribed line or F is common) it is possible to check that when they align the points are on the point of separation (Fig. 4.21). This method is quite satisfactory, but there have been instances where there have been inaccuracies in manufacture.

Dynamic – stroboscope (timing light) method

16 This check requires the use of a stroboscopic timing lamp, preferably of the xenon type (see Chapter 16 for more information). Before connecting the equipment, identify the timing marks on the flywheel or ATU and chalk or paint them white so that they show up under the stroboscopic light.

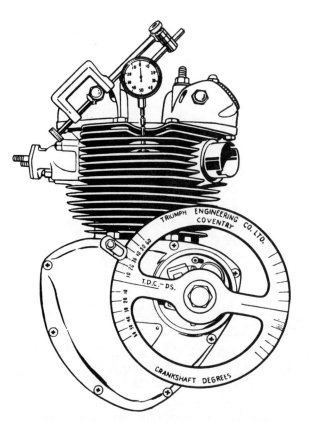

Fig. 4.20 Degree disc shown attached to the camshaft (Sec 10)

Fig. 4.21 ATU timing mark for cylinders 1 and 4 shown aligned with index mark (Sec 10)

17   The stroboscope should be connected as directed by its manufacturer and shone at the timing marks with the engine running at idle; the marks will appear frozen in position, and it will be possible to see any misalignment between fixed and moving marks (Fig. 4.22). If the marks do not align, stop the engine and make adjustment, repeating the test until the marks are accurately aligned.

18   The ATU operation can be checked by increasing the speed to about 3500 rev/min; at this point the marks corresponding to full advance should be in alignment. Lack of alignment indicates a fault in the ATU.

Ignition timing adjustment

19   If a check of the timing indicates inaccuracy, adjustment should be made. In almost all cases timing adjustment is made by rotating the baseplate on which the contact breaker is mounted after slackening the securing screws. Slots are usually provided to allow adjustment in small increments. Note that in cases where the baseplate is hidden behind the flywheel, removal of the flywheel may well be necessary for access.

20   On multi-cylinder engines, which have two or three sets of points, checking and adjustment will be necessary for each set. The order of adjustment is important because the first set of points is usually mounted directly on the baseplate, whereas the others have individual movement.

21   Often on small 2-stroke singles there is no provision for setting the timing other than by contact breaker adjustment. If a satisfactory gap cannot be obtained after timing adjustment, a new set of points is needed.

22   After all adjustments, recheck the ignition timing.

Fig. 4.22 Stroboscope in operation (Sec 10)

Chapter 5 Ignition: Magnetos

Contents

1 The Magneto

1 By 1920, most four-stroke motorcycles used a magneto for ignition and they were still in use into the 1960s. Even today, one special type, the flywheel magneto, remains in use for small engines. The magneto is an engine-driven generator designed to produce pulse voltages at specific times during rotation. The pulse voltage is sufficient to provide ignition sparks at one or more spark plugs.

2 All magnetos depend upon speed of rotation for spark voltage production since the internal coils will be subject to a magnetic flux

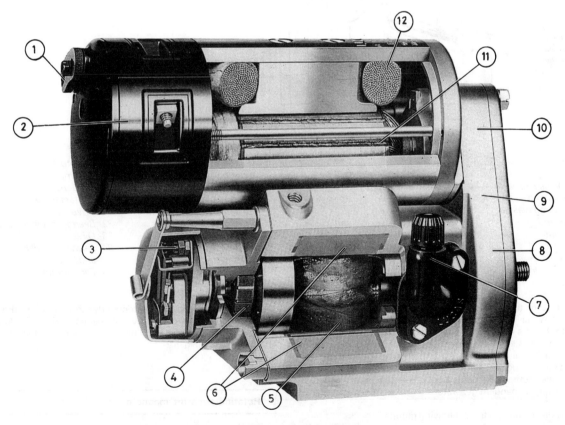

Fig. 5.1 Lucas Magdyno (Sec 1)

1 Dynamo output leads	4 Insulation washer	7 HT pickup	10 Dynamo gear
2 Dynamo commutator and brushes (beneath cover)	5 Armature	8 Main drive gear	11 Dynamo armature
3 Contact breaker	6 Magnets	9 Magneto drive	12 Dynamo field winding

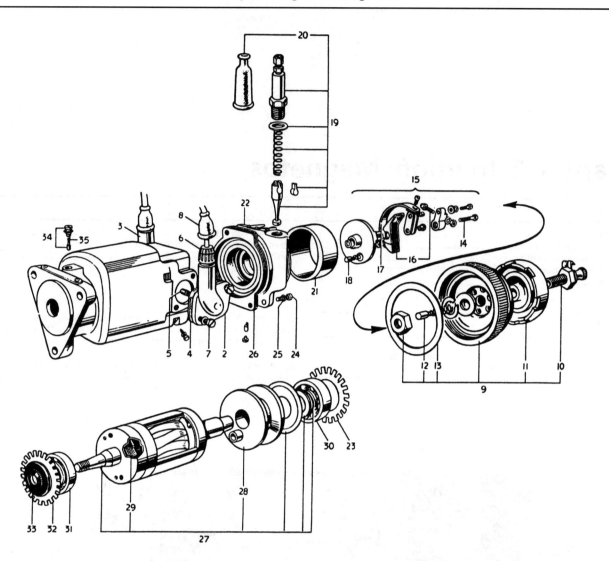

Fig. 5.2 Lucas twin-cylinder magneto, with manual advance (Sec 1)

2   Left-hand pick-up with brush
    and spring
3   Right-hand pick-up with
    brush and spring
4   Pick-up seating washer
5   Brush and spring
6   Moulded nut
7   Screw
8   Rubber cap
9   Contact breaker cover
    assembly

10   Terminal assembly
11   Moulded breather cap
12   Brush and spring
13   Rubber gasket
14   Screw
15   Contact breaker assembly
16   Contact set
17   Contact spring
18   Contact earthing (grounding)
     brush and spring

19   Manual advance control
     assembly
20   Rubber cap
21   Cam
22   End plate with bearing ring
23   Bearing insulating cup
24   Screw
25   Washer
26   Shim

27   Armature
28   Slip ring
29   Condenser
30   Contact breaker end bearing
31   Drive end bearing
32   Bearing insulating cup
33   Oil seal
34   Earth (ground) brush spring
     and holder
35   Earth (ground) brush

change as the rotor turns. It is the **rate of change** of magnetic flux through a coil which fixes the voltage generated, as explained in Chapter 2 and this is a disadvantage for ease of starting. It is essential that the magneto and external connections to the plug(s) are in good condition. The rival coil and battery system does not depend on how fast the engine can be kickstarted and has as a result, won the supremacy battle. However, it needs a good charged battery, whereas the magneto is an independent generator.

3   Magnetos divide into the three following groups.

    (a)   Rotating-armature.
    (b)   Rotating-magnet.
    (c)   Flywheel.

Of these, many variations appeared and some incorporated a battery charging facility. Very popular was the Lucas Magdyno in which a

rotating armature magneto carried a dynamo on top of the frame, the dynamo being gear driven by the magneto (Fig 5.1). Another type widely used was the Lucas twin-cylinder magneto which did not have a charging facility (Fig. 5.2).

2   Rotating-armature magneto

1   The essential components in this type are a rotating armature with primary and secondary windings, a contact breaker with a capacitor, a high voltage slip-ring and a strong permanent magnet (Fig. 5.3). The electric circuit is shown in Fig. 5.4.

2   As the rotating armature (rotor) passes under the magnetic poles

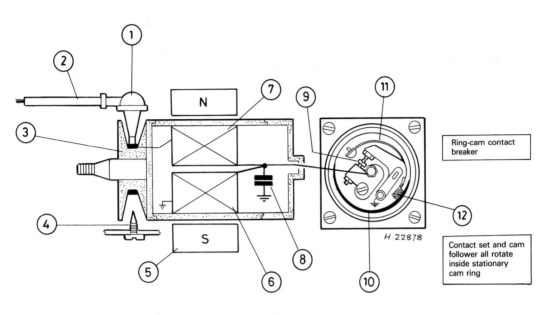

Fig. 5.3 Essentials of the rotating-armature magneto (Sec 2)

1   HT pickup
2   HT lead to spark plug
3   Brass slip ring in bakelite
    moulding
4   Safety spark gap screw
5   Strong permanent magnet
6   Primary winding
7   Secondary winding
8   Capacitor
9   Contacts
10 Cam profile
11 Leaf spring to keep cam heel in
    contact with cam profile
12 Cam heel

(Fig. 5.5, part A) a strong flux passes through the rotor and coils. Follow the motion to the point where the rotor edge is just leaving the N pole tip (Fig. 5.5, part B): the magnetic flux is now passing across to the rotor tip t_1 which is fast moving away anticlockwise (counterclockwise). At or about this point the flux coming out of the N pole into the rotor 'sees' an alternative path through the advancing rotor tip t_2 and suddenly jumps over to it (Fig. 5.5, part C). *Note that as far as the rotor and coils are concerned, the flux is now passing through it in the opposite direction.*

The **rate of** change of magnetic flux is very rapid and generates a maximum current in the primary winding, via the closed contact breaker.

At or near this point, the contact breaker points open and the high primary current is interrupted. The induced voltage in the rotor secondary winding is picked up by the slip ring brush and connected to the spark plug by the high tension (HT) cable. The ignition spark has occurred.

3   The contact breaker unit may be of the ring cam or face cam type. The former has a stationary ring with a contour such that the rotating cam heel opens and closes the contact at the correct point, as in Fig. 5.3, whereas the face cam unit has a contoured cam shape which is mounted at right angles to the drive shaft (and round it). A cam heel running on this contour again controls the opening and closure of contacts as seen in the Lucas Magdyno (Fig. 5.1).

4   Magnetos may have ignition advance provision in either manual or automatic form. Manual advance is by a cable attached to the contact breaker (stationary) plate (Fig. 5.6) which is operated by the rider from a handlebar control. Many a rider remembers being whacked by the kickstart pedal because he forgot to set the advance control to 'fully retarded' when starting!

Automatic advance may be achieved by using a centrifugal unit at the magneto drive end (Fig. 5.7). This works on the same principle as that already seen in coil ignition circuits (Fig. 4.16) and results in the magneto rotor being driven in advance of the drive gear rotation, according to speed.

5   At one end of the rotor is located an earthing (grounding) brush. This provides a proper path to the magneto body, since the alternative route would be via grease-packed bearings. The screw holding the brush and spring must be removed before taking the magneto apart. Sometimes the earthing (grounding) screw head is hidden under the serial number plate. In mentioning dismantling, it is also vital to take out the safety spark gap screw, for failure to do so will result in a fractured Bakelite slip ring (see Fig. 5.3).

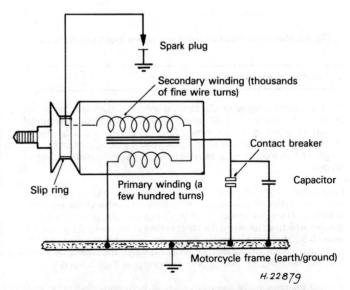

Fig. 5.4 Electric circuit of rotating-armature magneto (Sec 2)
The magneto shown is a form of high voltage generator. It achieves this by breaking the induced primary current, giving a pulse of emf in the primary winding. This is multiplied up by transformer action to give a secondary voltage big enough to give a plug spark

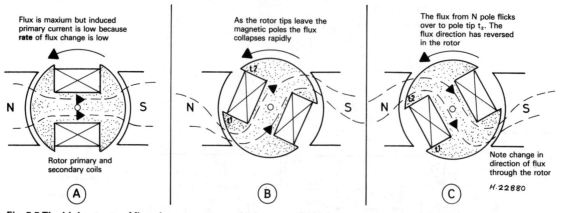

Fig. 5.5 The highest rate of flux change produces the best spark – the contact breaker must open near this point (Sec 2)

Stage A   Induced current in primary is low
Stage B   Flux collapsing – induced primary current rises rapidly
Stage C   Flux in rotor reverses – high primary current. Contact breaker opens between stage B and C, giving best spark

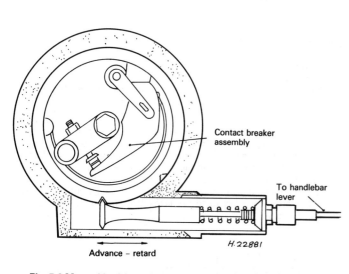

Fig. 5.6 Manual ignition advance and retard mechanism (Sec 2)

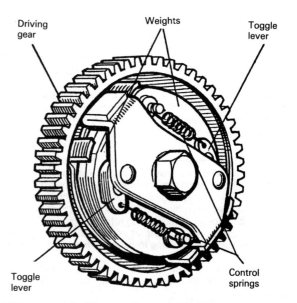

Fig. 5.7 Automatic ignition advance and retard mechanism (Sec 2)

3   Rotating-magnet magneto

1   The disadvantages of the rotating-armature magneto lay in the problems of rotating at high speed. Armature windings were under increasing strain as speeds were raised. Centrifugal loads tended to throw the windings outwards, so causing coil fractures; contact breaker surge or bounce could occur causing unwanted operation of the contact breaker.

Later magneto developments brought the rotating-magnet magneto in which the stationary primary and secondary coils were stationary on an armature. The rotor consisted of an Alnico (Aluminium-nickel-cobalt) magnet which ran between the stator laminations on which the coils are wound. Sudden flux reversal in the stator occurred as the poles passed under the stator laminations. Of small diameter, the rotational inertia was low, reducing the loading on the driving gear (Figs. 5.8 and 5.9).

2   Ball bearings carry the rotor shaft at both ends and on a shaft extension is the contact breaker, which is stationary, being operated by a shaft-mounted cam. There is no complication of the slip-ring and pick-up because the coils are stationary. HT spark current is picked up by a spring blade which is moulded into the end cover and makes contact with a round HT pickup.

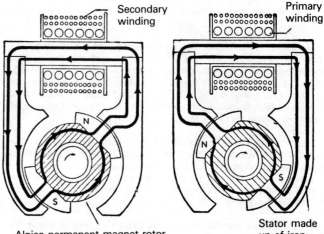

Fig. 5.8 Principle of rotating-magnet magnetos (Sec 3)

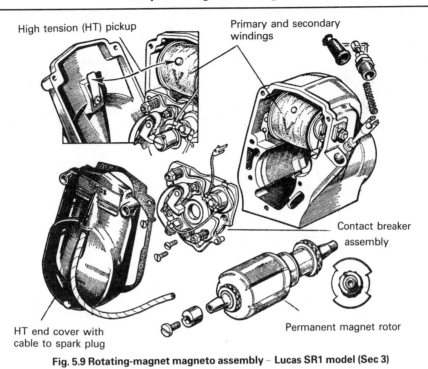

High tension (HT) pickup

Primary and secondary windings

Contact breaker assembly

Permanent magnet rotor

HT end cover with cable to spark plug

Fig. 5.9 Rotating-magnet magneto assembly – Lucas SR1 model (Sec 3)

Originally designed for racing, the rotating-magnet magneto came into use in road machines as the Lucas SR1 for single cylinder engines up to the SR4 for four cylinder models (Fig. 5.10).

4 Servicing notes – rotating-armature and rotating-magnet magnetos

1   Many magnetos can be made to work again simply by giving them a good clean, then dressing and setting the contact breaker points. With no manufacturer's information available try setting the contact breaker to 0.012 in (0.3 mm). Contacts may be cleaned by passing a strip of solvent-soaked paper through them.

2   Clean the slip ring with a solvent-damped rag and check that the HT pick-up carbon brush is in good condition.

3   Old horseshoe magnets made before circa 1935 tended to lose magnetism with time and use. Magdynos and magnetos later than this date do not normally suffer loss of magnetism. A weak spark can result from a weak magnet; turn over the magneto by hand and if there are two points per revolution where resistance to turning is felt, the magnets are good. If not, the magnets should be re-magnetised by a specialist.

4   Stripping down should be carried out with care; remember to remove the spark gap screw and the earthing (grounding) brush. Take care of shims for these are vital in setting end-play in the shaft; face-cam magnets are particularly fussy and the shims should be fitted to give zero end-play. Remove the Bakelite pickup complete; this may be

Fig. 5.10 Lucas SR1 (left) and SR4 (right) rotating-magnet magnetos (Sec 3)

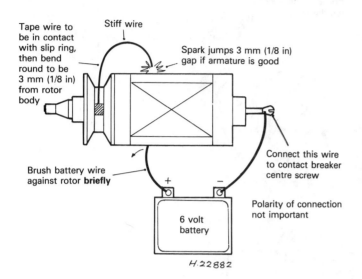

Fig. 5.11 Rotating-armature winding test (Sec 4)

require special extractors without which replacement is again best carried out professionally.

7   A simple test for armature windings is shown in Fig. 5.11. If a 6 volt battery is connected to the contact breaker centre bolt and the other battery lead flicked against the armature body, a spark should jump across the improvised spark gap. If the spark is good it is an indicator that all is well but even so, misfiring could occur at high speed because of internal sparking (tracking). No spark, however, does confirm that the windings are faulty and that the armature should be rewound.

5   Flywheel magneto

1   Used mainly on small engines, the flywheel magneto is a rotating magnet type usually found on two-strokes and on some competition four-stroke machines. It is also widely used on two-stroke lawnmowers and in other non-motorcycle applications. The essential difference between it and the rotating-magnet magneto described in Section 3 is that the magnets revolve around the stator windings and not inside them. Additionally the flywheel into which the magnets are cast has sufficient mass as to act as the main engine flwheel to carry the crankshaft over the compression resistance. (There is always an exception to the rule! One or two early models did have the stator outboard of the magnets).

2   Early flywheel magnetos had a coil for lighting (or battery charging), and an ignition coil plus contact breaker and capacitor (Fig. 5.12). This type was a complete unit with two outputs, one for charging (or lighting) and the other an HT cable going straight to the plug. Because it was self contained, it was supplied as a bolt-on package for engine manufacturers by such well known companies as Villiers, BTH, Wipac, Miller and others.

3   Later flywheel magnetos for motorcycles have an external ignition coil and work on the principle of energy transfer (see later). Internally the magneto has a coil for lighting (or charging), an ignition source coil for supplying the external ignition coil, plus a contact breaker and capacitor (Fig. 5.13). The rotating magnets are cast into a flywheel of sufficient mass to act as a crankshaft flywheel for small engines.

Developments have led to the CDI system which dispenses with the contact breaker and capacitor (see Chapter 6).

screwed to the body or clipped in place. On flange fitting types (as with the Lucas Magdyno) a paper or cork gasket is used – do not use gasket cement on reassembly since subsequent removal will be difficult.

5   The contact breaker should be removed after taking out the centre screw, noting which way the components are positioned, eg the flat spring on face-cam types. Look at the contacts (points) and if they are blackened this is an indication of capacitor problems. Usually it is better to send the magneto to a specialist for a new capacitor but the more adventurous may try replacing the faulty capacitor with a modern type of 0.2 μF (microfarad) size. (See references at end of chapter).

6   After carefully withdrawing the armature, inspect the windings visually and if the insulation is spongy there is the chance that after a hot run the shellac may jam the rotating armature – a rewind is essential. A broken slip ring side is not an uncommon fault and specialists will supply a replacement, but in general it pays to send a magneto with a faulty armature or slip ring assembly to a magneto repairer. Bearings

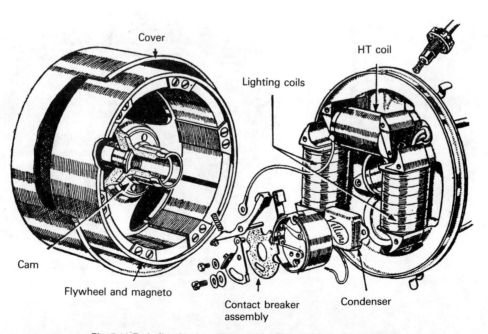

Fig. 5.12 Early flywheel magneto with HT and lighting coils (Sec 5)

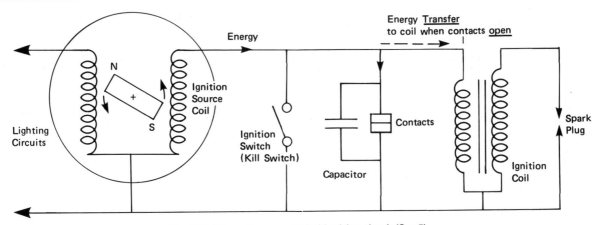

Fig. 5.13 Alternating current (ac) ignition circuit (Sec 5)

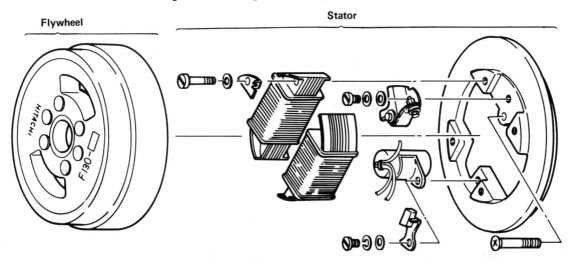

Fig. 5.14 Exploded view of Yamaha flywheel magneto (Sec 5)

Operation

4   The unit shown in Figs. 5.14 and 5.15 is a simple flywheel magneto for a small Yamaha motorcycle. Cast into the flywheel is a set of permanent magnets which pass over the stationary coils, generating an alternating voltage in them. Refer to Fig. 5.13 and note that the source coil is connected to a pair of contacts which, when closed, short circuit the alternating current to earth (ground).

At or near the point of maximum current flow (point M in Fig. 5.16) the contacts open. The current is abruptly transferred to the ignition coil primary winding, the voltage across it being stepped up by transformer action. This gives a secondary voltage sufficient for a good spark at the plug providing the contact breaker opening coincides with maximum source coil current or approximately so. It is because the energy from the source coil is **transferred** at the moment of contact breaker opening to the ignition coil primary winding, that the method is known as Energy Transfer.

5   Note the essential difference between Energy Transfer (ET) and conventional coil ignition. With ET the contact breaker is in parallel with the ignition coil primary; in conventional coil ignition it is in series (Fig. 5.17).

Timing

6   The magnet rotor is keyed to the crankshaft and as it turns the energy pulse generated in the stationary coils will occur over several degrees of rotation. In general, about + 10° makes not more than a 30% difference in plug voltage, this depending on the design. However, the fall off in plug voltage is not symmetrical around the magnetic neutral (the centre line between the magnetic poles) and drops away rapidly

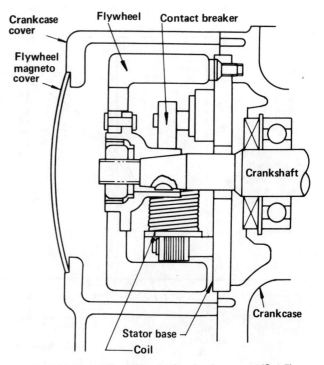

Fig. 5.15 Assembly of Yamaha flywheel magneto (Sec 5)

before magnetic neutral (see Fig. 5.18). It should be clear that the maximum spark voltage available does not occur at a fixed setting for all speeds and so a compromise is found by the manufacturer. It is important that the recommended timing point is used to maintain optimum performance and for many machines this is determined only by the correct setting of the contact breaker gap. A small error in the contact breaker gap is more serious in energy transfer than in conventional coil ignition systems.

ET Automatic advance for four-strokes

7   Four-stroke engines mostly require ignition timing control which will progressively advance the spark from somewhere around 200 rev/min up to about 3000 rev/min at the crankshaft. Automatic advance is achieved by a pair of bob weights which fly outwards by centrifugal force against spring tension as described in Chapter 4. As the weights move outwards the contact breaker is made to open earlier; the spring strength is all important and service manuals show that regular checks must be made on them.

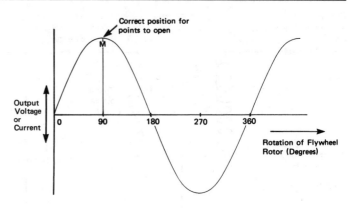

Fig. 5.16 Waveform of magneto source coil output (Sec 5)

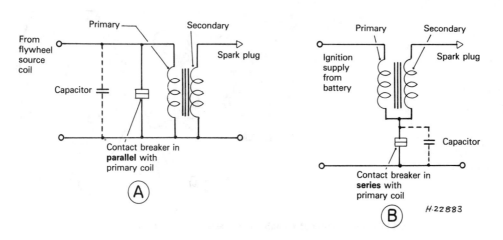

Fig. 5.17 Showing difference between Energy Transfer (A) and usual coil and battery ignition (B) (Sec 5)

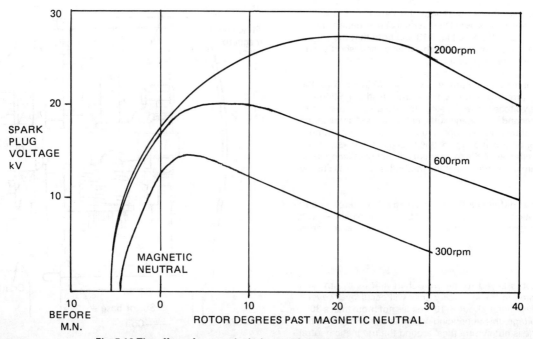

Fig. 5.18 The effect of magnetic timing on plug voltage at various speeds (Sec 5)

Because the spark intensity falls off so rapidly in ET systems only a limited amount of advance is possible and is substantially less than in coil and battery ignition. For this reason, automatic advance mechanisms are not interchangeable between ET and coil and battery machines. It is common for an ET automatic advance to be within the range 5 – 10° at the contact breaker, this corresponding to 10 – 20° at the crankshaft for a four-stroke engine.

6 Servicing notes – flywheel magneto

Servicing notes

1   Little needs to be done to a flywheel magneto apart from checking the contact breaker gap which averages out between the various makes from 0.010 – 0.015 in (0.25 – 0.38 mm). If the manufacturer's specification is not available it is best to try variations for best spark and performance. Older designs require removal of the flywheel rotor for which a puller will probably be required. When the flywheel is removed, bridge the magnetic poles with a keeper which can be any large chunks of ferrous metal such as spanners or even strip cut up for the job. Modern magnets do not require keepers according to manufacturers but habit dies hard and the advice is to use them anyway. When a flywheel is taken off it seems that ferrous filings appear as if from nowhere and stick to the poles – be careful to get rid of them before reassembly.

Common faults

2   **Weak magnets** – Poor sparking performance may be due to slow self demagnetisation of older magnets. Low turning resistance when the flywheel is turned by hand when on the shaft shows that the magnetic pole strength is low. The solution is to have the flywheel magnets remagnetised by a specialist in this work. Performance improvement after remagnetising can be quite dramatic!

3   **Coil leakage** – High voltage coils may eventually develop leakage giving rise to internal tracking so in effect the sparks are occuring in the coil rather than at the spark plug. The effects may be difficult to pin down and may show up as difficult starting or a petering out of the engine as the magneto warms up. A professional rewind is essential.

4   **Capacitor trouble** – As with most ignition equipment, the capacitor (condenser) may fail in one of three ways – short circuit, leaking or open circuit (see below).

With a short circuit there will be no spark and a test meter may show zero or low resistance from the live terminal to the case. A leaking capacitor gives rise to misfiring and rough running, first at high speed then as the fault worsens also at low speed. If the capacitor is open circuit there will be heavy sparking at the contact breaker points with signs of burning such as a white powdery appearance.

In all cases a replacement is essential. If a manufacturer's service replacement is not available an alternative capacitor may be be fitted in another position if necessary, provided it is proofed against the weather. An automobile capacitor may be used, or perhaps one from another source, providing it has a capacitance of 0.2 μF (microfarad) at 400 volt rating minimum.

7 Further reading

Readers interested in going further into magneto work are referred to the following sources:-

Restoring Motorcycles: Electrics by Roy Bacon.
The Vintage Motorcyclists' Workshop by 'Radco' (Haynes).
Classic Bike magazine, April 1992, article by Frank Farrington 'Classic Craftsmanship'.
For specialist repairers of magnetos see *Old Bike Mart*, PO Box 6, Chapel-en-le-Frith, via Stockport SK12 6LD.

Chapter 6
Ignition: Capacitor Discharge Ignition (CDI)

Contents

1 Deficiencies of the Kettering ignition system

1   The development of Capacitor Discharge Ignition (CDI) is one simple way of achieving a reliable spark up to high speeds using electronics. However, before looking at CDI in detail it is worth considering why contact breaker ignition has now been superseded.

Although the contact breaker plus coil and battery system has been in use for more than half a century, its shortcomings in performance and maintenance costs have long been appreciated. Mechanically, it is difficult to manufacture a cam, heel follower and spring mechanism which provide and maintain the required accuracies. Every few thousand miles it is necessary to reset the contacts to allow for heel wear; in addition the breaking of the coil primary current produces the effect of 'pitting and piling' because of metal transference with the spark.

It should be noted that to obtain enough energy for spark production (about 30 millijoules are required – for a definition of the joule see Chapter 2) the coil designer will allow as large a primary current as possible, consistent with reasonable life of the contact breaker points – but for long contact life the current should be small. The graph in Fig. 6.1 shows the general effect of break current on the life of points and that the designer does not have much latitude.

At high speeds the centrifugal force acting on the moving parts of the contact breaker assembly may be sufficient to cause the gap to increase beyond the design gap, due to flinging out when the heel loses contact with the cam.

2   These troubles have always been present but in recent times have become more undesirable due to engine design developments. Compression ratios have increased, demanding a higher spark voltage; additionally, higher maximum engine speeds are used needing a higher rate of sparking. All these limitations are best summarised as follows.

(a)   Plug fouling – For high compression ratios, petrol additives (lead salts) are used in the UK to prevent detonation. Unfortunately, these additives appear to contribute to fouling of plugs.

(b)   Mechanical limitations of contact breakers are now severe.

(c)   The time taken for 30 millijoules of electrical energy to build up between sparks limits the rate to about 400 sparks per second, or time per spark 0.0025 second. This may be too low a spark rate for high-speed multi-cylinder engines.

(d)   To overcome plug fouling, and to produce reliable sparks in cylinders of higher compression rates, a higher spark voltage of 15 to 30 kilovolts (kV) is required. Another reason for higher ignition system voltage is to do with both economy and the achievement of low pollution emission; weaker mixtures are now used and in turn are more difficult to ignite by sparks.

(e)   Contact breaker points pitting and burning due to the high coil primary currents used.

(f)   Inaccuracy occurring at high speeds due to backlash and whip in the contact breaker drive mechanism.

It is not surprising that ignition system designers have looked for alternative methods, and the arrival of the transistor and allied semiconductor devices has provided several solutions to the problem.

2 Capacitor Discharge Ignition (CDI)

1   Under ideal conditions less than 1 millijoule of energy will properly ignite the fuel:air mixture in the combustion chamber. The first part of the arc of perhaps only 1 microsecond duration ignites the mixture and the remainder of the spark contributes little or nothing. However, the practical condition is that the mixture may be wrong, or unevenly mixed, and it may be that the ignitable gas may not even have reached the plug electrodes at the time that the spark occurs. It is found that if the spark duration is made to last about 300 microseconds then the probability is that ignition will occur satisfactorily for all normal cylinder conditions.

2   A further desirable feature of the ideal spark in an engine is that the energy flow at the plug should reach a maximum in a very short period of time. This sudden rush of electrical energy will help to counteract plug fouling and may be regarded as a 'punch through' effect.

An ignition system which gives correct spark duration coupled with rapid rise of energy flow is the Capacitor Discharge Ignition system (CDI).

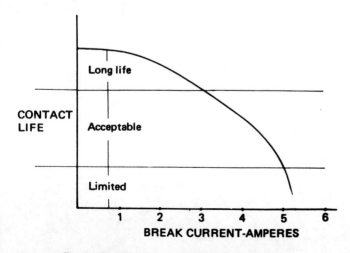

Fig. 6.1 Contact life versus break current (Sec 1)

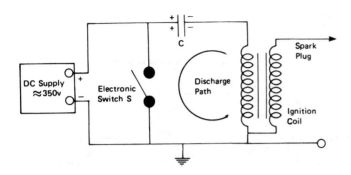

Fig. 6.2 Principle of Capacitor Discharge Ignition (CDI) (Sec 2)

3   The principle of CDI is illustrated in Fig. 6.2. If it is assumed that a dc supply is available to charge capacitor C to about 350 volts, then at the instant when a spark is required, the electronic switch S closes and capacitor C is discharged rapidly through the ignition coil primary winding. This pulse of current results in a high voltage to the secondary winding in excess of 40 kV to give a high intensity spark of short duration.

3   The electronic switch

1   Electronic switching is invariably by means of the thyristor, often called a Silicon Controlled Rectifier (SCR). Refer back to Chapter 2 for the basic principles of how the thyristor works, but in essence it is a switch which is either open circuit (ie no current can flow through it) or short circuit – just like a mechanical on/off switch.

2   To switch the thyristor ON, a very small current is fed into the gate terminal. This small current is derived from a sensor which detects the instant when a spark is required. Only when the capacitor has discharged itself fully through the thyristor and the ignition coil primary winding, does the thyristor resume the OFF position until the next gate

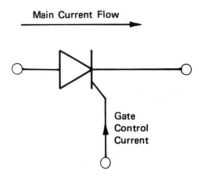

Fig. 6.3 Thyristor or Silicon Controlled Rectifier (SCR) (Sec 3)

signal arrives from the sensor. The symbol for the thyristor is shown in Fig. 6.3.

4   AC-CDI

1   AC-CDI means that an alternating voltage is taken from the ignition charge coil on the alternator or flywheel ac generator, then converted into direct voltage by a rectifier to charge up the capacitor (Fig. 6.4). The title AC-CDI is misleading, since the CDI capacitor must always be supplied with dc.

An alternating voltage with a peak of 350 volts (or lower in some designs) is required and will charge the capacitor up to this value in readiness for the point where the thyristor breaks down to the short circuit condition. The resulting pulse of current will pass round the ignition coil primary winding, generating a spark voltage in the secondary winding.

2   As the alternator rotor magnet passes under the pulse coil, a voltage pulse is generated which serves to trigger the thyristor.

The simple circuit in Fig. 6.4 has a movable pulse coil so that ignition

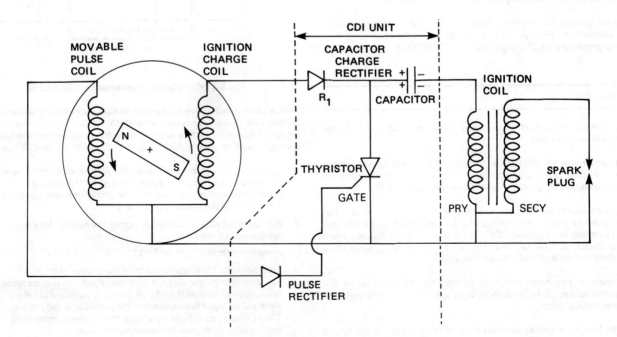

Fig. 6.4 Simplified CDI circuit using a flywheel generator (Sec 4)

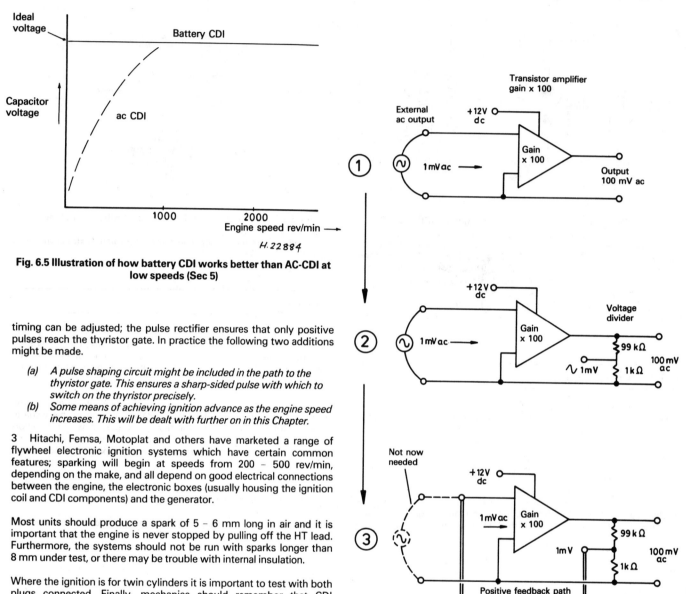

Fig. 6.5 Illustration of how battery CDI works better than AC-CDI at low speeds (Sec 5)

timing can be adjusted; the pulse rectifier ensures that only positive pulses reach the thyristor gate. In practice the following two additions might be made.

(a)   *A pulse shaping circuit might be included in the path to the thyristor gate. This ensures a sharp-sided pulse with which to switch on the thyristor precisely.*

(b)   *Some means of achieving ignition advance as the engine speed increases. This will be dealt with further on in this Chapter.*

3   Hitachi, Femsa, Motoplat and others have marketed a range of flywheel electronic ignition systems which have certain common features; sparking will begin at speeds from 200 – 500 rev/min, depending on the make, and all depend on good electrical connections between the engine, the electronic boxes (usually housing the ignition coil and CDI components) and the generator.

Most units should produce a spark of 5 – 6 mm long in air and it is important that the engine is never stopped by pulling off the HT lead. Furthermore, the systems should not be run with sparks longer than 8 mm under test, or there may be trouble with internal insulation.

Where the ignition is for twin cylinders it is important to test with both plugs connected. Finally, mechanics should remember that CDI systems generate a lot of energy and are DANGEROUS.

5   Battery CDI

1   An alternative method of supplying power to a CDI unit from the battery is now described.

The disadvantage of AC-CDI is that the starting-up spark voltage depends on how fast the engine can be turned over. At low rpm the battery-operated CDI gives a greater spark energy (Fig. 6.5).

Because the alternator does not now need an ignition charge coil, it can be designed to give a larger output for battery charging. Finally, the current demand for a battery CDI is lower than that of a transistorised ignition circuit at low rev/min. However, the starting success is dependent on having a well-charged battery!

2   A method has been found to convert the 12 volts dc of the motorcycle battery up to the high dc voltage (200 – 350 volts) required to charge the capacitor.

First, the 12 volts is applied to a transistor circuit designed to oscillate, ie to generate an alternating voltage. A built-in transformer then

Fig. 6.6 Principle for an invertor for CDI (Sec 5)

Follow steps 1 to 3 above to see how an oscillator-invertor works in battery CDI. This basic circuit is an invertor producing ac from a dc battery. The output voltage is stepped up by a transformer, then passed through a rectifier to give 200 – 350 volts dc to charge the CDI capacitor

1   *Consider a simple transistor amplifier with an alternating input voltage and a gain of 100. An ac input of 1mV (millivolt) will produce an ac output of 100mV. The amplifier power supply is 12 volts from the motorcycle battery*

2   *If a voltage divider is connected across the output, 1mV will appear across the 1KΩ*

   (Reason: $100mV \times \frac{1}{99+1} = 1mV$)

3   *Feed back the 1mV tapped off from the divider to the input. The amplifier is now supplying its own input and will continue to oscillate so long as the 12 volt supply is switched on.* **No external ac input is needed** *and the oscillator is self starting. The ac frequency is fixed by choice of amplifier components and is designed to give low radio interference*

Fig. 6.7 Schematic diagram of a CDI invertor (Sec 5)

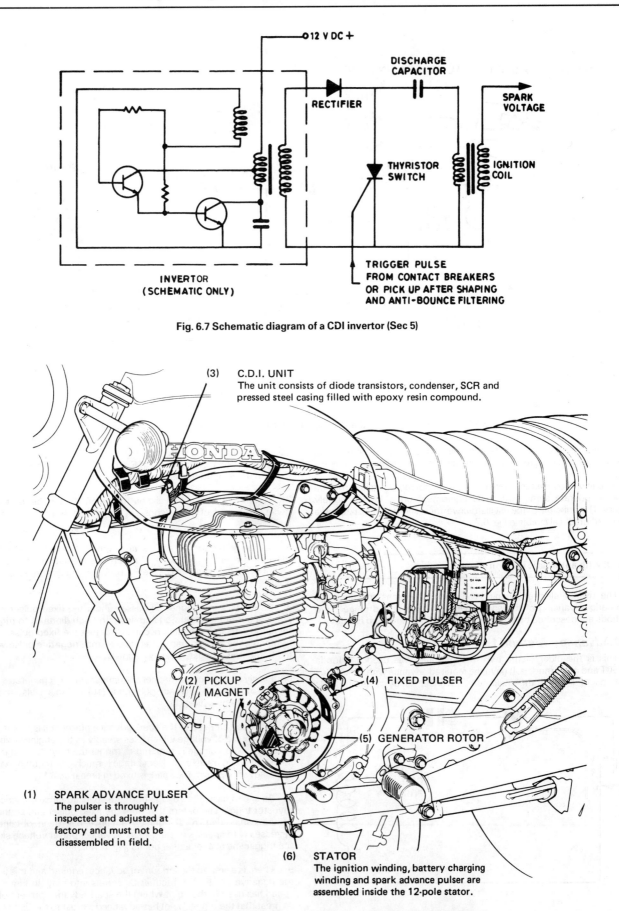

(3) C.D.I. UNIT
The unit consists of diode transistors, condenser, SCR and pressed steel casing filled with epoxy resin compound.

(2) PICKUP MAGNET

(4) FIXED PULSER

(5) GENERATOR ROTOR

(1) SPARK ADVANCE PULSER
The pulser is throughly inspected and adjusted at factory and must not be disassembled in field.

(6) STATOR
The ignition winding, battery charging winding and spark advance pulser are assembled inside the 12-pole stator.

Fig. 6.8 Layout of the CDI components on the Honda CB250/400T models (Sec 6)

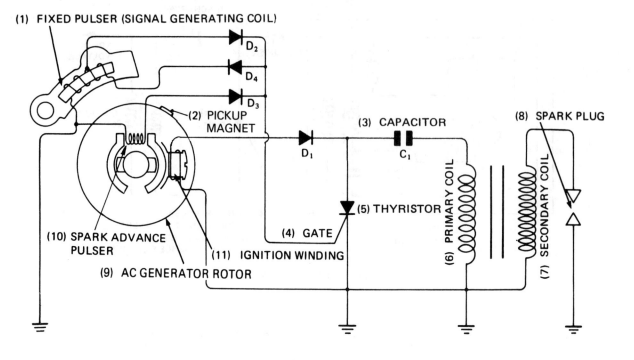

Fig. 6.9 Schematic diagram of the CDI system on the Honda CB250/400T models (Sec 6)

transforms the alternating voltage of this oscillator up to the required peak voltage, which is rectified to produce the required direct voltage.

This circuit is known as an invertor and in high powered versions may be made to operate some household equipment off a 12 volt supply battery. The principle of the oscillator/invertor is shown in Fig. 6.6, and a simplified practical circuit in Fig. 6.7.

6 CDI with automatic ignition advance

1 The use of electronic ignition in no way lessens the need for automatic advancing of the spark over the lower speed range. Two methods are described below which are both ingenious and effective.

CDI Advance – Method 1

2 This is the older of the two methods and was used on Honda CB250T and 400T models. It gave the required advance with speed plus a means of limiting the maximum advance, all by a set of coils

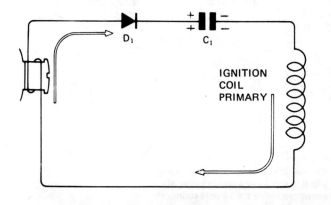

Fig. 6.10 Charging of the capacitor C_1 (Sec 6)

assembled within the generator. Fig. 6.8 shows the location of the CDI components on the machine and Fig. 6.9 the electrical circuit. Referring to Fig. 6.9, the operation is as follows.

3 The pick up magnet (2) is a button-magnet set in the rotor and this generates pulses of nearly constant magnitude in the fixed pulser coil (1).

4 As the generator rotor turns, an alternating current is generated in the ignition winding (11). This current is rectified by diode D_1 and charges the CDI capacitor C_1 (see Fig. 6.10). During this time the thyristor is OFF.

5 As the pick up magnet (2) passes under the fixed pulser coil (1) a pulse of current is generated and flows through diode D_2 to trigger the thyristor. The ignition spark occurs. Note that the fixed pulser coil has two parts, the second part generating a small **negative** pulse which is fed to the thyristor gate through diode D_4.

6 Finally as the pick up magnet continues rotation it generates a pulse voltage in the spark advance pulser coil (10) and this is also fed to the thyristor gate by a diode D_3.

7 The characteristic of the spark advance pulser coil is that it gives a broad + pulse of voltage which rises steeply as the engine speed rises. A certain fixed voltage is required to trigger the thyristor and it will be seen that when the fixed pulser voltage is much greater than that of the spark advance pulser, the spark is fixed in time (Fig. 6.11).

8 As speed rises, the voltage from the spark advance pulser cuts the thyristor trigger line before that from the fixed pulser and so the spark occurs earlier (Fig. 6.12). Ignition advance has been obtained and increases with speed since the spark advancer pulser voltage skirt cuts the trigger line at ever earlier points (Fig. 6.13).

9 There is a limit to the amount of advance required and this is where the negative pulse from rectifier D_4 comes into play. In Fig. 6.14 the speed has risen to the point where the spark advance pulser voltage is so great that the trigger point has advanced almost to the fixed position of the negative pulse from D_4. Here the negative pulse balances out the

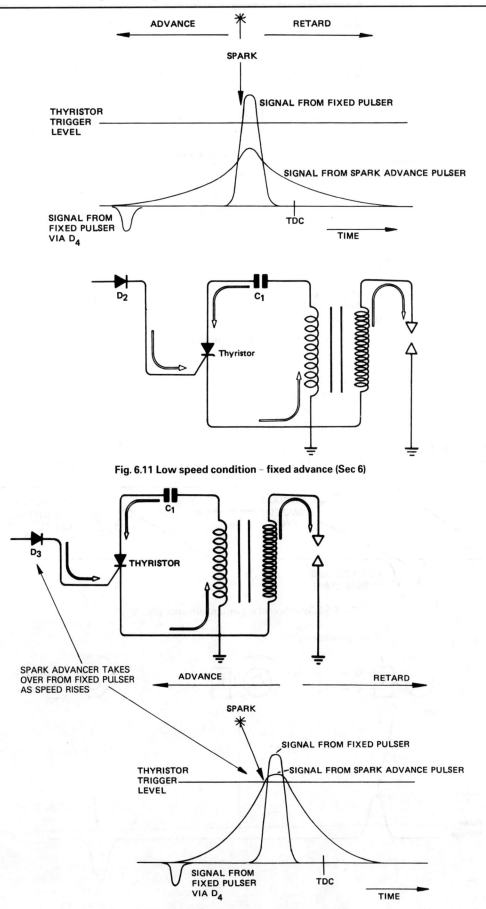

Fig. 6.11 Low speed condition – fixed advance (Sec 6)

Fig. 6.12 Advance condition just beginning (Sec 6)

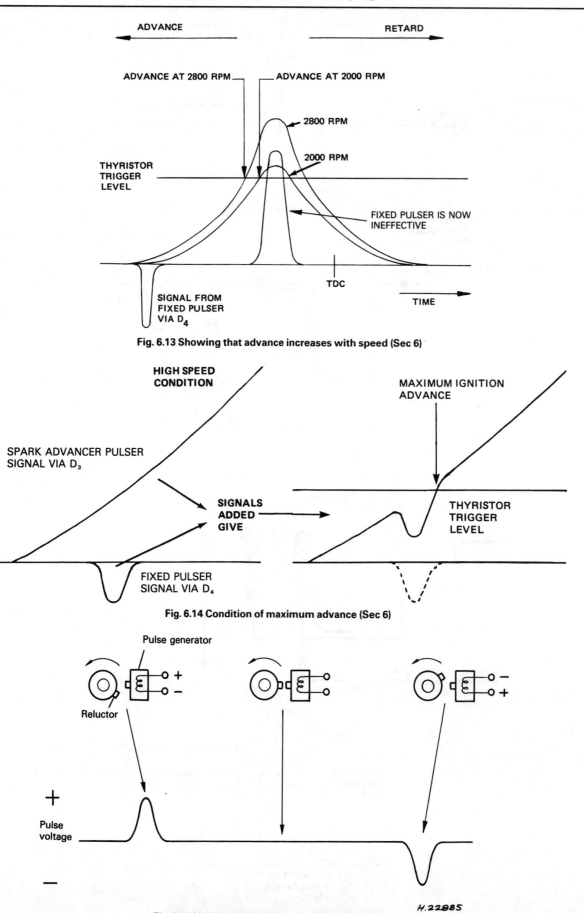

Fig. 6.13 Showing that advance increases with speed (Sec 6)

Fig. 6.14 Condition of maximum advance (Sec 6)

H.22885

Fig. 6.15 Voltage pulses from pulse generator (Sec 6)

positive output from the advance pulser rectifier D_3 and so further ignition advance is stopped.

CDI Advance – Method 2

10   The more recent method of obtaining ignition advance depends upon electronic circuitry.

11   Fig. 6.15 shows a pulse generator and the waveshape of the voltage produced in it as the rotor reluctor passes. (A reluctor is a steel projection which passes close to the pulse coil iron core, raising the magnetic flux level and thus inducing voltage pulses in the coil.) It will be seen that as the reluctor approaches the pulse generator, the magnetic flux across the gap will be increasing and as it moves away, the magnetic flux will be decreasing. This gives rise to a positive then a negative voltage pulse.

12   Inside the CDI unit the pulses are connected to two wave shaping circuits (Fig. 6.17). Wave shaper A detects the positive going pulse and produces a voltage wave with an initial step, then a linearly rising ramp shape until the negative pulse is received. The wave A then drops back to zero until the next positive pulse is received. *Wave A remains constant for all speeds.*

13   Wave shaper B takes the incoming pulses and is triggered when the negative pulse is received. It generates a linearly rising voltage waveform which continues until the next negative pulse arrives, but the slope of the waveshape B depends upon engine speed. *Wave B gets lower in height as speed increases.*

14   Waveforms A and B are connected to a logic-gate voltage comparator circuit. This circuit produces an output pulse to trigger the thyristor (SCR) subject to the following condition. *The comparator will send the spark signal to the thyristor when waveform A is greater than waveform B or when the negative pulse is received.*

15   Looking at the waveforms in Fig. 6.16, waveform B is shown for speeds increasing from N_1 to N_4. At N_1, waveform B is greater than waveform A, so the thyristor is triggered by the negative pulse at time T_1.

At N_2 the engine speed has risen and waveform B cuts waveform A giving a spark signal earlier to the thyristor at time T_2. When engine speed is at N_4 or greater, no further advance is possible because waveform A is not inclined and is inoperative. The result is that ignition advance occurs progressively from point T_1 up to T_4 and no further. As an example, T_1 may correspond to about 10° BTDC and T_4 to 35° BTDC.

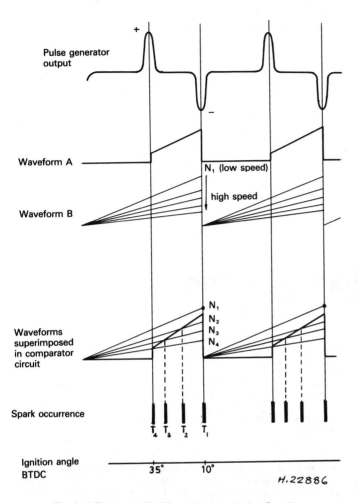

Fig. 6.16 Electronic ignition advance graphs (Sec 6)

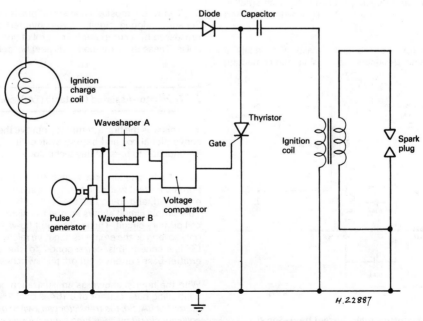

Fig. 6.17 Electronic ignition advance for CDI (Sec 6)

Chapter 7
Ignition: Transistor and digital ignition

Contents

1 Transistor ignition development

1   The first appearance of transistor-driven ignition for motorcycles was in the form of aftermarket kits or designs for DIY constructors.

Early circuits still employed the contact-breaker, but connected into a transistor circuit so that the current being broken was much smaller. Such circuit systems were known as TAC (Transistor Assisted Contacts).

2   Using a mechanically operated contact breaker was really a compromise and soon circuit designers were using non-contacting

sensors to pick up a signal indicating when sparking should occur. Circuits using transistors are prone to sharp pulse voltages or transients. Ignition coils are a prime source of spike pulse voltages and protection has to be given to the driving transistor(s) to avoid destruction. To some extent the development of modern sophisticated electronic systems proceeded in parallel with transistor devices which were less susceptible to transient failure.

3   Today, the most advanced and precise ignition systems are digital. Sensor analogue signals are converted to digital form and then processed by a computer for control of voltage and timing of the spark pulse. These three methods will now be looked at more closely.

2 Transistor-Assisted Contacts (TAC) coil ignition

1   This was the first attempt to improve the shortcomings of the (then) conventional coil and battery system; it is obsolete but forms a good introduction to present day technology.

Use of a transistor as a switch to break and make the ignition coil primary current was a first step; it is still necessary to turn the transistor on and off, and to do this the contact breaker (S) is retained (Fig. 7.1). This simple circuit shows an npn transistor connected into the ignition coil primary circuit. The load current flows from collector c to emitter e only so long as the emitter is negative relative to the base b. If the switch (S) is opened (this corresponds to the contact breaker) then the emitter-base current is cut off; this switches off the collector current.

With the figures shown as an illustration only, it will be seen that the controlling base current of 0.16A is only 2% of the controlled collector current of 8A. *So, the transistor can switch on or off a large current in the collector circuit by switching a much lower current in the base circuit.*

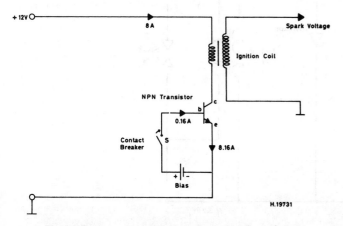

Fig. 7.1 Base current controls main current flow (Sec 2)

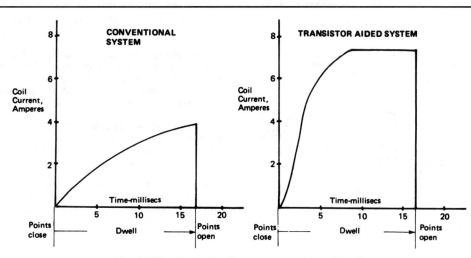

Fig. 7.2 Rise times of coil current comparison (Sec 2)

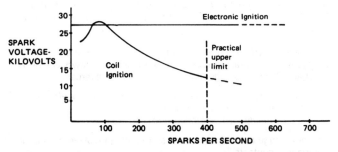

Fig. 7.3 Performance comparison between conventional and electronic systems (Sec 2)

The circuit arrangement is not really practical because of the need for an additional battery to bias the emitter to be negative with respect to the base.

Because the contacts now handle a low current, 0.16A in this case, the life is greatly extended and, moreover, no capacitor is required since the contacts are partly isolated from the ignition coil primary. It is claimed that a set of TAC points may have a life of 100,000 miles (160,000 km).

2 A factor to be considered when designing an ignition coil suitable for TAC is that of the primary coil inductance L, measured in henrys (see Chapter 2). Inductance depends, among other factors, upon the number of turns of a coil, and the energy stored in the magnetic field around the coil is:

$$W = \tfrac{1}{2}LI^2$$

where

W = energy stored (joules)
I = coil current (amperes)
L = coil inductance (henrys)

3 It is important to have the ignition coil primary current rise as quickly as possible when the contacts are closed, in order to build up energy ready for the next contact-break. Inductance in an electrical circuit is similar to the inertia of a flywheel. As a heavy flywheel takes time to accelerate, so current rise takes time in an inductive circuit (Fig. 7.2 and see Chapter 2).

The primary current rise time is significantly reduced allowing a higher maximum rate of sparking (see Fig. 7.3). Designers have, therefore, taken the opportunity to set the value of the ignition coil current higher than that in conventional coils – about 8 amperes instead of 3 amperes in one particular design. This allows the inductance (and therefore number of primary turns) to be reduced and results in a

secondary-to-primary turns ratio of about 250:1 or even 400:1 compared with about 66:1 in a conventional coil. The low primary resistance will also reduce the resistive power loss in the coil.

4 It might reasonably be asked what other advantage this gives. The answer is that if current is changed rapidly in an inductive circuit, transient voltages are generated across the inductive coil and these could be hazardous to electronic components elsewhere in the electrical system. It is therefore of advantage to keep the primary coil inductance low.

5 This rise-time of coil current after the contacts have closed has been a limiting factor to the maximum possible spark rate, since at high engine speeds the next spark was due before the current could rise to its maximum value. The reduced primary inductance of ignition coils driven by transistors has meant much improved performance, as shown by the typical graphs of Figs. 7.2 and 7.3. The retention of good sparking voltage at high engine speeds is required for efficiency and economy.

6 Several advantages stem, therefore, from the use of transistor-assisted contact breaking, which include a higher maximum sparking rate, and less plug fouling and contact wear leading to longer intervals between service.

The disadvantage of retaining mechanical contacts remains, however, and no motorcycles are now fitted with TAC as original equipment. Aftermarket conversion kits are still popular with the DIY market, but most now dispense with contacts and substitute a sensor.

3 Basic TAC ignition circuit

1 A drawback of the circuit shown in Fig. 7.1 is the need for a separate battery in the base control path. In practice, the supply of current for both the base and collector branches is drawn from the same battery; all that is needed is a pair of resistors across the main battery supply, their resistance being calculated to make the centre tap correspond to the voltage required at the base. An illustration of this idea is given in Fig. 7.4.

2 The first approach to transistor ignition was to relieve the contact breaker of interrupting current in an inductive circuit. Fig. 7.4 shows a practical circuit using an ignition coil of 400:1 ratio. The transistor is protected from inductive transient voltages by the Zener diode connected across it; when the Zener conduction point is reached (56 volts) the transistor is effectively bridged by a low resistance path until the offending voltage disappears.

3 When the points are closed, R_1 and R_3 act as a voltage divider and thus bias the transistor so that it is switched on. Current flows round the main path of R_1 through diode D_1, the transistor (emitter to collector) and through the ignition coil primary winding back to the battery.

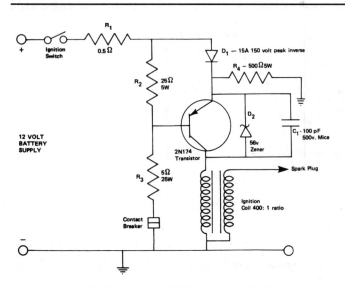

Fig. 7.4 Single transistor TAC ignition circuit (Sec 3)

4   At break point, the chain R_2 and R_3 is broken and bias is removed from the transistor, causing it to switch off; a small current continues to flow through diode D_1 and R_4 the result being that the emitter is about 0.7 volt **negative** with respect to the base. This ensures abrupt cut-off of coil current, the effect of which is to generate a spark voltage in the secondary winding. The unit must be constructed on a heat sink (an aluminium plate to disperse the heat) and can then be encapsulated in epoxy resin to give protection from damp.

---

4   TAC ignition – dual transistor circuits

---

1   Using only one transistor of the power type is feasible but a better solution is to use a second transistor to receive the open-close signal from the contact breaker and then to drive the power transistor which controls the on-off current to the ignition coil.

The main advantage of a two-transistor switch is its comparatively high

switching speed, but further, it operates at a lower temperature than if a single power switching transistor is used.

2   Two transistors T_1 and T_2 are shown in Fig. 7.5 and the direction of the arrows on their emitters shows that T_1 is of the pnp type and T_2 is npn. (It should be recalled that a pnp transistor is ON when the emitter voltage is + relative to its base, and the npn transistor is ON when the emitter voltage is – relative to its base).

With the contact breaker closed, the current flow through R_1 and R_2 will produce volt-drops as shown in Fig. 7.5. The volt-drop across R_2 is sufficient to switch T_1 to ON. T_1 collector current will give volt-drops on R_3 and R_4. That across R_4 will switch T_2 to ON.

When the contact breaker opens there is no forward bias to T_1 which shuts OFF. This removes the forward bias from T_2 which also switches OFF, so no collector current flows through the ignition coil primary winding. The induced voltage in the secondary winding of the ignition coil provides the spark at the plugs.

3   At the point when ignition occurs, there will be a high emf generated in the ignition coil primary winding of the order of a few hundred volts, enough to destroy transistor T_2. The Zener diode ZD is chosen to conduct at about 100 volts and so protects T_2 from large voltage spikes.

The bias chain R_1R_2 is made up of resistor values to give correct bias to T_1. R_6 sets the contact breaker current to about 250 mA, sufficient to burn off dirt and corrosion. R_5 is a ballast resistor to limit primary coil current.

4   Many variations of this circuit have been used, but although good results may be obtained with TAC, the following drawbacks of using mechanical contacts to generate the ignition signal remain.

(a)   Need for regular servicing due to cam-follower heel wear.
(b)   Contact bounce at high speeds.
(c)   Relatively high manufacturing cost.

The next stage in solid state transistor ignition involved getting rid of mechanical contacts.

---

5   More about sensors

---

1   A sensor is a conversion device which will measure or detect a

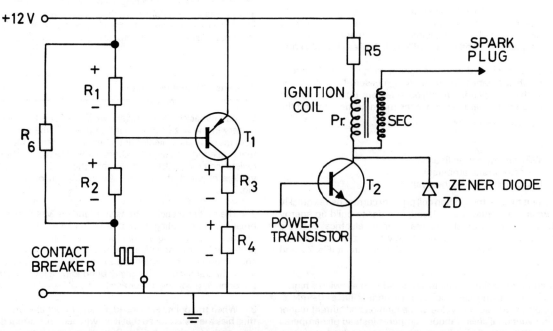

Fig. 7.5 TAC circuit using complementary transistors (Sec 4)

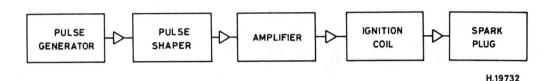

H.19732

Fig. 7.6 Pulse-triggered electronic ignition (Sec 5)

quantity and produce a corresponding electrical signal. Quantities measured in motorcycle and automobile engineering are, commonly, speed, position, temperature, pressure, liquid or air flow and oxygen content of exhaust gases.

2   For the purpose of ignition, to trigger the spark some form of sensor is required to produce an electrical signal at the instant when the spark is required. The contact breaker is a crude sensor which carries out on this function, but a non-contacting trigger device has the following advantages.

(a)   Elimination of contact wear, bounce or mechanical free play; thus the timing will remain accurate.
(b)   Spark timing can be made accurate over all speed and load conditions by electronic control.
(c)   The fall-off of spark energy with speed can be eliminated by electronic control of the dwell period.

The sensing device is sometimes called a **pulse generator** or a **signal generator**.

3   Pulse generators fall usually into 3 types:-

(a)   Optical.
(b)   Hall Effect.
(c)   Variable reluctance.

In general, the pulse signals are too small for direct use and do not always have the optimum waveform, so circuits will **shape** the incoming signal and then **amplify** it as shown in the block diagram of Fig. 7.6.

Optical pulse generator

4   An engine-driven segmented chopper disc breaks an infra-red beam normally focussed onto a photo-transistor (Fig. 7.7). The infra-red is produced by a gallium arsenide semiconductor diode. During the period when the beam is on the photo-transistor the coil current is ON; as a vane cuts the beam, the photo-transistor sends a pulse (Fig. 7.8) which, after amplification, shuts off the coil primary current and the spark is generated at the plug.

Several variations of this arrangement exist; the pulse may be generated at the instant when the vane allows the beam to pass through to the photo-transistor; another possibility is the use of a light emitting diode (LED) instead of an infra-red diode.

Hall effect pulse generator

5   This device consists of a silicon chip through which a small current is passed between opposite edges. When a magnetic field passes through the major surface of the chip, a voltage appears between the other two edges (Fig. 7.9). This is the Hall voltage and is used to trigger the ignition spark when the magnetic field is changed, this being achieved by a metallic trigger vane segment disc (Fig. 7.10). The magnetic field is usually provided by a small permanent magnet on the opposite side of the gap from the Hall chip. Note that the vane will break the magnetic field as it passes in the gap between the permanent magnet and the Hall element.

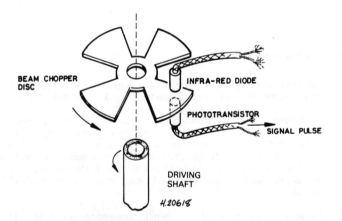

Fig. 7.7 Optical pulse generator (Sec 5)

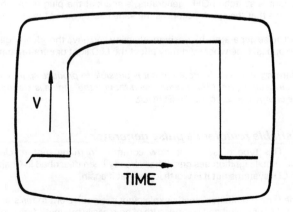

Fig. 7.8 Trace produced by optical generator (Sec 5)
Courtesy FKI Crypton Ltd

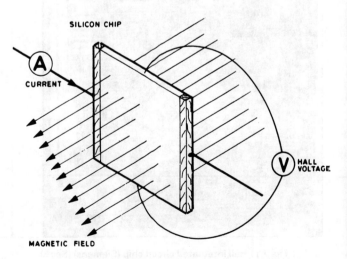

Fig. 7.9 Illustrating Hall-effect voltage (Sec 5)

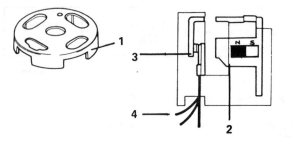

1   Trigger vane segment
2   Permanent magnet
3   Sensor element (Hall chip)
4   Sensor wires

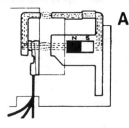

A. No interruption - magnetic field passes
through sensor. Switch is ON

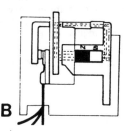

B. Vane interrupts magnetic field
Switch is OFF.

Fig. 7.10 Effect of trigger vane in Hall sender (Sec 5)

Typically the chip will take a current of about 30mA, delivering a 2mV Hall voltage signal with a positive temperature coefficient, ie the Hall voltage increases with an increase of temperature. The chip is usually built into an integrated circuit, providing signal shaping and amplification.

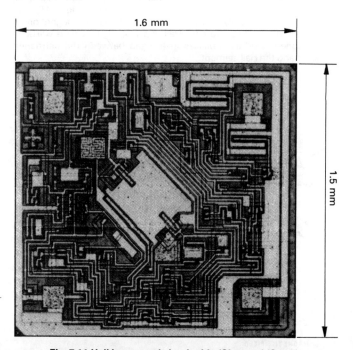

1.6 mm

1.5 mm

Fig. 7.11 Hall integrated circuit chip (Siemens) (Sec 5)
The Hall generator is located in the centre

The example shown is a Siemens Hall-IC chip, the Hall generator being located in the centre of the chip; note the size – 1.5 x 1.6 mm! (Fig. 7.11).

Fig. 7.10 shows that at A the magnetic field crosses the air gap when the vane is not inbetween the gap faces and the Hall chip gives an output voltage; at B the vane is between the air gap faces and provides a path for the magnetic flux, shielding the Hall chip so the output voltage falls to a low level (Fig. 7.12). The voltage waveform is roughly rectangular and is processed by the integrated circuit to give a sharp ON-OFF output.

The rotor vane is shaped so as to give the required ratio of ON/OFF. This gives a pre-set dwell angle which can be varied by the electronic circuit into which the pulse signal is fed.

Finally, when the Hall voltage is switched ON (= high) the ignition coil current is switched OFF, generating a spark at the plug from which it follows that **the spark** occurs as the vane passes out of the airgap.

Hall pulse generators have a high reliability and have the advantage over the optical type where dirt may affect the LED light or infra-red path.

Warning: *It should be noted that it is possible to produce spark voltage when working on a Hall system even though the engine is stationary – the energy delivered is DANGEROUS.*

Variable reluctance pulse generator

6   This type of sensor is now common in many motorcycle and automobile ignition designs. It has already been described in Chapter 6 on CDI systems but it is worth looking at it again.

The term 'reluctance' needs explaining; it is equivalent to resistance in the electric circuit and is a measure of how easily magnetic flux can pass round a magnetic circuit. If the cross-sectional area of the iron path is small the reluctance will be higher than that for a large cross-sectional

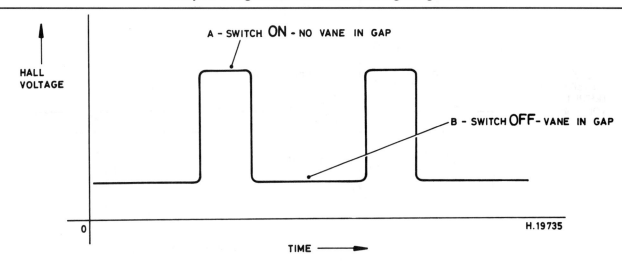

Fig. 7.12 Output waveform of Hall pulse generator (Sec 5)

area; equally an airgap will introduce reluctance into the magnetic flux path. A large airgap will produce high reluctance and a lower magnetic flux and vice versa if the airgap is small.

Going back to the fundamentals of electromagnetism, it will be remembered that if a coil is subjected to a change of magnetic field, voltage will be induced. The voltage generated will depend upon the following.

(a) *The rate at which the magnetic field changes.*
(b) *The number of turns of wire in the coil.*
(c) *The direction of flux change, ie increase or decrease.*

This principle is used in a device to trigger an ignition spark. The magnetic field is varied by altering the reluctance of the magnetic circuit (see Fig. 7.13).

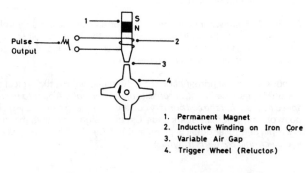

1. Permanent Magnet
2. Inductive Winding on Iron Core
3. Variable Air Gap
4. Trigger Wheel (Reluctor)

H.19733

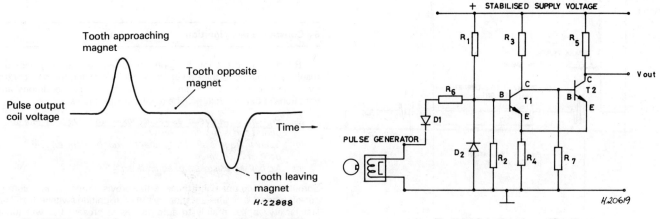

Fig. 7.13 Variable reluctance pulse generator (Secs 5 and 6)

As a trigger wheel tooth approaches the iron core of the pick-up winding, the flux rises rapidly only to fall as rapidly as the tooth moves away. The maximum voltage is generated just before and just after the teeth are opposite each other. The output is a form of alternating voltage which is passed through a pulse shaping circuit and on to the power transistor switch controlling the ignition coil current.

The output voltage will vary in two ways with a speed increase:

(a) *The frequency will increase.*
(b) *The magnitude will increase from a fraction of a volt upwards.*

Both these changes can be sensed and used by the electronic module into which the pulse generator output is fed.

The idea of using the flywheel teeth is also used on certain models, in which a sensor counts the teeth as a series of impulses and can then pass this information to the computer module to read speed and estimate advance required.

6   Pulse shaping

1   The signals produced by sensors have to some extent a smooth change (see Fig. 7.13) and are not sharp enough to produce a sudden clean cut-off of ignition coil current; additionally, the sensor voltage can vary with speed.

One solution is to pass the sensor voltage into a Schmitt trigger circuit which will produce a sharp square wave of constant peak voltage. The

Fig. 7.14 Schmitt trigger (Sec 6)

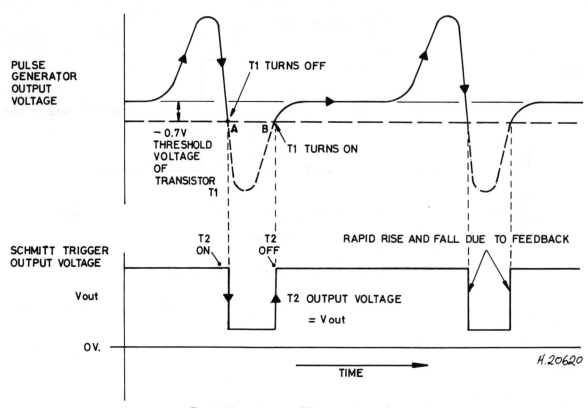

Fig. 7.15 Input/output of Schmitt trigger (Sec 6)

Schmitt trigger employs two transistors in which voltage signals from the second are sent back to the first (Fig. 7.14).

This is known as feedback and results in an extremely rapid switching action from ON to OFF and vice versa (Fig. 7.15). (In equipment literature similar pulse shapers are sometimes called flip-flops).

7   Dwell control

1   In contact breaker ignition, the DWELL ANGLE (the angle over which the contacts are closed) is fixed by the shape of the lobe(s) and the gap setting of the contact points. However, the DWELL PERIOD is not fixed and will decrease as the engine speeds up and it is the dwell period in time that determines how far the ignition coil primary current can build up before the next spark.

2   Fig. 7.16 shows a simplified waveform of coil secondary voltage. The high peak is the voltage provided by the ignition coil secondary winding; once the spark has begun, a lower, flat voltage plateau shows the voltage required to maintain the spark.

At point A the coil primary current is switched on and the typical dwell period begins. *Dwell control consists of moving point A back to the left as speed rises so that the coil primary current has time to rise.* The limit is the point of time when the spark ends. Circuit design to achieve this control is simple and fuller detail is given in the Author's *Automobile Electrical and Electronic Systems* (Haynes).

![Fig. 7.16 Coil secondary voltage]

Fig. 7.16 Coil secondary voltage (Sec 7)

8   Constant energy ignition

1   By monitoring the ignition primary current and feeding back the result as a voltage to the power transistors supplying the coil, control over the coil current is maintained over all engine conditions and variations of battery voltage. The results are as follows.

(a)   Primary current reaches a safe maximum value for a defined period and is limited to this value.
(b)   Spark voltage is almost constant throughout the engine performance range.
(c)   No ballast resistors are required.

Sometimes accompanying these is the provision for primary current cut-off when the engine is stationary but with ignition switched on. This last facility applies mainly to automobiles at present but will surely apply to motorcycles eventually.

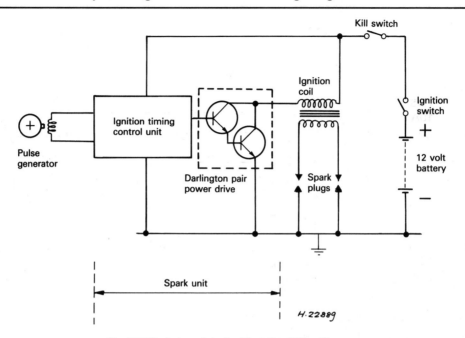

Fig. 7.17 Basic transistor ignition circuit (Sec 9)

9 Honda transistor ignition

1 Manufacturers' drawings generally show the sub-circuits described so far as one block diagram which may be labelled SPARK UNIT (for example) or ECU (Electronic Control Unit).

The spark units will each contain a pulse shaper, advance and dwell controls, an amplifier with a power stage for driving primary current into the ignition coils and a voltage stabiliser to ensure that a constant supply voltage is delivered to the electronic circuits irrespective of battery voltage variations.

2 A basic block diagram (Fig. 7.17) shows all this as an ignition timing control circuit and a Darlington pair power drive (see Chapter 2). Note the technique of using two spark plugs in series; although both will spark simultaneously, only one will fire a cylinder, the other spark being redundant in another cylinder not ready for combustion (a **wasted spark**).

3 A Honda diagram (Fig. 7.18) shows a four cylinder arrangement as

used on the CB750/900, NTV600, CBX750 and VT500 motorcycles. Note that one ignition coil drives spark plugs in 1 and 3 cylinders, and the other coil drives 2 and 4. To achieve this only two spark units and two pulse generators are needed.

4 An interesting variation is the Honda Gully Transistor Ignition system used on the VFR750FJ (Fig. 7.19). This uses one ignition coil per spark plug and a further pulse generator on the inlet front bank cam. Pulses from this sensor are used to indicate to the spark unit which coil to fire next in the ignition sequence. If the cam pulse generator fails, the engine will not run, so avoiding possible engine damage.

When the starter button is first pressed the engine turns over without firing until the spark unit receives its first signal from the cam pulse generator. Thus the ignition starts at the correct point in the cycle to match the engine rotation.

5 It is to be noted that these ignition circuits have provision for ignition advance with rise of engine speed only. No account is taken of load, ie how far the throttle is open and the result is an advance angle curve which is a good compromise but cannot be perfect.

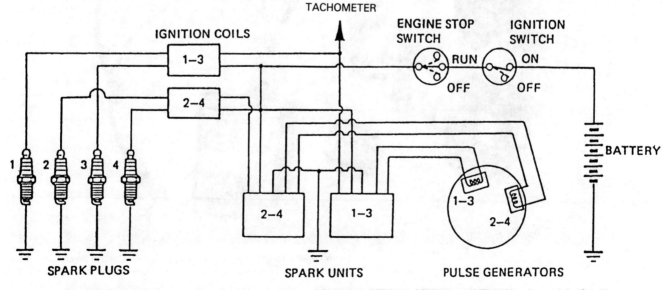

Fig. 7.18 Four cylinder transistor ignition as used on CB750/900, NTV600, CBX750 and VT500 Honda models (Sec 9)

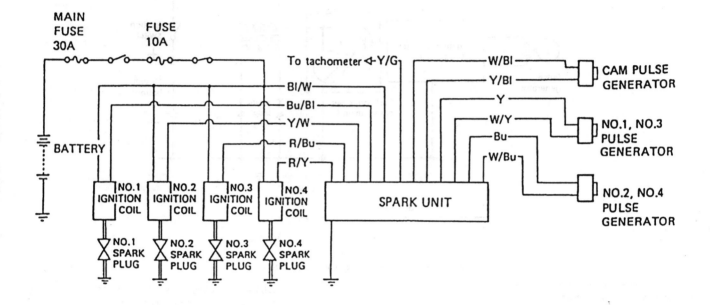

Fig. 7.19 Honda Gully transistor ignition system (Sec 9)

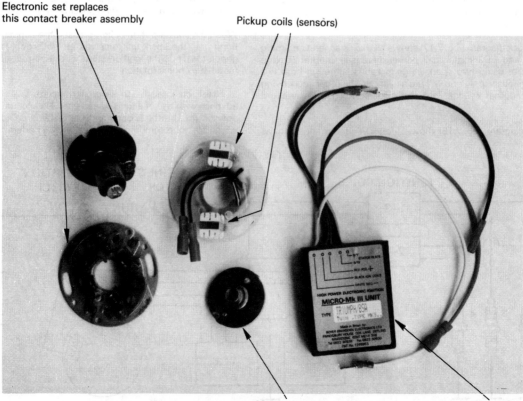

Fig. 7.20 Boyer-Bransden ignition system components (Sec 10)

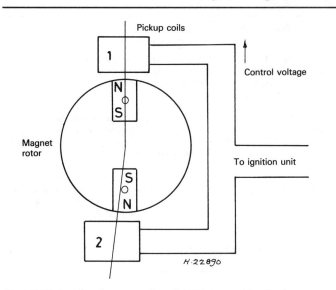

Fig. 7.21 Pulse signals are equal each 180° even with misalignment (Sec 10)

___

10 Aftermarket electronic ignition kits

___

Boyer Bransden ignition system

1   Originally designed for Boyer's production racing 500 and 650 Triumph twins, this system gained deserved popularity for conversion of British machines from Lucas 4CA and 6CA contact breaker units to electronic ignition.

Today, units are supplied for a wide range of British, German and Japanese motorcycles.

2   The mark 3 system converts a contact breaker twin into an electronic ignition machine with automatic speed advance. The camshaft-driven magnetic rotor turns beneath two sensor coils mounted at 180° to each other on a printed circuit board. These components replace the contact breaker mounting plate, the centrifugal advance unit and cam (Fig. 7.20).

Any variation or misalignment of coils, magnet or shaft balance out and pulses at 180° intervals are identical. This gives a high degree of accuracy of firing when the engine has been finally strobe-timed (Fig. 7.21).

3   Fig. 7.22 shows the layout of the electronic ignition set, shown here working off + 12 volts and driving two 6 volt ignition coils in series. Variations available include –12 volts supply and/or a single 12 volt ignition coil.

Operation

4   Looking at Figs. 7.22 and 7.23 together; the input pulse (A) has a positive and negative voltage wave (like a rough sine wave) and then a relatively long gap before the next pulse.

5   The pulses are amplified and passed through a limiting circuit resulting in a positive going pulse with a flat top (B). The point at which the square wave pulse rises and then cuts off is determined by the rise and fall of the input waveform A. Control of the rise point fixes the ignition advance angle.

6   Pulse (B) is fed into the flip-flop stage resulting in a sharp cut off of output voltage at point (C) at the leading edge of pulse (B). This corresponds to the instant of ignition sparking.

When pulse (B) returns to zero, the flip-flop voltage abruptly switches on and remains on until the next (B) pulse is received.

7   The output of the flip-flop now enters the dwell control circuit which ensures that the ignition coil primary current is switched on early enough to build up magnetic energy for the next spark.

An output power stage controls the ignition coil primary current switching (D) and is so arranged that the coil is switched off when the engine is stationary.

8   Note that contained in the amplifier-limiter is a circuit which responds to the input frequency and voltage and sets the points of the input wave at which wave B rises and falls.

After setting the timing at low speed, this circuit will produce a progressive advance of 10° camshaft from 1000 – 4500 rev/min up to a maximum of 15°.

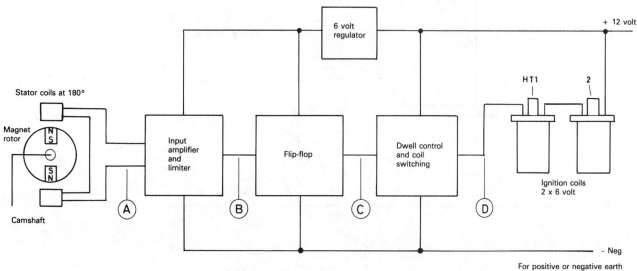

Fig. 7.22 Wiring diagram for Boyer-Bransden ignition system as fitted to British twin-cylinder models (Sec 10)

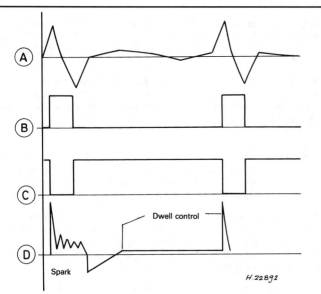

Fig. 7.23 Control box waveforms in Boyer-Bransden ignition (Sec 10)

See text for details

Lucas Rita ignition system

9   A number of variations of this Lucas transistor ignition set have been produced but essentially it consists of a sensor (called a pick-up in the information sheet) with a rotating reluctor feeding an amplifier. The amplifier drives one or two ignition coil primaries. In the circuit shown in Fig. 7.24 for a Norton Commando, two 6 volt coils have primary windings connected in series. The reluctor has to be set carefully for both the reluctor/sensor gap and for the correct firing position.

11   Digital ignition

1   Quite different from other methods, this system uses information on the engine status in the form of square on-off pulses and employs a digital computer to process this information to control the ignition timing with precision.

2   The key to this precision lies in the pre-programmed memory in the computer which has in store all correct ignition advance figures corresponding to engine speed and in some cases load and engine temperature among other possible parameters.

3   Several motorcycle engines are controlled by digital ignition circuits which take into account speed only and give good results. More complex systems exist, which allow for load (eg throttle opening), temperature, etc., and both will be considered in this chapter.

12   Ignition advance v engine design

1   When an engine is first built, the manufacturer will run it over the speed range and find, experimentally, the best angle of ignition advance for each speed.

At every spot value of speed, the ignition advance required is noted and a graph plotted like that shown in Fig. 7.25. This procedure will then be repeated for a series of throttle opening positions giving rise to a family of ignition advance graphs.

2   Ignition advance by centrifugal weights on a distributor or ignition camshaft is a poor match, with at best two different slopes between low speed and the point where the graph flattens out. Fig. 7.25 is an example of the actual engine requirement at one load and the best that a mechanical advance system might provide.

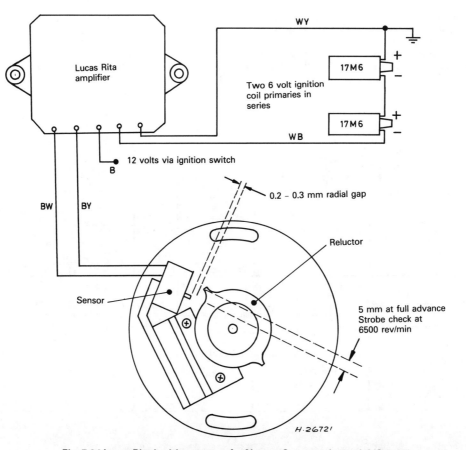

Fig. 7.24 Lucas Rita ignition system for Norton Commando model (Sec 10)

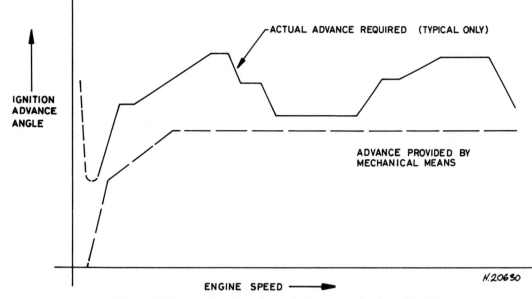

Fig. 7.25 A shortcoming of mechanical advance mechanisms (Sec 12)

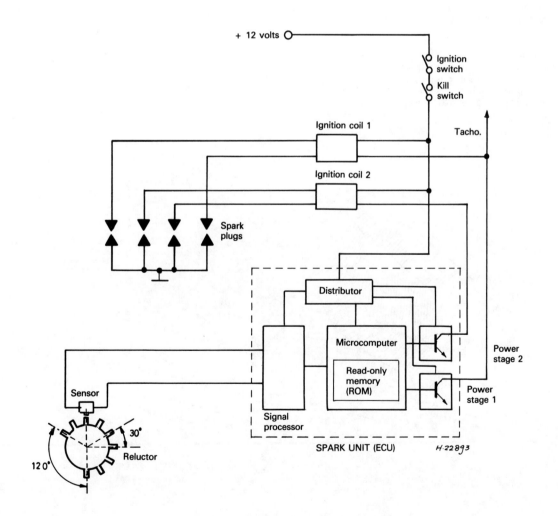

Fig. 7.26 Honda's digital ignition system (Sec 13)

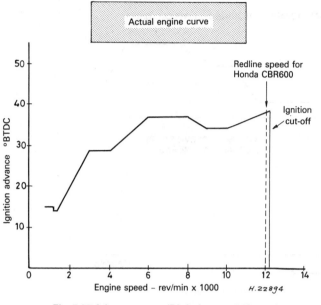

Fig. 7.27 Advance curve (Digital control) (Sec 13)

3   The digital system can store the ideal advance angle against speed in the memory ROM (Read Only Memory). Signals from the crankshaft speed sensor are fed into the microcomputer giving crankshaft speed; from this the computer will send ignition firing signals to the ignition coils.

4   It is not sufficient for the sensor to inform the computer about speed alone. The crankshaft position is also required and this is measured either by a special position-sensor or using a rotating reluctor which has certain teeth missing to identify to a single sensor where the piston is located. This can be Top Dead Centre (TDC) or sometimes 90° BTDC.

13   Digital ignition – speed control only

1   Fig. 7.26 shows a computer controlled digital ignition system as used on Honda 4-cylinder models CBR600/1000F (later models), VFR400R/750/750R, and ST1100.

The reluctor has nine projections and a single sensor. The angle between the ninth projection and the first is 120°, the others being 30° apart. This gives a means of finding the crank angle and the starting point for the ignition sequence. Pulses from the sensor first pass through a signal processor where they will be amplified and sharpened up into square-topped pulses.

2   As the 120° gap passes the sensor, no pulse voltage will be generated; when the first of the nine teeth passes under the sensor, the firing sequence commences. The 120° gap resets the computer (like pushing the reset button on a tripmeter) and the sequence repeats.

The rate at which teeth pass the sensor is measured by the computer as engine speed. Information stored in the ROM is interrogated and a figure for ignition timing will be retrieved and passed to one of the two power stages and an ignition coil.

Any engine can be controlled by this system by changing the ROM and position of the sensors.

3   Ignition timing will be precisely that required for optimum engine performance throughout the complete speed range, a typical curve being shown in Fig. 7.27.

4   Ignition cutout provision is built into the memory to prevent engine overspeed. This is achieved in two stages and in the case of the CBR600F motorcycle the computer cuts off ignition in cylinders 2 and 3 at 11,900 rev/min and cuts off cylinders 1 and 4 at approximately 12,500 rev/min. 'Redline' speed for the CBR600F is 12,000 rev/min.

5   To prevent the ignition coils overheating if the engine stops and the ignition switch remains on, an inhibitor circuit in the computer will cut power to the coils below a pre-determined speed (90 – 110 rev/min).

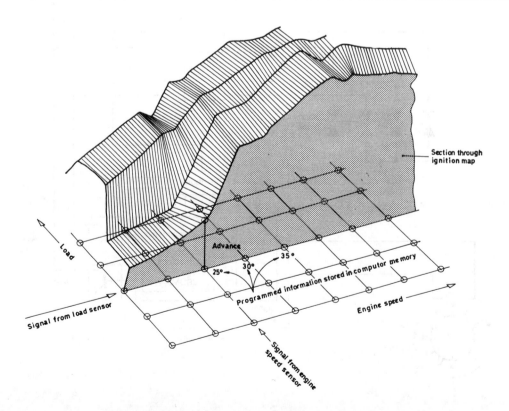

Fig. 7.28 Ignition map and stored information concept (Sec 14)

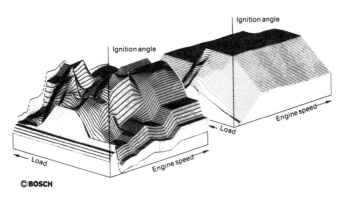

Fig. 7.29 Optimized electronic ignition advance map (left) compared with the ignition map of a mechanincal spark advance system (right) (Sec 14)

14   Mapped digital ignition

1   If a family of ignition advance/speed graphs were plotted separately for each position of throttle opening, there would be a large number of sheets to look up. Imagine them compressed together; the resulting block of graphs is now three dimensional as shown in Fig. 7.28. Here, three values are displayed. Ignition advance vertically, load and speed horizontally at right angles. Two spot values of load and speed are shown entered by the arrows. Where they cross on the horizontal grid, erect a vertical line to cut the solid surface. The height gives advance angle. The surface is like a 3 dimensional contour map and for this reason is known as **mapped ignition**. In practice the ignition map may be made up of 1000 – 4000 individual recallable ignition angle advance points.

2   It is interesting to see the difference between the optimum advance curve and the best that might be obtained by a mechanical contact breaker and advance system (Fig. 7.29). Clearly, if a digital ignition can 'read' the ideal graph, the result is a big improvement.

3   The condition of overrun is programmed specially for the purpose of fuel shut off above a certain speed when coasting downhill. A switch to signal this condition may be linked to the throttle.

4   When the engine runs, sensor signals enter the ignition control unit (or ECU or Spark Unit – all the same thing!) and are processed to give digital pulses.

These signal pulse voltages are then interpreted against the pre-programmed Read Only Memory (ROM) which fixes the correct ignition timing. Firing pulses are then sent to the transistor drive stages (usually Darlington Pairs) which operate the ignition coils.

15   Computerised ignition processing

1   In Section 13 the speed-only digital control was outlined. Here we move a stage further forward to consider computer control of ignition involving extra engine parameters.

2   Information may be fed into the computer in the form of electrical signals representing the following.

   (a)   Engine speed and crank position.
   (b)   Engine load.
   (c)   Coolant temperature (on liquid-cooled motorcycles).
   (d)   Battery voltage.
   (e)   Inlet air temperature and knock detectors may be found on more advanced systems.

3   Since computers handle digital pulses only, any electrical signals which are constant or slowly varying (ie analogue signals) will have to be converted to a corresponding train of square-topped digital pulses by an AD converter (AD means analogue to digital).

4   Engine speed/position signals are usually in pulse form and require no AD conversion, but load, temperature and battery voltage are in analogue form and need AD conversion.

The variables listed in paragraph 2 above are now looked at in more detail by reference to Fig. 7.30.

Engine load

5   Inlet manifold vacuum gives a measure of load as is well known in the case of the car distributor vacuum unit. In a motorcycle there are other ways of measuring the vacuum – for instance by an aneroid capsule similar to that in a barometer, but with the addition of an electrical sensor sensitive to movement.

If air temperature is measured electrically and this signal also is fed to the computer, an allowance can be made for variation of air density with

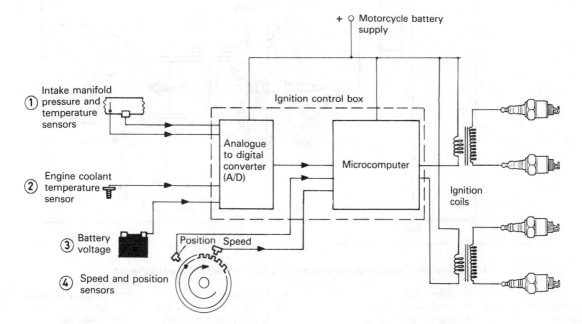

Fig. 7.30 Schematic layout of digital electronic ignition system (Sec 15)

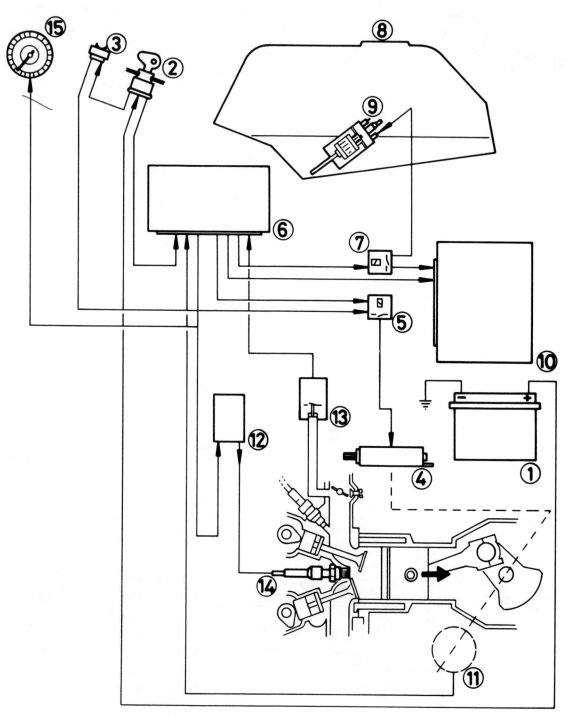

H.19486

Fig. 7.31 Ignition system components on the BMW K75 and 100 models (Sec 15)

1 Battery	5 Starter relay	9 Fuel pump	13 Vacuum switch (where fitted)
2 Ignition switch	6 Ignition control unit	10 Fuel injection control unit	
3 Starter button	7 Injector relay	11 Ignition trigger assembly	14 Spark plug
4 Starter motor	8 Fuel tank	12 Ignition HT coil	15 Tachometer

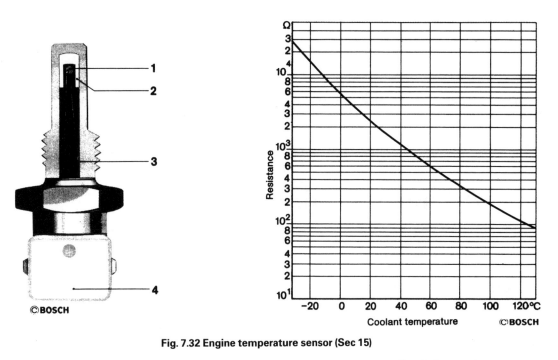

Fig. 7.32 Engine temperature sensor (Sec 15)

1 Negative temperature coefficient semiconductor resistor (NTC bead)	2 Insulation 3 Sealing compound	4 Electrical connection

The graph shows the resistance change with temperature of NTC bead (negative temperature coefficient)

temperatures. This information is particularly needed for fuel injected engines. It must be realised that it is **air mass flow** that we really want to measure and a better way of doing this is by a hot wire or hot surface airflow sensor, these devices being designed to take into account air temperature and density (see Chapter 8 for details).

An interesting way of dealing with engine load in the part load condition occurs with pre 1985 BMW K100 models in which a vacuum switch was located in the inlet manifold (Fig. 7.31). On part load the switch brought in a second advance curve but in practice this had so little effect that it was omitted on later models.

Engine temperature
6   Temperature sensors are usually of the semiconductor type, known as thermistors, which have displaced earlier thermocouple units for situations below 200°C (400°F).

The bead of semiconductor material has a marked negative temperature coefficient of resistance, and a working range of at least –20°C to +130°C. It is suitable for measuring coolant temperature and is mounted in a screw-in capsule (Fig. 7.32) in a water channel in the cylinder block. The sensitivity is good for accurate temperature measurements to within 0.05°C.

Battery voltage
7   This is a correcting quantity; if the battery voltage deviates from a set standard, the time allowed for energising the coil (dwell period) is

lengthened or shortened so that constant energy conditions are obtained.

Engine speed and crankshaft position
8   Sensors of the Hall type or variable reluctance type have already been met in Section 5 of this Chapter.

---

16 Ignition and fuelling

---

1   In Chapter 3 we have seen that both ignition and fuelling affect performance and pollution levels.

Along with the developments in ignition has come an increasing use of electronically controlled fuel injection, giving much better use of fuel than is usually achieved with a carburettor.

2   Fuel injection is explained in the following chapter and it is interesting to see that initially ignition and fuel injection were controlled as separate units.

Now it is possible to combine the two controls into one electronic system which will manage both ignition advance and fuelling. It is known as Engine Management and is still relatively new in motorcycle applications (see Chapter 9).

Chapter 8 Fuel injection

Contents

1 Fuel metering

1   The petrol/gasoline engine requires a supply of fuel in the form of a vapour of air and fuel in a ratio within the range 12:1 to 17:1, the first being a rich mixture and the second a weak or lean mixture.

From the beginning of petrol/gasoline engine technology this has been achieved, not always with precision, by the carburettor. Now anti-pollution regulations require exact metering of fuel, particularly where catalytic converters are used, and have brought about a surge in fuel injection automobile engine production. The motorcycle engine is also appearing with fuel injection, particularly on larger models.

2   Although the carburettor is now available with electronic controls to improve precision of fuel metering, fuel injection is rapidly gaining ground. It is by no means a new idea – much pioneering work being done by Bendix in the 1950s. The principal advantages of fuel injection are as follows.

(a)   *Increased power output per unit of displacement.*
(b)   *Higher torque at low engine speeds.*
(c)   *Improved cold start, warm-up and acceleration.*
(d)   *Lower pollution levels from the exhaust.*
(e)   *Lower fuel consumption.*

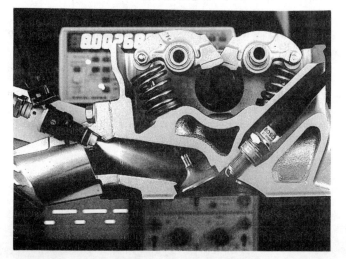

Fig. 8.1 Indirect fuel injection (Sec 2)

Disadvantages of the carburettor can be summed up as follows.

(a)   *Volumetric efficiency is limited by the venturi constriction and fuel mixture pre-heating requirement. Volumetric efficiency is the ratio:*

    Volume of mixture actually taken in : Swept volume

    and is about 70% using conventional carburation.
(b)   *It is virtually impossible to distribute the mixture evenly between cylinders. One result is the use of a richer mixture than might otherwise be required so that the cylinder(s) receiving the weakest mixture do not suffer from detonation.*
(c)   *In cold conditions, fuel wets the walls of the induction manifold causing running difficulties.*

2 Fuel injection

1   There are several ways in which fuel may be injected; the first consideration is whether injection should be directly into each cylinder (direct injection) or into the airstream before entering the cylinder via the inlet valve(s) (Fig. 8.1).

Direct injection has been ruled out in present designs because of complexity. Fuel would need to be injected at high pressure by an expensive and noisy pump; also the injection pulses would need to be synchronised with the engine cycle.

Indirect injection in which the fuel is sprayed at one or more points in the air intake system operates at lower pressures, and the injectors can be triggered simultaneously with no engine-cycle synchronisation.

2   With indirect injection there are then two ways of supplying the fuel to the injectors.

Continuous injection – Fuel is sprayed continuously while the engine is running, the quantity of fuel being governed by changes in the fuel pressure. However, the ratio of idle to full load fuel consumption can be 1:60 with high accuracy at the low end being required. Pump and system design is complex and is not a favoured option.

Intermittent injection – Fuel is sprayed at regular intervals at constant pressure (see later). The quantity of fuel is determined by the length of spraying time. These spraying pulses may take place EITHER without regard to the opening of the inlet valves (simultaneous) OR being correctly phased in relation to the opening of the inlet valves (sequential).

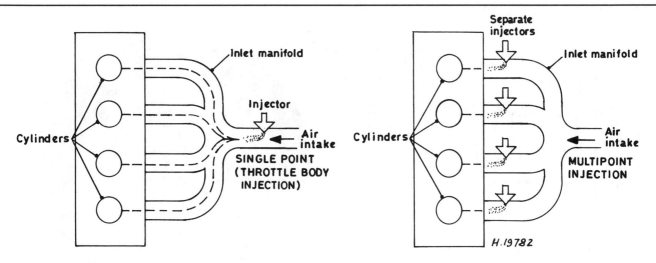

Fig. 8.2 Positions for fuel injectors (Sec 2)

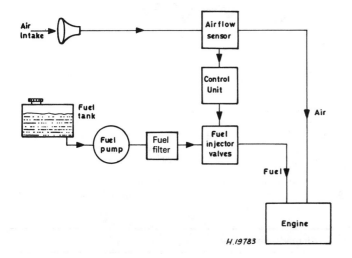

Fig. 8.3 Principle of fuel injection (Sec 2)

3   Finally, designers have to choose between the use of only one injector per engine (single-point injection) or one injector per cylinder (multi-point injection) (Fig. 8.2).

4   Past and present designs favour multi-point injection on motorcycles, but there is no technical reason why single-point injection should not be used in the future.

The single point injector valve is located above the throttle valve and is a relatively low-cost system. Because the injector is so located it is sometimes known as throttle-body injection (TBI). Multi-point injection is in use in the majority of systems, particularly where the extra cost is not an overriding consideration. Whichever method is used, the basic principle is illustrated in Fig. 8.3.

3   Flap sensor air metering

1   In order that the electronic control system can provide the correct amount of fuel it is necessary to measure the amount of air taken by the engine.

The airflow (flap) sensor in use for some years is shown in Fig. 8.4. It is located in the air intake and the flap (2) will rotate due to airflow against a spring return. It is balanced by a similar flap in a damping chamber which not only balances the main flap but damps out any tendency to oscillate.

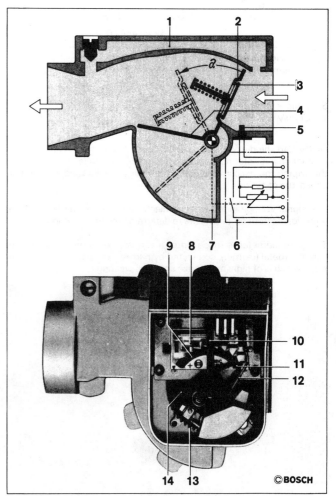

Fig. 8.4 Airflow (flap) sensor (Sec 3)

1   Bypass
2   Airflow sensor flap
3   Non-return valve
4   Compensation flap
5   Temperature sensor
6   Potentiometer circuit
7   Damping chamber
8   Ceramic substrate with resistors R0 ... R10 and conductor straps
9   Wiper track
10 Wiper tap
11 Wiper
12 Safety switch for the fuel pump. Off position at a = 0°
13 Ring gear for spring preloading
14 Return spring

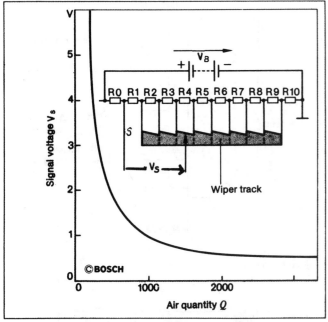

Fig. 8.5 Airflow meter output characteristic (Sec 3)
*Potentiometer circuit and voltage characteristic of the airflow sensor.
The characteristic is a hyperbola since $V_s = 1/Q$*

S	Conductor straps	V_s	Tapping point voltage
V_B	Supply voltage		

On the flap spindle outside the airflow chamber is an arm with a wiping contact on a resistor potentiometer (Fig. 8.5). The voltage picked up by this wiping contact corresponds to the angle of the flap and this in turn is a measure of airflow.

The signal voltage is fed into the Electronic Control Unit (ECU) along with signals from other sensors to determine the fuel injection.

The potentiometer is made up of a series of resistors R0 to R10 of ceramic-metal (cermet), connected by narrow conductors to the wiper track which is of high impedance and hard wearing.

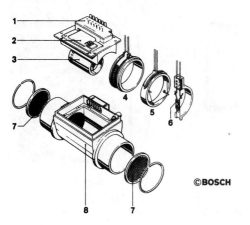

Fig. 8.7 Hot wire air mass flow meter assembly (Sec 4)

1	Printed board	3	Inner tube
2	Hybrid circuit. In addition to the resistors of the bridge circuit, it also contains the control circuit for maintaining a constant temperature and the self-cleaning circuit	4	Precision resistor
		5	Hot wire element
		6	Temperature compensation resistor
		7	Guard
		8	Housing

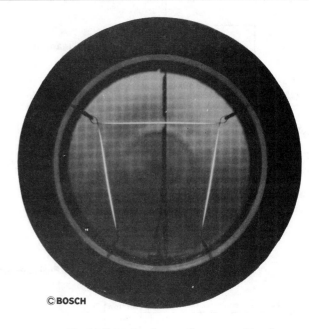

Fig. 8.6 Hot wire air mass flow meter (Sec 4)

Signal voltage is high as the air quantity Q goes down resulting in the graph shown in Fig. 8.5.

2   The airflap sensor is simple and reliable but suffers from the disadvantage that it measures the volume of intake air. Air to fuel ratios are in terms of mass (weight) and the flap meter readings will require correction for air density. An air temperature sensor is mounted at the air intake to the flap sensor, the signal being processed by the ECU.

3   The flap is bypassed by a channel for idle air and an adjusting screw partially closes an orifice to regulate the idle mixture (Fig. 8.4. item 1).

4   Air mass-flow meters

1   The disadvantage of the airflap sensor lies in the fact that it measures volume of air intake and not the mass (weight). Errors are introduced according to altitude, since the density of air falls with increasing altitude and, in addition, the airflap sensor is subject to slight pulsation errors due to sudden opening or closing of inlet valves. (Remember: Mass = Volume x Density).

2   One solution lies in the hot wire air mass meter which will measure the air mass directly, independent of air density (altitude) changes (Figs. 8.6 and 8.7). In addition, there is no pulsation error. This type of sensor

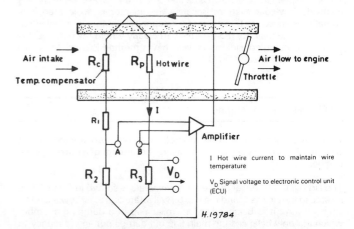

Fig. 8.8 Hot wire air mass meter electrical circuit (Sec 4)

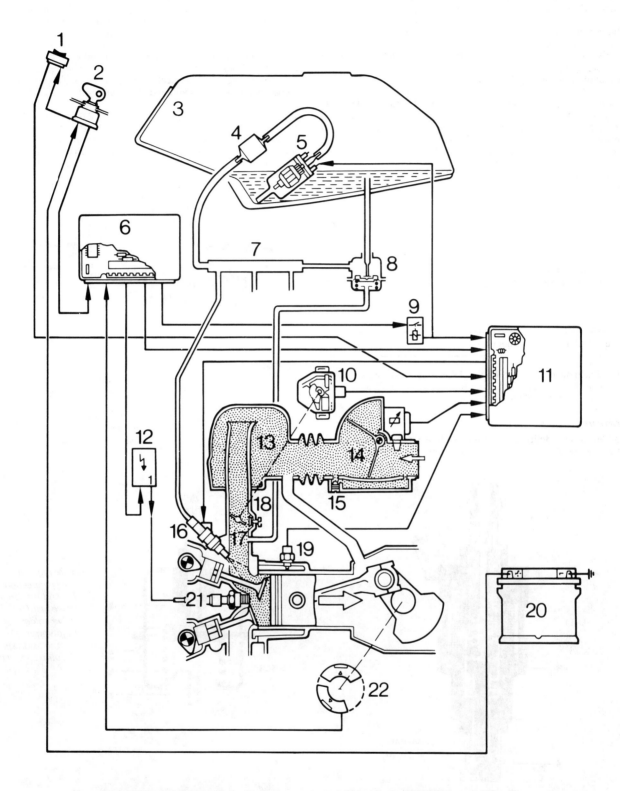

Fig. 8.9 Bosch LE-Jetronic fuel injection system as fitted to the BMW K75 model (Sec 5)

1	Starter switch	7	Fuel supply rail
2	Ignition switch	8	Pressure regulator
3	Fuel tank	9	Injection relay
4	Fuel filter	10	Throttle butterfly switch
5	Fuel pump	11	Electronic Control Unit
6	Ignition control unit		(ECU)

12	HT coil
13	Air collector
14	Airflow meter
15	Bypass air screw
16	Injector
17	Throttle butterfly

18	Idle adjusting screw
19	Coolant temperature
	sensor
20	Battery
21	Spark plug
22	Hall-effect trigger

uses a heated wire of 70μm diameter mounted in a measuring tube in the incoming airstream before the throttle valve.

3   The hot wire air mass meter works on the constant temperature principle. The hot platinum wire is one arm of a Wheatstone Bridge which is kept in balance by changing the heating current so that the temperature (about 100°C, 212°F) of the hot wire is a constant amount above that of the incoming air (Fig. 8.8).

As airflow increases the wire cools and the resistance falls. This unbalances the bridge, the difference voltage between A and B being fed into an amplifier, the output of which supplies the bridge so heating up the wire and increasing its resistance until balance is restored. The range of heating current is from 500 – 1200mA.

The increase of current will flow through the precision resistor R_3 and the voltage drop across it is read as a signal by the ECU in calculation of the fuel to be injected.

The hot wire sensor is presently used in automobiles but is included here because it will surely supersede the air flap valves in motorcycle fuel injection.

Readers wanting more information on mass flow sensors should refer to the Author's book *Automobile Electrical and Electronic Systems* (Haynes).

---

5   Bosch LE-Jetronic fuel injection

---

1   This Bosch system is used on the BMW K-series engines. Fig. 8.9 shows the system fitted to the K75 models and serves here as a model to explain the principles of intermittent multi-point fuel injection.

Operation

2   Fuel and air are admitted as a correct mixture with engine speed and intake air volume as the main controlling factors.

The volume of air supplied to form the combustion mixture is drawn in by the engine and varied by the angle of the throttle butterflies (17). The fuel injection system then supplies the correct amount of fuel in the form of a spray from an injector (16) located in the inlet tract.

3   The three injectors (one for each cylinder) have nozzles which are opened and closed by solenoids wound in the injector units (Fig. 8.10). All three injectors are electrically connected in parallel so opening at the same time once per revolution of the crankshaft.

When open, fuel is sprayed at a pressure of 2.5 bar (36 lbf/in²) until the electric signal current in the solenoids is cut off by the control unit, the 'on' period being between 1.5 and 9 milliseconds (ms). The fuel spray mixes with the incoming air as both move towards the inlet valve, giving a precisely metered combustion mixture. The complete system has three areas as follows.

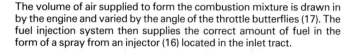
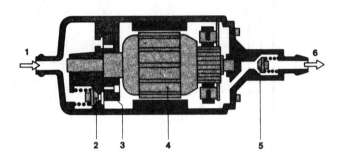

©**BOSCH**

Roller cell fuel pump
1   Intake (suction) side
2   Pressure limiter
3   Roller cell pump
4   Motor armature
5   Non-return valve
6   Pressure side

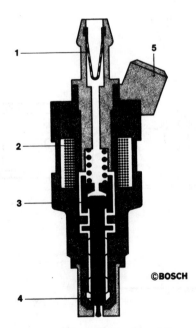

Fig. 8.10 Fuel injector cross-section (Sec 5)
With no current in the solenoid, the needle valve is held against its seating by a spring. When the coil is energised the needle valve is lifted 0.1 mm. The pintle atomises the fuel into a fine spray

1 Filter	*4 Needle valve*	
2 Solenoid winding	*5 Electrical connection*	
3 Solenoid armature	*6 Pintle*	

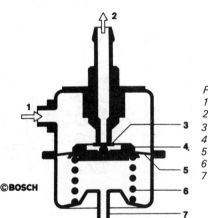

©**BOSCH**

Pressure regulator
1   Fuel connection
2   Fuel return connection
3   Valve plate
4   Valve holder
5   Diaphragm
6   Compression spring
7   Vacuum connection

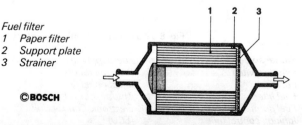

Fuel filter
1   Paper filter
2   Support plate
3   Strainer

©**BOSCH**

Fig. 8.11 Fuel system components (Sec 5)

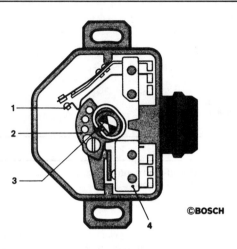

Fig. 8.12 Throttle butterfly valve switch (Sec 5)

1   *Full-load contact*
2   *Contact path*

3   *Throttle valve shaft*
4   *Idle contact*

Fuel system

4   Fuel is pumped from the tank by a roller-cell pump (5) through a fuel filter (4) into a fuel rail (7) at the end of which is a fuel pressure regulator (8).

In order to keep the injector pressure differential constant despite variations of inlet manifold depression with load, the fuel pressure regulator senses the difference between pumping pressure and that of the inlet manifold.

Excess fuel is returned to the tank, the continuous flushing keeping the fuel cool and avoiding pockets of fuel vapour.

Filtering of the fuel is important in case dirty fuel gets into the tank; the filter has a $10\mu m$ pore-size paper cartridge requiring eventual replacement. Details of the roller cell pump, pressure regulator and the fuel filter are shown in Fig. 8.11.

Air intake system

5   The airflow meter (14) has already been described in Section 3 of this Chapter.

As the airflow varies so will the angle of the airflap (14). A potentiometer is mounted on the airflap spindle, and a voltage picked off by a sliding contact connected to the spindle will signal the quantity Q of air being taken in by the engine.

The airflow meter has a by-pass screw (15) which may be adjusted externally and is used to set the CO emission of the exhaust gases.

Electronic control system

6   The volume of fuel injected per crankshaft revolution into all the intake tracts simultaneously is fixed by the time over which the injectors are open. To control this open period, an Electronic Control Unit (ECU) (11) passes current pulses to the injector solenoid windings (16) which pull open the nozzles. The time length of these pulses depends upon the following five factors.

(a)   *Engine speed information from the Hall-effect trigger (22) via the ignition control unit (6).*
(b)   *Special cold start and normal start programmes initiated by operating the starter switch (1).*
(c)   *Engine load information from the throttle butterfly switch (10). To achieve maximum power output on full load, the engine must have a richer mixture than when on part load. This switch signals to the ECU (11) that enrichment is required (Fig. 8.12). The idling state is shown when the idle switch closes.*
(d)   *Air volume as indicated by the airflow meter (14).*
(e)   *Engine temperature, measured by the coolant temperature sensor screwed into a coolant channel (19).*

Chapter 9 Engine management

Contents

1 Combined control of ignition and fuelling

1   The motorcycle engine has two supplying units for the production of power, one being the supply of atomised fuel in correct quantity and correct air:fuel ratio, the other being the supply of an igniting spark at the correct timing. For most of this century, these two provisions of fuelling and sparks have been dealt with separately. However, Chapter 3 *Ignition and Combustion* shows that the relationships of optimum power, fuel economy and exhaust pollution involve both fuelling and ignition.

2   Digital ignition circuits use a microcomputer in the ignition control unit and this computer is capable of controlling other tasks in addition, ie it has spare capacity.

Up to this stage of development, fuel injection control units, although fully electronic, did not use digital methods but, instead, multivibrator technology, and these were not compatible with the ignition control boxes.

3   Bosch developed a digital electronic control system for fuel injection and combined it with the digital ignition control to form a simple controller – this is the Motronic system. It uses one control unit to sense the necessary engine conditions and to produce ignition pulses and fuel injector pulses accordingly.

4   Although Motronic has been in use for some time, it has now been applied to the 16-valve models in the BMW range.

2 Performance mapping

1   Three-dimensional mapping has been discussed in Chapter 7 to explain the interlink between engine speed, load and ignition (advance) angle.

2   With the memory capacity available to the microcomputer, further sets of three-dimensional information can be stored which relate to additional variables. Two examples are shown in Figs. 9.1 and 9.2. The Lambda map shows how engine speed and load relate to λ, the Lambda factor. (Remember Lambda λ is 1.0 for air:fuel ratio of 14.7:1. Higher than 1.0 is a weaker mixture and lower is a richer mixture.) The value of Lambda λ is critical to keep pollution levels low and assumes special importance where a catalytic converter is fitted.

Another set of information which a control unit may store is the relationship between engine speed, battery voltage and dwell angle (Fig. 9.2). It is possible in the more complex engine management units to store and use other interdependent quantities such as engine speed, load and warm-up enrichment.

The sensors which measure all these variables are often the same type used in both fuel-injection and ignition: it is a matter of natural development that one set of sensors and one control unit should suffice.

3 Open- and closed-loop control

1   When the engine maps are drawn up the results are stored in the permanent memory (ROM) of the micro-processor. The engine will be operated according to the figures in store for any value of speed or load. However, an assumption is made that the engine remains in the same condition as when the performance maps were plotted.

2   This cannot be so, for as the engine wears there will be wear on the piston, valve guides and throttle spindles so that the air intake, for example, will soon become different from what the micro-processor believes it to be from the sensor inputs. This situation is one of **open-loop control**, meaning that there is no check on the actual performance of the engine or the actual exhaust emission. Similarly, the

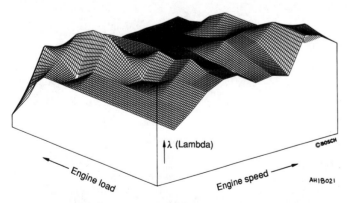

Fig. 9.1 Lambda map (Sec 2)

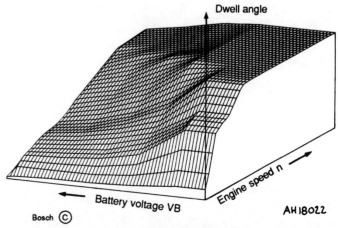

Fig. 9.2 Dwell map (Sec 2)

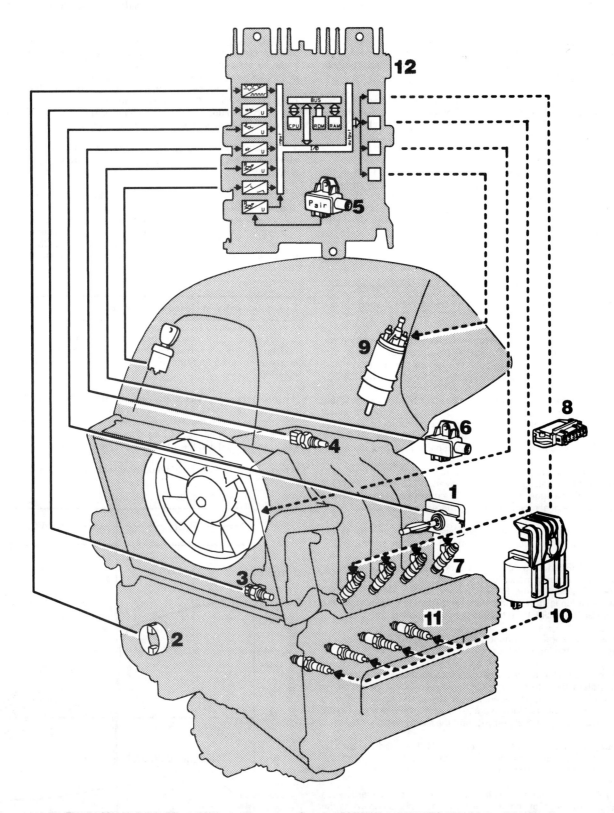

Fig. 9.3 Motronic engine management system as fitted to BMW K1 and K100RS 16-valve models (Sec 4)

1	Throttle butterfly angle sensor	4	Air temperature sensor	7	Fuel injectors
2	Hall ignition sensors	5	Air pressure sensor	8	Power amplifier
3	Engine temperature sensor	6	Variable resistor	9	Fuel pump

10	Ignition coils
11	Spark plugs
12	Motronic control unit

ignition performance could go off tune resulting in loss of power (retard) or engine knock if the errors result in advancing ignition too far.

3   The solution to these possible problems lies in measuring the performance with sensors, the signals from which can be fed back to the Electronic Control Unit (ECU). The ECU can then adjust timing or mixture to standard values.

4   Engine knock can be detected by a vibration sensor attached to the cylinder block, and incorrect mixture by a Lambda sensor situated in the exhaust gas stream. Feedback by these sensors gives a **closed-loop control** system which holds the required values throughout the life of the engine and takes into account engine deterioration with time.

5   At the time of writing, knock sensors appear to be used in the automobile and not on the motorcycle, but the technology of knock control is firmly established and could well appear in a motorcycle engine management system at any time. Lambda sensors are used for closed-loop control in fuelling and, as stated, find special use in exhaust systems with catalytic converters.

---

4   Bosch Motronic – BMW 16-valve models

1   This digital control is the first engine management system applied to a production motorcycle.

Referring to Fig. 9.3, note that the four-cylinder engine has ignition and fuel injection controlled by the single Motronic control unit (12). The system is of the open-loop type, but a closed-loop version is available with a catalytic converter and Lambda exhaust sensor (see Section 5).

2   The vertical row of boxes on the left side of the Motronic control unit (12) are signal processors. Inputs from sensors are fed into signal processor circuits to ensure that all outputs to the computer are in the form of digital pulses. In the case of the Hall ignition sensors (2), the input will be in pulse form already and only shaping will be required.

Other inputs may be steady or slowly varying voltages; these are said to be in analogue form and will need to be converted into equivalent digital values by an analogue to digital (AD) converter. AD converters constitute those signal processor boxes where inputs are analogue.

The digital outputs of the signal processor boxes are fed to the input/output rail for transporting to the main heart of the computer.

3   The ROM (Read Only Memory) contains performance maps for optimum engine performance corresponding to any possible set of conditions. Adjacent is the RAM (Random Access Memory) where signal information is stored temporarily and taken out again to aid the CPU (Central Processing Unit) to carry out calculations.

All of this information movement is carried by the BUS between CPU, ROM, RAM and the Input/Output rail.

4   When the CPU has made the necessary calculations for ignition and injection pulses, this information is fed to the set of boxes shown on the right of the control unit. These are output stages and activate ignition and fuelling components. Outputs are to the ignition power amplifier (8), the fuel injectors (7), the fuel pump (9) and the electric fan.

5   Inputs are, most importantly, from the Hall ignition sensors (2) which give speed and top-dead centre information, and from the throttle butterfly angle sensor (1).

The angle of throttle opening (alpha) and the engine speed n are, when multiplied, a measure of the air intake volume. This is known as the alpha-n principle and dispenses with the usual airflow meter.

Correction is necessary for air temperature measured by a Negative Temperature Coefficient capsule NTC (4) and engine temperature by another NTC (3) mounted in the coolant jacket.

Finally, to allow for altitude variation, an air pressure sensor (5) is built into the Motronic control unit.

A variable resistor (6) enables carbon monoxide emissions to be adjusted at idle.

6   Output stages from the Motronic control unit control fuelling, fan and fuel pump. In the case of ignition, pulses are sent from the output stage to a power amplifier (8) (mounted on the battery carrier for cooling) which switches current to the ignition coil primaries (10), the secondary windings being connected by high voltage cable to the spark plugs (11). Injectors (7) are controlled to give half the required volume of fuel every revolution of the crankshaft, with provision for doubling of fuel pulse frequency while the engine is being started.

7   Fuel cut-off when coasting operates providing the engine speed is above 2000 rev/min and the engine temperature is higher than 70°C (158°F).

8   Fail-safe provision allows for a possibility of an absent input signal due to a fault condition. The computer switches to a pre-programmed substitute value so that ignition and injection continue without interruption. Missing signals from sensors are registered in a fault memory and will be read out at the next service by BMW diagnostic equipment. No substitute signal is available for the engine speed sensor.

---

5   Lambda exhaust closed-loop control

1   In Chapter 3, the pollutant products of combustion were discussed and the catalytic converter was shown to be a highly successful solution in reducing toxic outputs to within the limits specified by most countries.

It is an overriding proviso that an engine fitted with a catalytic converter must run on unleaded fuel and have an air:fuel ratio at which combustion will be theoretically complete. This Stoichiometric ratio is 14.7:1 by mass, meaning 14.7 kg of air to 1 kg of fuel. It is convenient to call this figure 1.0 and the international symbol is Lambda (λ).

A comparison is given overleaf between actual numerical ratios and the

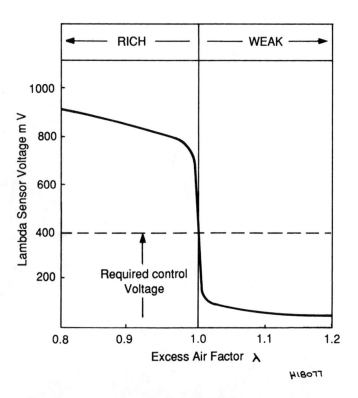

Fig. 9.4 Lambda sensor voltage characteristic at 600°C (1112°F)
(Sec 5)

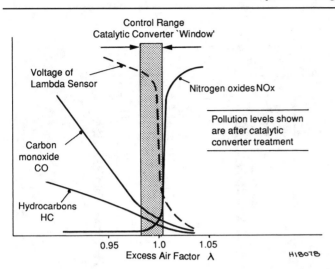

Fig. 9.5 Lambda sensor voltage curve and pollutants in exhaust (Sec 5)

corresponding Lambda figure. In some literature λ is called the Excess Air Factor.

Air/fuel ratio	11.76	13.23	14.7	16.17	17.64
Excess Air Factor	0.8	0.9	1.0	1.1	1.2

2   So far, the fuel injection systems described have no check on the results of injector control as far as exhaust emissions are concerned and are only measured when the engine is serviced. Such a system is said to have open-loop control.

3   To measure the state of exhaust gases, a Lambda sensor (sometimes called an exhaust gas oxygen (EGO) sensor) is fitted in the exhaust (muffler) pipe. This sensor measures the oxygen left unburned in the exhaust gases (a measure of excess air factor) and generates a signal voltage (Fig. 9.4) which is fed back to the Electronic Control Unit (ECU) as an additional unit of information.

In turn the ECU will correct the fuel injection to ensure that the excess air factor is within a narrow range around unity (ie λ = 1); this range is called the catalytic converter window (Fig. 9.5). Because the output information (ie state of exhaust gas) is fed back to the ECU which in turn controls the output, this is an example of closed-loop control (Fig. 9.6).

4   The graphs in Fig. 9.5 show that carbon monoxide quantities rise sharply just below λ = 1.0 and nitrogen oxides rise rapidly just above

λ = 1.0. From this it will be seen that maintaining the Stoichiometric ratio at λ = 1.0 is vital to the success of the catalytic converter.

6   Operation of the Lambda sensor

1   The sensor is an exhaust gas oxygen measuring device which works like a small battery. It is about the size of a spark plug, screws into the exhaust (muffler) system and is exposed to the full flow of the exhaust gases. The presence of oxygen in the exhaust gases means that the mixture is weak (λ greater than 1.0), whereas no oxygen indicates a rich mixture (λ less than 1.0).

2   The Lambda sensor (or exhaust gas oxygen sensor, EGO) uses a ceramic body made of zirconium dioxide (ZrO_2) in the shape of a long thimble; the outer surface is exposed to the exhaust gases and the inner surface is in contact with the outside air (Fig. 9.7).

The zirconium dioxide is covered inside and out with two thin layers of porous platinum which act as electrodes from which the output signal voltage is taken. Extra protection is given by coating the surface exposed to the exhaust with a layer of porous alumina through which the exhaust gas can penetrate.

The zirconium dioxide acts as the (solid) electrolyte; the inside surface is exposed to air which has 21% oxygen content and the outer surface is exposed to the exhaust gas.

The sensor develops a voltage between the inner and outer surfaces according to the difference of oxygen concentration and the voltage is collected at the two platinum electrodes (Fig. 9.8).

3   When the engine is working with a rich mixture the voltage generated will be about 900 millivolts (mV). This drops abruptly at the Stoichiometric point and levels off to about 50 mV in the weak region.

The change is abrupt so that the sensor acts almost like an on-off switch and the signals it sends to the ECU, together with wave re-shaping and the rapid correction produced by the ECU, mean that the signal is like an on-off square wave maintaining the excess air factor at very close to λ = 1.0 (Fig. 9.9).

4   The output voltage is strongly influenced by temperature since the electrolyte ZrO_2 does not become conductive below 300°C (572°F); ideally the sensor should work at about 600°C (1112°F). In addition, the response time at 300°C (572°F) is several seconds but at 600°C (1112°F) the sensor reacts in less than 50 ms.

For these reasons the location of the sensor is critical – too far away

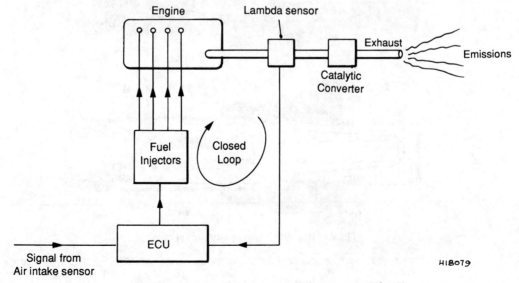

Fig. 9.6 Lambda closed-loop excess air factor control (Sec 5)

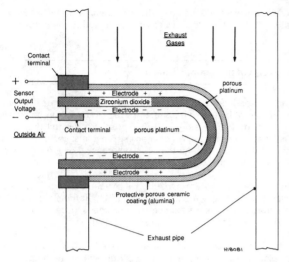

Fig. 9.7 Schematic of Lambda sensor (Sec 6)

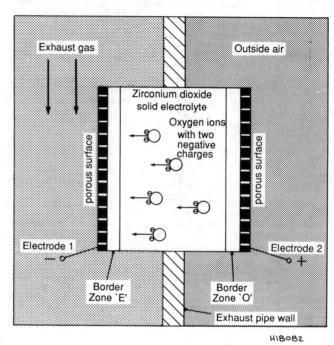

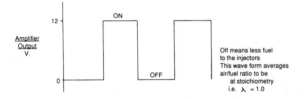

Fig. 9.8 Lambda sensor operation (Sec 6)

When in the vicinity of the electrode surface, residual oxygen is bound to hydrogen, carbon monoxide and hydrocarbons. If the mixture goes from weak to rich, border zone E becomes depleted of oxygen. Large numbers of oxygen ions migrate to electrode 1, causing this to go negative relative to electrode 2. This gives the sensor voltage used in the Lambda closed-loop control system

Fig. 9.9 Control waveforms in Lambda control system (Sec 6)

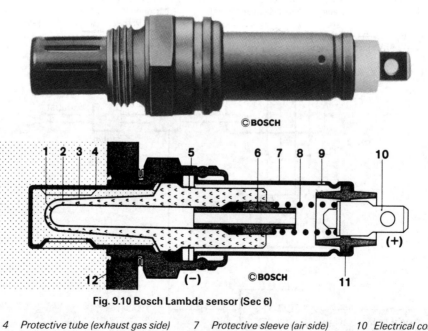

Fig. 9.10 Bosch Lambda sensor (Sec 6)

1 Electrode (+)	4 Protective tube (exhaust gas side)	7 Protective sleeve (air side)	10 Electrical connection
2 Electrode (–)	5 Housing (–)	8 Contact spring	11 Insulating part
3 Ceramic body	6 Contact bush	9 Ventilation opening	12 Exhaust (muffler) wall

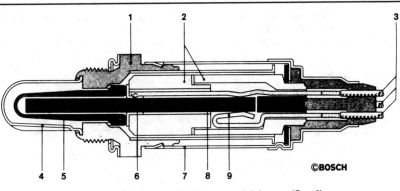

Fig. 9.11 Lambda sensor with heater (Sec 6)

1	*Sensor housing*	4	*Protective tube with slots*
2	*Protective ceramic tube*	5	*Active sensor ceramic*
3	*Connection cable*		

6	*Contact section*	8	*Heating element*
7	*Protective sleeve*	9	*Clamp terminals for heating element*

from the engine and the sensor would not work, too near and on long hot runs the sensor would be destroyed. (Note – maximum temperature should not exceed 850°C, 1562°F). A Lambda sensor is shown in Fig. 9.10.

Some units have a built in heater (Fig. 9.11) for use under low engine load conditions; the heater is switched off on high loading. The location is still important but the Lambda control is up to temperature and working after 25 seconds.

Properly installed the heated Lambda sensor has an expected life of

62,000 miles (100,000 km). Unleaded fuel must be used to avoid damage to the active outer platinum electrode.

7   Catalytic converter

BMW system
1   This was the first motorcycle catalytic converter with Lambda closed-loop control to be offered.

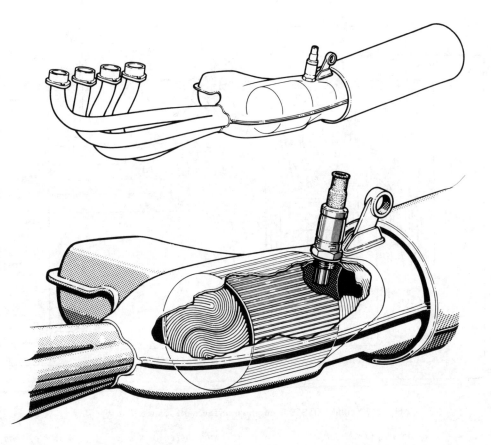

Fig. 9.12 BMW catalytic converter with Lambda sensor (Sec 7)

The converter (Fig. 9.12) uses a metallic base (or monolith), BMW claiming that this gives a greater exhaust gas through-flow than the ceramic-based type (see Chapter 3) and that the unit reaches operating temperature quicker.

With dimensions of 85 x 74 mm (3.3 x 2.9 in), the cylindrical catalyst holder is located within the exhaust system and insulated from the outer skin of the exhaust.

2   The catalyser uses precious metals applied to the surface of the monolith in order to stimulate the chemical reactions which oxydise the noxious exhaust gases. Palladium causes oxydisation of hydrocarbons (HC) and carbon monoxide (CO), while the rhodium acts to reduce oxides of nitrogen (NOx). (Palladium is an alternative agent instead of platinum).

3   Fig. 9.12 (reproduced with kind permission of BMW) shows the physical layout and the Lambda sensor, which is a heated type. Feedback from this sensor to the Motronic control unit ensures that the engine always runs at Stoichiometric conditions ($\lambda = 1$).

4   The following advantages over open-loop systems are worth restating.

(a)   *Efficient exhaust emission control.*
(b)   *Long term optimum engine settings are maintained.*

(c)   *Fuel consumption rarely alters during the life of the catalytic converter.*
(d)   *Lambda control largely compensates for the effects of engine wear.*

Yamaha system

5   The Yamaha GTS1000 motorcycle features a closed-loop engine management system. This follows the principles outlined earlier in this chapter, the arrangement being shown in Fig. 9.13. Note the small differences in terminology such as the Lambda sensor which is referred to by its common name of oxygen (O_2) sensor, and the electronic ignition supply is here termed the igniter.

6   A graphic illustration of how precise control of the correct air:fuel ratio is maintained is given in Fig. 9.14.

A fuel cut-off device comes into operation when the engine speed is high and the rider has closed the throttle to decelerate. Under these conditions the electronic signal from a sensor attached to the throttle shuts off the injection of fuel. This action prevents generation of carbon monoxide (CO) and hydrocarbons (HC) as only air is then drawn into the combustion chamber.

The additional advantages are prevention of overheating and reduction of fuel consumption.

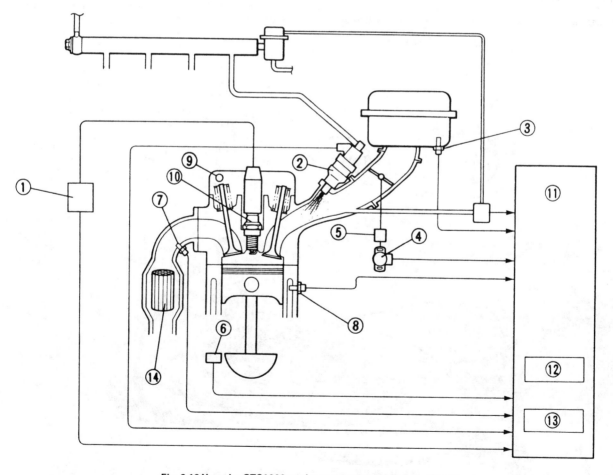

Fig. 9.13 Yamaha GTS1000 engine management system (Sec 7)

1 Ignition coil	5 Intake pressure sensor	9 Camshaft sensor	13 Atmospheric pressure
2 Injector	6 Crankshaft sensor	10 Spark plug	sensor
3 Intake temperature sensor	7 Oxygen (O_2) sensor	11 ECU	14 Catalytic converter
4 Throttle sensor	8 Water temperature sensor	12 Igniter	

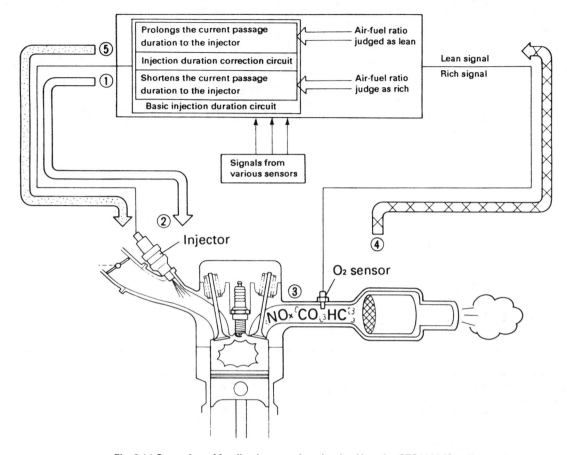

Fig. 9.14 Operation of feedback correction circuit – Yamaha GTS1000 (Sec 7)

1   *The ECU decides the basic injection quantity based on the input signals from various sensors, and gives instructions for current passage duration to the injector*

2   *Current passes through the injector which injects fuel accordingly*
3   *Combustion/exhaust takes place*
4   *The oxygen sensor detects the residual oxygen concentration in the exhaust gas. It sends the lean signal/rich signal for the fuel:air ratio based on this data*

5   *The ECU adds fine compensation to the basic injection timing, based on the signals received. It decides the injection quantity for the next stroke and gives instructions to the injector*

By repeating the operations described, the theoretical air-fuel ratio is maintained

Chapter 10 Spark plugs

Contents

1 The Spark plug

1   In principle, the spark plug is a simple device for providing a pair of electrodes within the cylinder space. A high voltage provided by the ignition system is applied to the electrodes causing a spark at the correct time and in the correct position to ignite the fuel-air vapour.

It was invented by Jean Lenoir in 1860 and although in principle it remains the same today, in practice it is the result of much research and technological innovation.

2   A spark plug operates in the combustion chamber of the engine under severe conditions. For example, the combustion chamber temperature can reach 2500°C (4532°F) and pressures of 700 lbf/in² (50 kg/cm²).

The plug is exposed to sudden changes in temperature and pressure; going abruptly from the temperature of burning fuel to the relatively low temperature of the incoming mixture.

It must endure high voltage, mechanical vibration and corrosion attack from the combustion gases.

2 Construction

1   Plugs are made up of three main components – the shell, electrodes and insulator (Fig. 10.1).

Shell

2   Made of steel, the shell has a thread to screw it into the cylinder head while the upper part has a hexagon. The surface is electroplated nickel to deter corrosion, keep the thread free, and to prevent seizure. Prevention of seizure is most important with alloy cylinder heads. The insulator is inserted into the spark plug shell, then swaged and heat-shrunk in position by inductive heating under high pressure.

Electrodes

3   The electrode materials are vital to correct plug operation for they must be suitable for easy spark emission, and resistant to high temperature and chemical corrosion.

The centre electrode is held in place in one of several ways. Bosch use a conducting glass seal, and NGK and Champion use a powdered seal which caulks the electrode/insulator and insulator/steel body gaps.

Nickel alloys are suitable for electrodes but in some plugs the nickel alloy has a core of copper to assist in conducting away the heat.

The earth (ground) or side electrode is welded to the steel body and is commonly of rectangular section.

4   The Champion double copper plugs have a copper core for both the centre and earth (ground) electrodes, the latter having a trapezoidal cross-section to give a larger area over which the spark may jump. It is claimed that this plug runs 100°C (212°F) cooler than plugs with a solid nickel-alloy earth (ground) electrode (Fig. 10.2) and because the wear rate of the copper-cored earth (ground) electrode is reduced, it is possible to use electrode gaps of up to 0.15 mm (0.006 in) greater than with conventional solid electrode plugs.

It is now accepted that a wider spark plug gap improves both the engine start-up characteristic and the ability to give efficient ignition to leaner fuel:air mixtures.

Insulator

5   The job of the insulator is to ensure that the high voltage pulse will not leak to earth (ground) within the plug body. It also has an effect on heat dissipation and partly determines the 'heat range' of the plug.

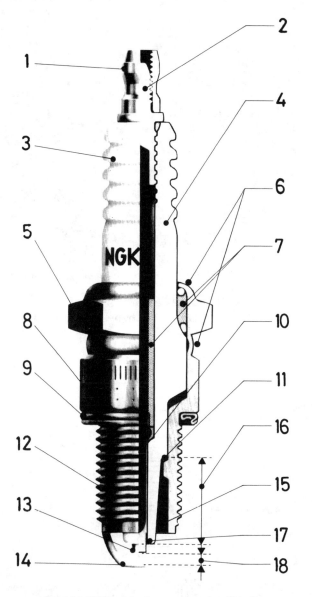

Fig. 10.1 NGK spark plug construction (Sec 2)

1	Terminal	9	Sealing washer
2	Terminal stud	10	Copper core
3	Insulator ribs	11	Inner gasket
4	Insulator (top portion)	12	Threaded portion
5	Metal shell	13	Centre electrode
6	Caulking (to ensure gas-tight seal)	14	Earth (ground) electrode
7	Packing powder (to prevent leakage)	15	Gas volume
		16	Insulator nose length (determines heat rating)
8	Plated finish (to prevent corrosion)	17	Insulator (firing end)
		18	Electrode gap

Alumina ($Al_2 O_3$) plus a filling agent is used to form the insulator which starts as a blank and is then fired in a high temperature furnace, during which a shrinkage of 20% takes place (Fig. 10.3). The exposed surface is glazed to prevent adherence of dirt, which could provide a leakage path. The effective length is increased by providing five ribs over which leakage current would have to travel.

The insulator houses the centre electrode and the terminal stud. In summary it must possess the following qualities.

(a)   Mechanical strength.
(b)   High insulation resistance.
(c)   Good thermal conductivity.

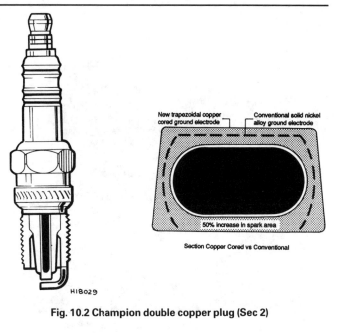

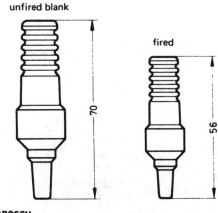

Fig. 10.2 Champion double copper plug (Sec 2)

unfired blank

fired

Fig. 10.3 Spark plug insulator before and after firing (Sec 2)

3   Heat range

1   The firing end of a spark plug must operate between the temperature limits of 400 – 800°C (750 – 1470°F) approximately. Below 400°C (750°F) the plug cannot burn off the carbon deposits generated by combustion, and much above 800°C (1470°F) there is increasing oxide fouling and electrode burning. At 950°C (1740°F) the plug tip becomes so incandescent that premature igniting of the fuel vapour occurs (pre-ignition) resulting in damage to the piston and the plug itself (Figs. 10.4 to 10.6).

Between 400 – 800°C (750 – 1470°F) the plug is self cleaning – the essential condition for good running and long service intervals.

2   Heat flow from the plug has been measured by manufacturers with some accuracy and it is known that about 91% is transmitted via the screw thread and gasket to the engine body, with the remaining 9% lost by radiation and convection from the plug shell and the exposed insulator (Fig. 10.7).

3   The figures do not take into account the cooling effect of the fresh inflowing vapour, but do give an informative picture. It is clear, for instance, that correct fitting and tightening down is vital, since the attached gasket (if fitted) is responsible for nearly half of the heat transmission – failure to maintain good seating contact could result in an overheated plug.

Fig. 10.4 Pre-ignition damage to plug (Sec 3)

Fig. 10.5 Piston crown holed by pre-ignition (Sec 3)

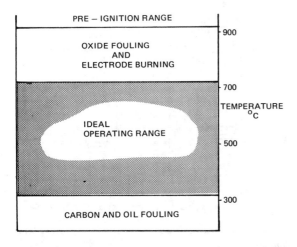

Fig. 10.6 Plug operating temperatures (Sec 3)

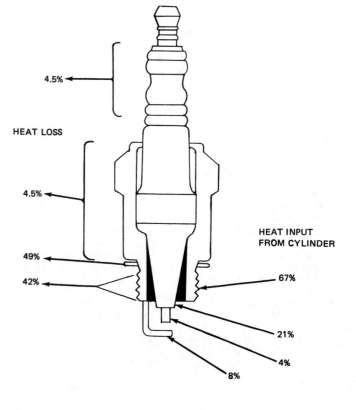

Fig. 10.7 Heat flow in a spark plug (Sec 3)

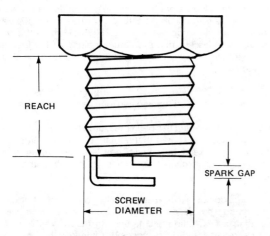

Fig. 10.8 Vital dimensions of a spark plug (Sec 3)

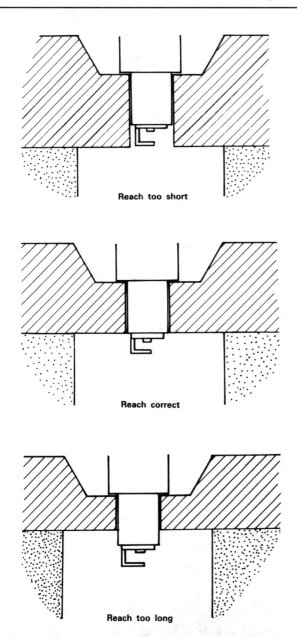

Fig. 10.9 The importance of correct plug reach (Sec 3)

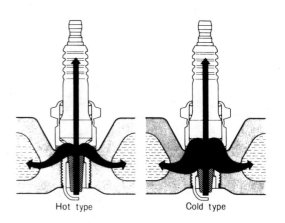

Fig. 10.10 Heat flow in hot and cold plugs (Sec 3)

compression engine has lower combustion chamber temperature and so a hotter grade of plug would be chosen so that the plug tip temperature could be maintained above the oil fouling level (Fig. 10.6).

A hot engine uses a cold plug.
A cold engine uses a hot plug.

Note that sometimes hot plugs are referred to as 'soft' and cold plugs as 'hard'.

8   The working temperature of a plug (heat range) depends upon four factors – see Fig. 10.11.

(a)   *Choice of material used for the insulator and the design of electrodes. Electrodes with materials of high thermal conductivity or copper-cored types will conduct heat well.*
(b)   *Insulator nose length will affect tip temperature. This is the length from the tip of the insulator to the point where it can transfer conducted heat to the body.*
(c)   *Insulator projection into the combustion chamber is linked to the cooling effect of the incoming fuel vapour. The term 'turbo action' is used to describe the effect of the incoming charge and better resistance to fouling is claimed.*
(d)   *Insulator/shell space is important because gas circulates in this 'gas volume'. Exchanges of heat between incoming vapour and outgoing gas will take place here. Enlarging this volume improves the ability of the plug to resist low temperature fouling. Due to the clearance gap there is improvement in charge cooling effect on the insulator nose and allows the use of a longer insulator nose. Enlarging the clearance also increases the amount of deposits that can be accepted before the fouled plug condition occurs.*

4   Clearly no one plug can be correct for all operating conditions and some manufacturers distinguish between plug choice for round-town work or for sustained high speed travel. The important dimensions of a spark plug are at the bottom end, and Fig. 10.8 shows vital statistics that MUST be correct.

5   It is essential for correct plug tip temperatures that the electrodes should JUST project into the cylinder. If the plug reach is too short, the spark is shielded from the fuel vapour; bad misfiring will result and be accompanied by carbon build-up. If the reach is too long, the electrodes will run hot and there is also the chance that the screw threads of cylinder and plug may be damaged by overheating or even by impact with the piston (Fig. 10.9).

6   Plugs dissipate heat from the centre electrode via the nose of the insulator surrounding it. A short insulator will pass heat to the steel shell more readily than a nose insulator which is relatively long and thin (Fig. 10.10).

7   A high compression engine generally has hot operating conditions and requires a plug with good heat dissipation. Conversely, a low

4   Plug examination

1   The state of a spark plug that has been in service will indicate the condition in the engine and some examples are shown in the colour photographs on page 91.

5   Ignition timing

1   Incorrect ignition timing will have a marked effect on plug temperatures.

While advancing ignition beyond manufacturer's figures may show a small power increase, the temperature rise will be disproportionately greater, giving rise to problems on sustained full load (Fig. 10.12).

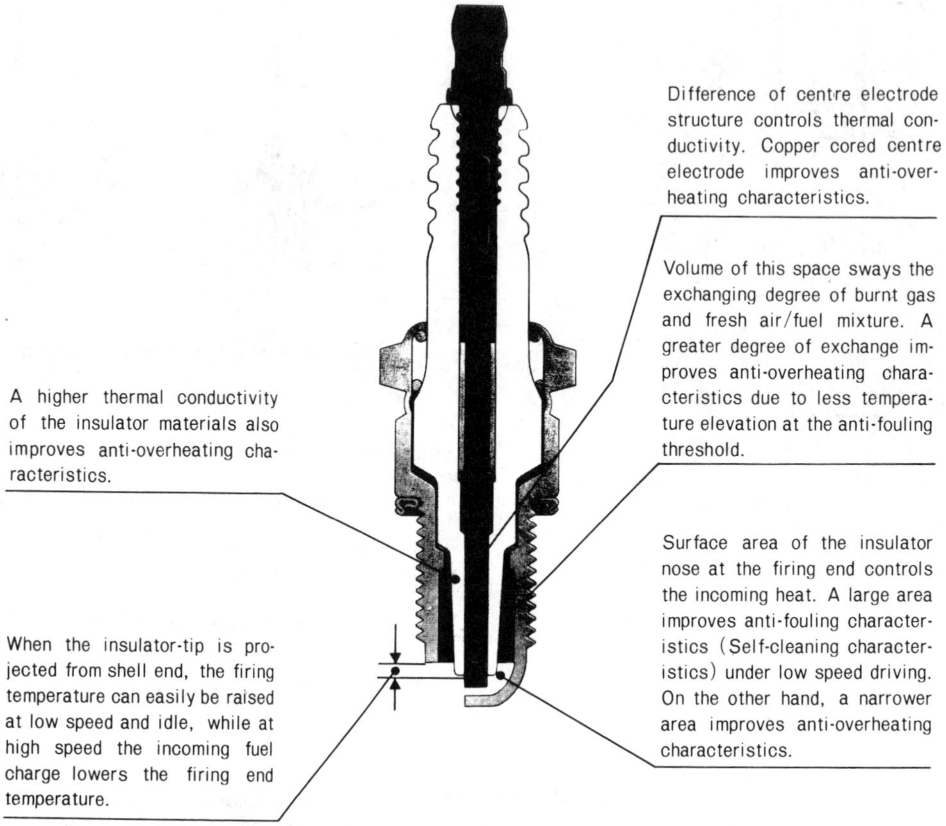

Difference of centre electrode structure controls thermal conductivity. Copper cored centre electrode improves anti-overheating characteristics.
Volume of this space sways the exchanging degree of burnt gas and fresh air/fuel mixture. A greater degree of exchange improves anti-overheating characteristics due to less temperature elevation at the anti-fouling threshold.
A higher thermal conductivity of the insulator materials also improves anti-overheating characteristics.
Surface area of the insulator nose at the firing end controls the incoming heat. A large area improves anti-fouling characteristics (Self-cleaning characteristics) under low speed driving. On the other hand, a narrower area improves anti-overheating characteristics.
When the insulator-tip is projected from shell end, the firing temperature can easily be raised at low speed and idle, while at high speed the incoming fuel charge lowers the firing end temperature.

Fig. 10.11 Influence of design on the heat range of a spark plug (Sec 3)

PER CENT INCREASE
12
10
8
6
4
2
PLUG TEMPERATURE
POWER OUTPUT
2
4
6
8
10
12
TIMING OVERADVANCE – DEGREES

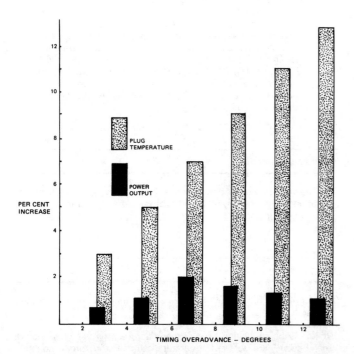

Fig. 10.12 Effects of ignition advance on plug temperature (Sec 5)

SUPER
SUPER
©BOSCH

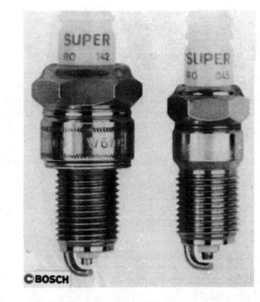

Fig. 10.13 Spark plugs with flat (left) and conical (right) seats (Sec 6)

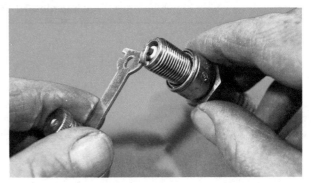

Spark plug maintenance: Checking plug gap with feeler gauges

Altering the plug gap. Note use of correct tool

Spark plug conditions: A brown, tan or grey firing end is indicative of correct engine running conditions and the selection of the appropriate heat rating plug

White deposits have accumulated from excessive amounts of oil in the combustion chamber or through the use of low quality oil. Remove deposits or a hot spot may form

Black sooty deposits indicate an over-rich fuel/air mixture, or a malfunctioning ignition system. If no improvement is obtained, try one grade hotter plug

Wet, oily carbon deposits form an electrical leakage path along the insulator nose, resulting in a misfire. The cause may be a badly worn engine or a malfunctioning ignition system

A blistered white insulator or melted electrode indicates over-advanced ignition timing or a malfunctioning cooling system. If correction does not prove effective, try a colder grade plug

A worn spark plug not only wastes fuel but also overloads the whole ignition system because the increased gap requires higher voltage to initiate the spark. This condition can also affect air pollution

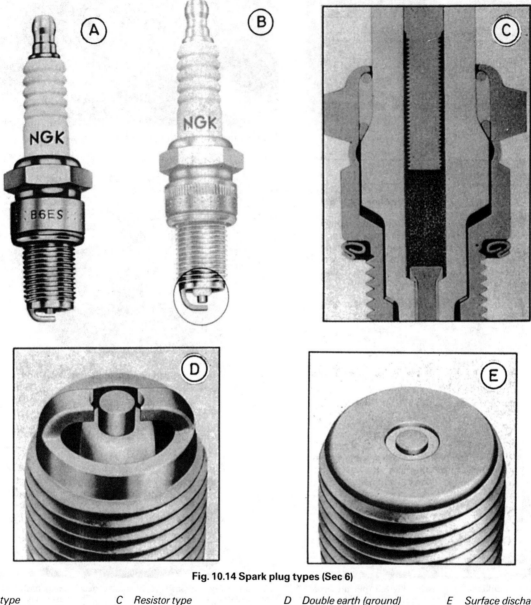

Fig. 10.14 Spark plug types (Sec 6)

A   Standard type
B   P-type (extended insulator nose)

C   Resistor type

D   Double earth (ground)
    electrode type

E   Surface discharge type

6   Types of spark plug

1   Plugs have seats which are either flat or conical (Fig. 10.13).

The **flat** seat uses a gasket washer which is attached permanently to the plug body, and it is important that the plug is screwed properly into the cylinder head. Too loose and the effect can be pre-ignition because there is no proper conductive path for heat: too tight and threads of both plug and cylinder head could be damaged (see Section 8).

Conical (or taper) seating plugs do not use gaskets and can be made with a smaller body shell: they are becoming increasingly popular. Special care must be taken when fitting (see Section 8).

2   **The standard plug** has the spark gap just protruding from the bottom of the plug thread (Fig. 10.14, item A). The standard insulator nose plug is suitable for older engine designs.

3   **P-type plugs** (an NGK term) have a projecting insulator nose (Fig.

10.14, item B). Better fouling protection and anti-pre-ignition characteristics are claimed for this type of plug, since the nose temperature is raised quickly at idle and low speeds to be within the self cleaning heat band. At high speeds the incoming charge has a cooling effect. This type of plug is suited to modern engine design.

4   **Resistor plugs** have a carbon compound resistor often of about 5KΩ resistance in the centre core (Fig. 10.14, item C). This gives good radio interference suppression because it is more effective to have a suppression resistor close to the source of radiation – namely the spark.

5   **Double earth (ground) electrode plugs** are used for rotary engines in which plugs are more intensely heated than those in reciprocating engines (Fig. 10.14, item D). The gap growth-rate is low using multiple electrodes and a lower production of carbon monoxide is claimed.

6   **Surface discharge plugs** are designed for CDI (Capacitor Discharge Ignition) systems and give good sparking even under conditions of fouling (Fig. 10.14, item E).

Fig. 10.15 Corona discharge and flashover (Sec 7)

7 Corona discharge and flashover

1 If conditions are damp or the plug ribbed insulator is dirty, then in the dark a pale blue light may be seen around the HT cable connector and/or the plug insulator when the engine is running. This is due to ionization of the air which splits up into free electrons and positively charged ions in the area of high electric stress. It is known as Corona discharge. It can also sometimes be seen on high voltage cable insulators in wet weather.

The effect on ignition is minimal unless the Corona reaches the terminal stud allowing flashover to the metal shell. This gives an engine misfire (Fig. 10.15).

2 On examination of a spark plug a discoloration on the insulator surface may be seen which looks as if gas has leaked between the insulator and the shell, as shown in Fig. 10.16. This discoloration is generally called 'Corona stain'.

It is due to oil particles, hanging in the air around the insulator surface,

being attracted by the corona discharge; these become charged and adhere to the insulator surface.

The corona stain causes no deterioration in the function of the spark plug. The corona stain does not cause flashover since it has sufficient insulation, but moisture adhering to the insulator will cause flashover.

8 Spark plug servicing

1 Plugs should be checked regularly at 3000 mile (4800 km) intervals, or as recommended by the machine's manufacturer, for performance to be maintained. Properly serviced plugs have a gradual deterioration and a finite life.

Depending upon riding style, the economical limit of plug life is 6,000 – 10,000 miles (10,000 – 16,000 km) for a 4-stroke engine. Due to the oily nature of the 2-stroke engine, plug life is reduced markedly to 4,000 – 6,000 miles (6,500 – 10,000 km). Note that the use of unleaded fuel (where possible) will greatly increase spark plug life.

Fig. 10.16 Insulator staining due to corona discharge (Sec 7)

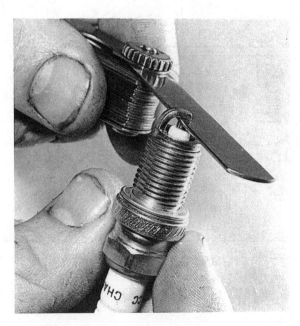

Fig. 10.17 Measuring the plug electrode gap using a feeler gauge (Sec 8)

Fig. 10.18 Measuring the plug electrode gap using a wire gauge (Sec 8)

Fig. 10.19 Adjusting the plug electrode gap using a special tool (Sec 8)

2   Plug cleaning may be carried out by hand but workshops frequently use an abrasive grit blast machine. It is most important to clean away all traces of grit afterwards with compressed air. Note that some plug manufacturers specifically advise against cleaning due the likelihood of

damage to the firing ends. Considering the relative cheapness of spark plugs, renewal is often the best course of action if there is any doubt about their condition.

3   When removing a plug, unscrew it a few turns using a proper spark plug spanner (wrench) and blow or brush away any grit or rust particles lying round the plug well. Do not, under any circumstances, allow foreign matter to drop into the engine through the plug hole.

4   Cleaning manually is best carried out with a fine wire brush, going over the external thread, plug tip and earth (ground) electrode CAREFULLY; a harsh abrasive brush may damage the plug. After cleaning check that no whiskers from the wire brush remain in the plug. Clean the insulator with a rag moistened with solvent to prevent spark tracking paths developing.

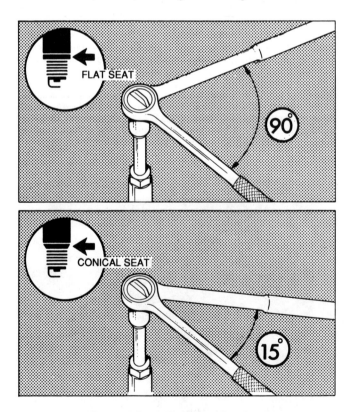

Fig. 10.20 Spark plug tightening (Sec 8)

5   Gap resetting should be carried out using a combination tool with an electrode adjuster and feeler gauge. Note that flat feeler gauges are not ideal for this job in case of irregular electrode wear (Figs. 10.17, 10.18 and 10.19).

6   Refitting needs care, especially with alloy heads. After cleaning the plug thread with a brass wire brush smear a TRACE of graphited or copper-based grease on the thread and start the plug carefully by hand. Withdraw immediately if unusual resistance is felt – this may be due to cross threading. One manufacturer (Bosch) states that their NEW plugs are already lubricated but grease should be applied for all used plugs.

Plugs should ideally be tightened to the torque setting specified by the machine's manufacturer. The following rules will be satisfactory if a torque setting is not provided (Fig. 10.20).

    (a)   *Flat seat plugs – Screw the plug in by hand as far as it will go. Apply and turn the plug spanner (wrench) until first resistance is felt and then for a NEW plug turn through 90°. Used plugs should be turned 30° only to tighten since the gasket will have been compressed previously.*

    (b)   *Conical seat plugs – Turn by 15° after the first resistance is felt. This applies to new and used plugs.*

Chapter 11
Charging: Direct current (dc) generators

Contents

1 Introduction

1   The use of a generator to charge a motorcycle battery goes back to the early part of the century, but widespread use of the direct current dynamo began in the 1920's when the Lucas Magdyno first appeared (see Fig. 5.1 in Chapter 5).

2   It is interesting to note that the voltage generated in the dynamo armature is alternating and appears as direct voltage at the output terminals only after passing through a commutator. This is a mechanical means of reversing the negative alternating wave so that the output is a series of uni-directional pulses which are a form of direct current and suitable for battery charging. We shall examine in some detail how the dynamo works, going right back to basics.

2 Electromagnetic generation

1   When a wire is moved through a magnetic field, a voltage is induced proportional to the following (Fig. 11.1).

   (a)   The velocity (v) at which magnetic lines of force are cut.
   (b)   The strength of the magnetic field (B).
   (c)   The length of the wire (l) actually in the field

$$\text{induced emf. } e = Blv \text{ volts.}$$

This is the basic equation on which all generators, both ac and dc, operate.

2   The strength of the magnetic field (B) is usually measured in Teslas, the length of wire (l) measured in metres and the wire velocity (v) in metres per second at right-angles to the magnetic field.

3   This arrangement does not make a practical generator and so the wire was next arranged as a parallel sided loop and the voltage picked off by slip rings with carbon brushes pressing lightly on them. Rotating the coil between the poles of a magnet means that the coil sides are first moving up through the field and then down. Not surprisingly, the voltage generated changes direction and is thus said to be **alternating**.

4   Fig. 11.2 shows the coil in various positions but it is to be noted that when the coil sides are sweeping past the N and S poles (where the flux density is greatest) the voltage is maximum, and is zero at points a, c and e where the coil sides are running parallel to the magnetic flux lines. This type of generator is an **alternator**.

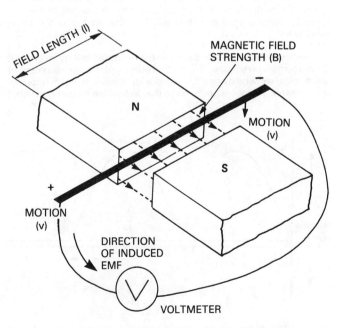

Fig. 11.1 Inducing emf in moving conductor (Sec 2)

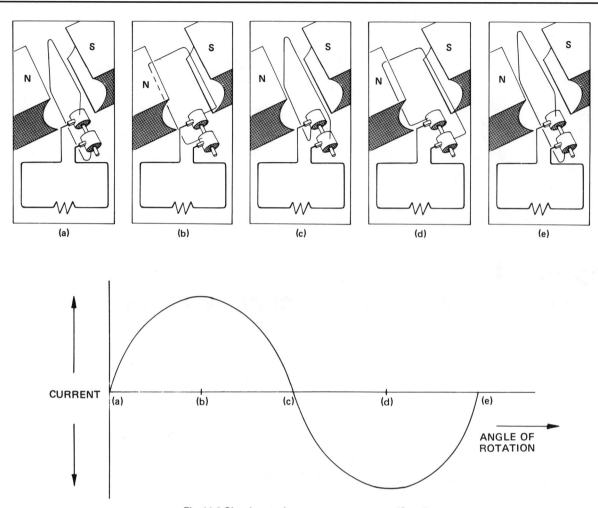

Fig. 11.2 Simple rotating-armature generator (Sec 2)

3   Converting ac to dc

1   The simplest way of converting the alternating current (ac) into direct current (for battery charging) is to remove one half of the sine wave of current, so that pulses will flow but always in the same direction.

2   An improvement would be to use the discarded half by inverting it to add to the current flow (Fig. 11.3). Today, with the development of electronics, we would use a semiconductor rectifier, but generators on early motorcycles were designed so that alternating current generated in the armature coils was rectified by mechanical means for battery charging.

This was achieved by the commutator (the word commute meaning 'to change'). Instead of slip rings, a single split ring was used so that the two halves were insulated from one another (Fig. 11.4).

3   If you imagine the coil turning slowly through 360° then as the coil sides are exactly halfway between the magnetic poles, the brushes are just passing over the commutator joint. Thus current in the armature coil is reversing in direction but simultaneously the connections to the external circuit are being reversed so that the current in the load is always in the same direction: namely it is direct current, with a waveform as in Fig. 11.3, and may be used to charge a battery.

4   In practice, a single coil would give insufficient voltage to be of use, so a series of coils is wound round the armature perimeter and the ends are connected to a commutator which has many segments. The result of this arrangement is that at any one time a constant number of coil sides are passing the N and S poles; the voltage and current are both nearly constant but with a ripple which depends on how many conductors and slots are used.

Fig. 11.5 shows a typical armature and it should be noted that the coils are wound in slots of a laminated iron armature. The reason for the iron-cored armature is to create a path for the magnetic lines of force to go through and so the field is stronger and more concentrated.

5   Referring again to Fig. 11.3 the output wave form of the simple single-coil generator is shown. Comparison with that shown in Fig. 11.6 illustrates that the multicoil armature gives a higher output which is nearly constant.

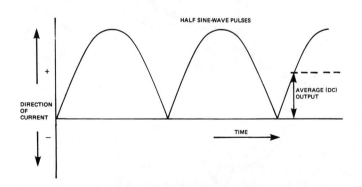

Fig. 11.3 Uni-directional (dc) output from single-coil armature (Sec 3)

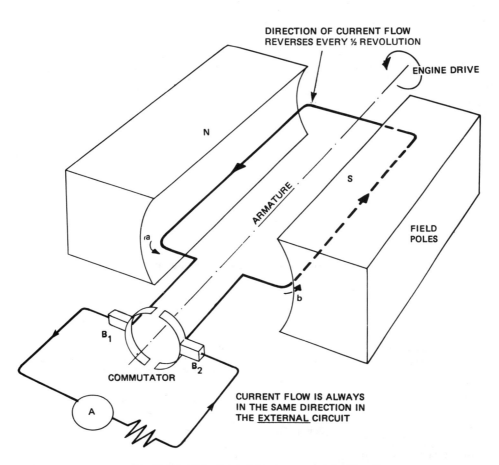

Fig. 11.4 Rectification by simple commutator (Sec 4)

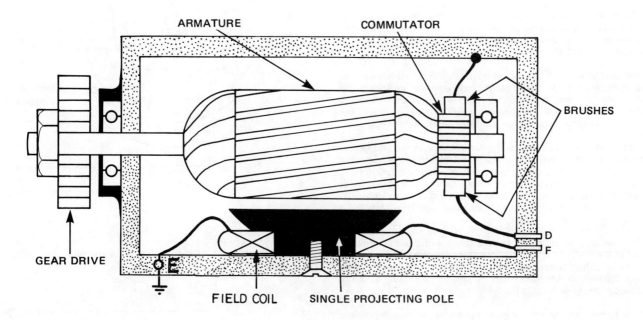

Fig. 11.5 Direct current unipole generator – schematic presentation (Sec 4)

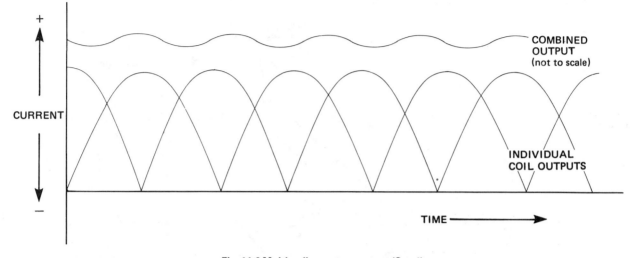

Fig. 11.6 Multi-coil armature output (Sec 4)

4   The dc generator – excitation and control

1   Permanent magnets are not used in motorcycle dc generators because it is possible to obtain stronger fields using electromagnets and, moreover, the magnetic field strength is then controllable.

2   A field winding wrapped round the poles may be supplied with a small current from the armature and hence this type of generator is said to be a self-excited shunt generator (shunt meaning 'in parallel' as are the armature and field coils). The arrangement is shown in Fig. 11.7 together with the conventional diagram for a shunt generator. Two poles are shown in the schematic diagram and the coils wound over them are in series and constitute the **field winding**.

3   The Lucas E3 type dynamo was standard equipment for many years and used only one projecting pole (Fig. 11.5). It is always necessary to have magnetic poles in pairs but in this model the frame forms the opposite pole. Rather incorrectly, therefore, this dynamo was referred to as a UNIPOLE type.

4   When a dc shunt generator is driven by a motorcycle engine the armature rotates, and because of the residual magnetism left in the poles, there will be a small voltage induced which will appear between the armature D and E terminals.

The field coil terminal F is connected externally direct to D (via a pair of contacts in the regulator box) and so the induced armature voltage will drive a small current down the field winding, thus creating more magnetic flux and a rise in armature voltage. In turn, this gives a higher field current, a higher magnetic flux and a higher armature voltage.

You might ask, why does this voltage not continue to rise and rapidly burn out the field winding? The answer is that the iron of the field poles eventually becomes magnetically saturated, providing a natural limit to the armature voltage which is fixed to an extent also by the resistance of the field winding. Even so, the voltage attained could cause the field winding to fail and dynamos must not be run at high speed without a control box.

5   If the dynamo were run at a constant speed, with F and D terminals connected but with no external load, then the characteristic of armature voltage against field current would be similar to that of Fig. 11.8. Points B, C and D correspond to the terminal voltage for decreasing values of resistance added in series with the field.

6   Note particularly that point A gives a generated voltage dependent on the residual magnetism of the field iron. Sometimes a generator put into service may have insufficient residual magnetism to start up or may

generate with reversed polarity. To correct both situations it is usual to *flash* the field windings by connecting F and E *momentarily* to a battery; if the generator is for negative earth (ground) working then the battery connection would be F+ and E– and vice versa for positive earth (ground) systems. In Section 6, where the cut-out is discussed, it will be seen that this can be done in situ by pressing the cut-out contacts together for a very short time when the ignition is switched off.

Field Windings (in practice many more turns are used)

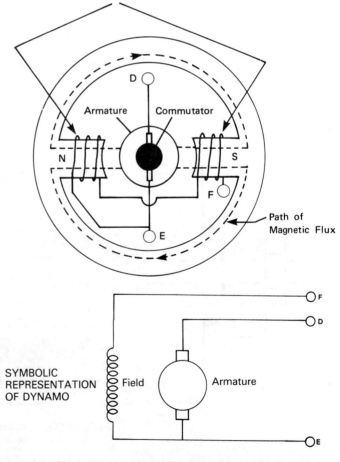

SYMBOLIC REPRESENTATION OF DYNAMO

Fig. 11.7 Self-excited dc shunt generator (Sec 4)

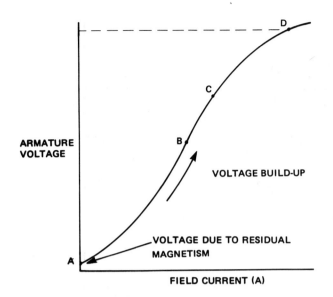

Fig. 11.8 Direct current dynamo no-load characteristic (Sec 4)

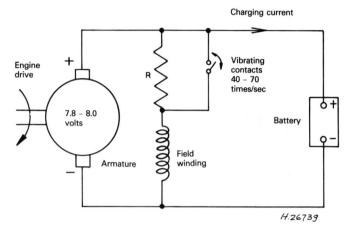

Fig. 11.9 Principle of the voltage regulator (Sec 5)

5 Voltage regulation

1   The dynamo will be driven by the motorcycle engine over a wide speed-range. Correspondingly the generated voltage will be variable and, without some form of control, the battery and electrical equipment would be destroyed. The voltage required to charge a 6 volt motorcycle battery is approximately 7.8 – 8.0 volts and the device designed to keep the dynamo at this voltage over the speed range is the **regulator**.

Most dynamo-equipped motorcycles used 6 volt systems, but the same principle of a somewhat higher dynamo voltage than battery voltage would be applicable in a 12 volt system.

2   The simplest form of regulation is that in which a resistor is periodically connected in series with the field winding. Inserting the resistor will reduce the generator voltage and conversely, when the resistor is shorted out, cause an increase.

3   Fig. 11.9 shows a simplified arrangement in which the field resistor (R) is switched in and out of circuit between 40 and 70 times per second, so the generated voltage rises and falls between certain limits, the average of which is that required for charging.

4   Fig. 11.10 shows a simple regulator circuit, featuring an electromagnet which overcomes the pull of a restraining spring on the iron armature at the voltage setting of 7.8 – 8.0 volts and opens the contacts, thus switching in the additional field resistor (R). As the voltage falls the magnetic pull on the regulator armature decreases and the contacts again close when the spring pull overcomes the magnetic force. Thus the dynamo voltage hunts between two limits, but so long as the average voltage is within the specified limits all is well. The value of R is between 27 – 45 ohms depending upon the model of regulator.

5   You may ask, what happens if engine speed slows to the point where the dynamo voltage is less than that of the battery? The battery will drive current back into the dynamo, and there must be some device which breaks the connection between the dynamo and battery when this happens. This device is called the CUT-OUT as is discussed in the following section.

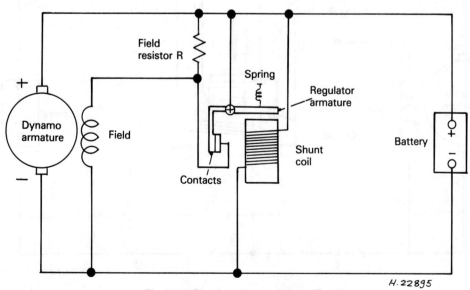

Fig. 11.10 Simple voltage regulator (Sec 5)

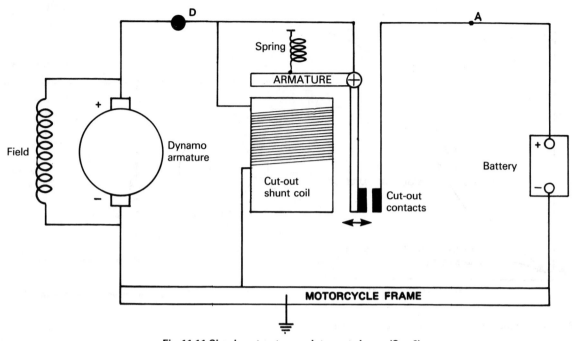

Fig. 11.11 Simple cut-out – regulator not shown (Sec 6)

6 The Cut-out

1   Rather similar to the regulator in its mode of working, the cut-out consists of an electromagnet which pulls in its armature at a pre-set dynamo voltage. When this happens, a pair of heavy duty contacts connect the D terminal of the dynamo to the battery. In traffic at tickover speeds, the dynamo voltage drops below that of the battery and the cut-out drops out, thus disconnecting the battery from the dynamo.

2   Fig. 11.11 shows the general idea, although as with the regulator, there are certain practical improvements that can be made to ensure best working, these being dealt with in the following sections. The regulator and cut-out are usually contained in one control box.

7 Compensated Voltage Control (CVC)

1   There are serious shortcomings of the simple voltage regulator since, as its name implies, it controls the dynamo voltage and not the current. When a battery is discharged this would result in a very large current from the dynamo, which could damage the dynamo, regulator and battery. What is needed is a device which will sense the output current and introduce a fall in the dynamo terminal voltage as the current to the battery increases. This is called Compensated Voltage Control (CVC) and is achieved by winding a few turns of heavy gauge wire over the regulator electromagnet and passing the dynamo charging current through them (Fig. 11.12).

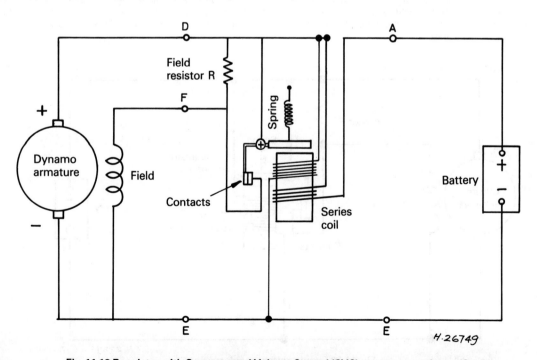

Fig. 11.12 Regulator with Compensated Voltage Control (CVC) – cut-out not shown (Sec 7)

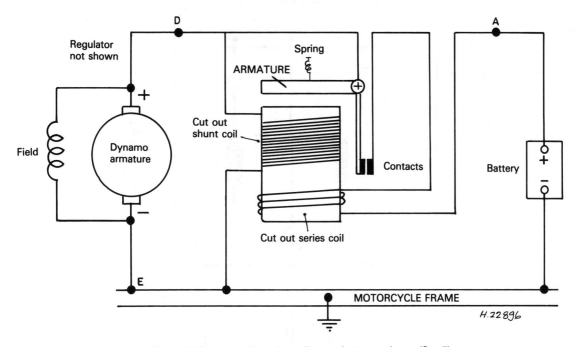

Fig. 11.13 Cut-out with series coil – regulator not shown (Sec 7)

2   The magnetic effect is to assist the main winding in opening the regulator contacts at a lower voltage. As the battery charges up, the terminal voltage will rise and the charging current will decrease.

3   The cut-out electromagnet also has a series winding of heavy gauge wire wound over the main shunt winding. Charging current passes through this series winding. The main shunt winding senses the dynamo voltage and pulls in the contacts at about 6.5 volts so that the dynamo connects to the battery and charging occurs (Fig. 11.13).

Charging current passing out to the battery creates a magnetic field in the series winding which assists that of the main shunt winding. The effect is to *reinforce* the pull on the armature, so keeping the contacts more firmly together.

4   However, when the dynamo speed drops to tickover, the generated voltage drops below that of the battery and current reverses, flowing back into the dynamo. This reverse current, flowing through the series winding, creates a magnetic field which *opposes* that of the main shunt winding and throws open the cut-out contacts. The contact-opening voltage is between 4.8 – 5.5 volts according to the control box model and the temperature.

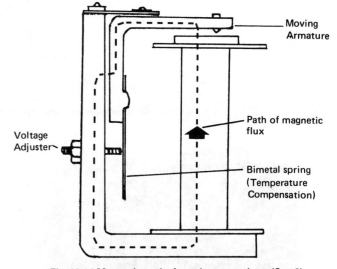

Fig. 11.14 Magnetic paths for voltage regulator (Sec 8)

8   Temperature compensation

1   The effect of a temperature rise is to increase the resistance of the main shunt coils of both the regulator and the cut-out. Higher coil resistance means that the dynamo voltage must rise to push through the current necessary to open the contacts (regulator) or close the contacts (cut-out).

2   In practice, the armature return springs are flat strips made in bimetal form which bend with temperature change and accordingly change the spring pressure. Fig. 11.14 shows the arrangement of bimetal spring temperature compensation and the complete magnetic circuit.

9   Complete control box

1   Control boxes containing a regulator and cut-out for use with a two brush dynamo were produced by Lucas from 1936. The popular MCR1 used a wire wound resistor of about 30 ohms and continued in use until the 1950's, when the similar MCR2 replaced it. One difference was the resistor which now became a round carbon disc fixed to the frame. Its ohmic value was slightly higher at about 40 ohms.

In 1954 the RB107 was introduced and used in great numbers, the last of the range was the RB108 of 1960 which was finally superseded by alternator systems.

2   Fig. 11.15 shows the circuit diagram for a complete control box with connections to the dynamo, and Fig. 11.16 is the RB107 in cutaway form.

REGULATOR   CUT-OUT

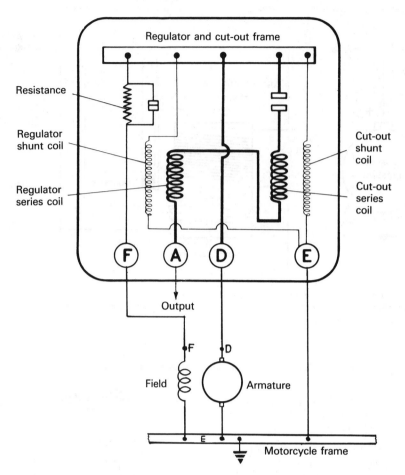

Fig. 11.15 Circuit of compensated voltage control box with connections to dynamo (Sec 9)

Fig. 11.16 Lucas RB107 control box (Sec 9)

10   Dynamo construction and overhaul

1   The two brush dynamo came into service in 1936 to replace the earlier three brush dynamo. This became the standard charging set (with certain variations) up to the time when it was superseded by the alternator.

Construction

2   Fig. 11.17 shows the construction of the E3 series used as part of a Magdyno. Early models E3 and E3HM were of 35 watt output and negative earth (ground) up to 1951, when positive earth (ground) systems were introduced; up to 1949 the commutator end bearing was of the plain type but this was changed to a ball bearing for the 1950 range onward. At the same time, the dynamo was lengthened and the output uprated to 60 watts (E3L and E3LM).

Larger 3.5 inch diameter dynamos with 75 watt output were also introduced for motorcycles with coil ignition (C35S series).

3   Servicing is mainly concerned with cleaning away brush dust, checking bearings for wear, brushes for free movement and remaining length, electrical testing of field and armature. See the appropriate sub-section for details.

Testing

4   A preliminary check on the electrical health of a dynamo is to see if it will run as a motor.

Join D and F and apply 6 volts to D and earth (ground); if the dynamo runs it is a good indication that all is well. This test is not conclusive,

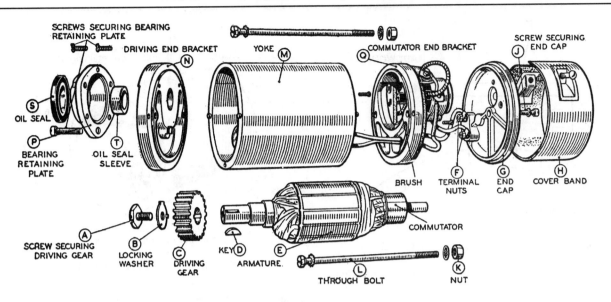

Fig. 11.17 Lucas dynamo (E3 series) (Sec 10)

however, because a dynamo may run as a motor even if there is an armature winding fault which would prevent it generating, but it does at least indicate that the field connections are correct.

Overhaul

Commutator and brushes

5   Commutators wear after a long period of use and may be cleaned up by the use of a thin strip of glasspaper wrapped completely round the commutator bars. Thorough cleaning-off with methylated spirits (stoddard solvent) is essential to remove abrasive particles.

If the bars are too badly scored for this treatment then the commutators must be dry skimmed (ie no lubricant) on a lathe. The insulation (mica) must then be undercut to a depth of about 0.02 inch (0.5 mm) using a hacksaw blade with the blade teeth ground to the correct width (Figs. 11.18 and 11.19).

After undercutting the commutator bar insulation (mica), all burrs must be removed with a Swiss file and the commutator polished with very fine glasspaper, or burnished with a small block of hardwood (Fig. 11.20).

6   Brushes should always be renewed when the dynamo is overhauled, but for routine checks only renew if the hairspring holding the brush down is close to the brush carrier.

Genuine Lucas brushes are pre-formed but it is safest to bed-in all new brushes. This is done by wrapping a strip of fine glass paper (abrasive side outwards) round the commutator and pressing the brush lightly down while the commutator is rocked in the direction of rotation. Bedding-in is complete when full contact over the brush working face is evident.

Armature

7   To check an armature it is necessary to strip it out of the casing, taking care when withdrawing it to safeguard the brushes which should be lifted back and held in position (or taken out of their carriers).

With a test meter on high ohms range (or use a battery in series with a bulb) test the insulation between the commutator and the iron armature laminations. The insulation resistance should be very high and if low (or the bulb lights) there is a short between the windings and frame.

If all is in order, use the test meter on low ohms range to check the resistance between adjacent commutator bars all round. Each reading should be the same; if one is higher then that armature coil is open-circuit. Checking for shorted turns ideally needs a growler in which the armature is slowly rotated by hand between a V-block laminated core which has a mains ac primary winding on it. When shorted turns on the armature span the growler laminations, the buzzing note changes because the shorted turns are like a heavy load on the growler secondary.

Finally check for solder splashes in the frame. It may be that a connection between the commutator bars and windings has been electrically overloaded. Re-soldering might be possible but if any faults

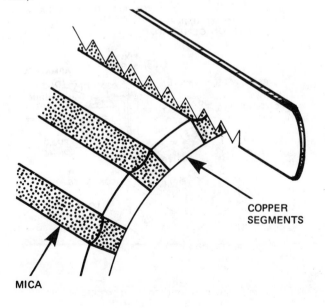

Fig. 11.18 Undercutting mica between commutator bars (Sec 10)

Fig. 11.19 Mica undercutting measurement (Sec 10)

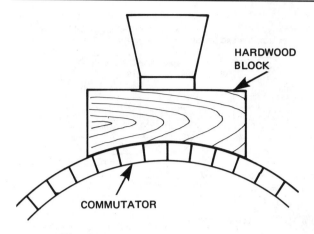

Fig. 11.20 Burnishing the commutator (Sec 10)

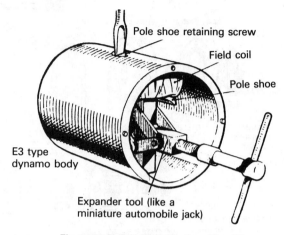

Fig. 11.21 Refitting a pole shoe (Sec 10)

are found in an armature it is advisable to send it to a professional repairer.

Field coil

8   Check by high range ohmmeter that the insulation resistance between the windings and frame is high.

Next measure the resistance of the field coil which for early E3 models is 3.2 ohms and 2.8 ohms from 1950 on. A single shorted turn, enough to stop the dynamo working, would not show up conclusively on this test but an open circuit would.

If a field coil rewind is necessary, the awkward part is removal and refitting the field pole shoe. It is put on very tight in manufacture and the fixing screw then caulked by pin-pinching the case metal into the head slot.

To refit, an expander of some sort must be used (Fig. 11.21) to force the pole shoe hard up against the case – so unless the workshop equipment is available it is again best to send it to a professional.

Bearings

9   Examine the armature and field poles to see if rubbing has occurred. If bright patches are evident, the bearings have probably worn. Early models used a bush at one end and a ball bearing at the other. Later units had ball bearings at both ends.

The sintered bronze bush requires soaking in thin oil overnight before installation, whereas the ball bearing(s) should be lightly packed with high melting-point grease (HMP).

---

11   Control box settings

1   The most frequently found types of control boxes containing both cut-out and regulator are the Lucas MCR1, MCR2 and the RB107 (Figs. 11.22, 11.23 and 11.16). The settings to be checked are as follows.

   (a)   *Voltage of the regulator.*
   (b)   *Cut-in voltage of the cut-out.*
   (c)   *Drop-out voltage of the cut-out.*

For full servicing, the gap settings of points and armatures should also be checked (refer to the two books listed in Section 12).

Voltage regulator setting

2   Voltage regulator setting is checked by slipping a piece of paper between the cut-out contacts so that no charging can occur. Connect a voltmeter between D and E and then start the engine, running up speed slowly until the voltmeter needle flicks showing that the regulator is working.

The voltage should be within the limits shown in the table at the end of this Section. Should adjustment be needed, stop the engine so that the regulator voltage does not alter, adjust the voltage adjuster screw

slightly and test the voltage again after restarting the engine. When the setting is satisfactory, tighten the locknut on the adjuster screw.

Cut-out settings

3   Connect a centre-zero ammeter in the lead to the battery and remove the paper from between the contacts.

Start and run up the engine slowly until the cut-out points close and a charge is noted on the ammeter. The voltage at which this occurs should be noted. If incorrect, stop the engine and make a small adjustment to the cut-out screw (in for high voltage). Repeat the check until the correct cut in voltage is obtained.

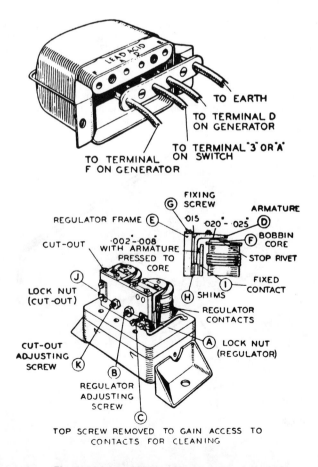

Fig. 11.22 Lucas MCR1 control box (Sec 11)

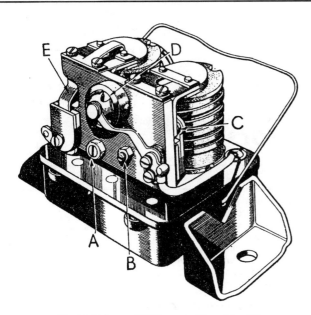

Fig. 11.23 Lucas MCR2 control box (Sec 11)

A   *Cut-out adjuster*
B   *Regulator adjuster*
C   *Regulator contacts*

D   *Field resistor*
E   *Cut-out contact blade*

When the revs are allowed to drop slowly, there will be a reverse current before the cut-out contacts open. This should not exceed 5 amperes (MCR2 and RB107). Take off the lead from the A terminal and connect a voltmeter from A to E. Run up the engine speed and let it drop slowly until the cut-out contacts open – note the voltage at which this occurs. Check the test results with the table below.

Voltage settings for Lucas control boxes

Check	MCR1	MCR2	RB107
Cut in voltage	6.2 to 6.6	6.3 to 6.7	6.3 to 6.7
Drop out voltage	3.5 to 5.3	4.5 to 5.0	4.5 to 5.0
Reverse current (amperes)	0.7 to 2.5	3.0 to 5.0	3.0 to 5.0
Regulator voltage @ 20°C (68°F)	7.8 to 8.2	7.6 to 8.0	8.0 to 8.4

The voltage settings are temperature dependent, being higher if the temperature falls and vice versa if it rises. For example, the RB107 regulator setting has a voltage rise of 0.2 volt per 10°C (50°F) drop in temperature.

12   Further reading

1   For further reading, see the following references.

Restoring Motorcycles: Electrics by Roy Bacon (try Public Library)

The Vintage Motorcyclists' Workshop by Radco (Haynes)

Old Bike Mart (a good source for specialist repairers)

Chapter 12 Charging: Alternators

Contents

1 Introduction

1 The dc generator (dynamo) was standard in all but small motorcycles until 1953, when Lucas fitted the Triumph Speed Twin

with an alternator. From then on, the alternator reigned supreme and underwent several stages of development so that today it is a high efficiency assembly of first class design.

2 It is worth looking at the shortcomings of the dc generator. First, the current from the armature had to be collected from the commutator by brushes. This was a considerable technical achievement but, nevertheless, meant that maintenance for wear on brushes and commutator was necessary. A characteristic feature of the alternator is that the armature in which the output current is generated is always stationary and hence an improvement in efficiency is possible (Fig. 12.1).

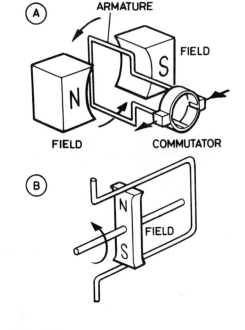

Fig. 12.1 Essentails of the dynamo (dc) and alternator (ac) (Sec 1)

A *Dynamo (stationary field)*   *B* *Alternator (rotating field)*

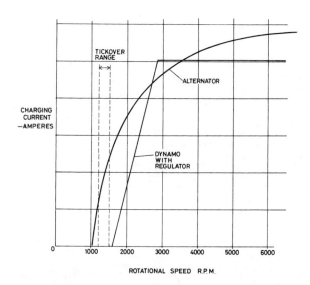

Fig. 12.2 Generator output comparison between dynamo and alternator (Sec 1)

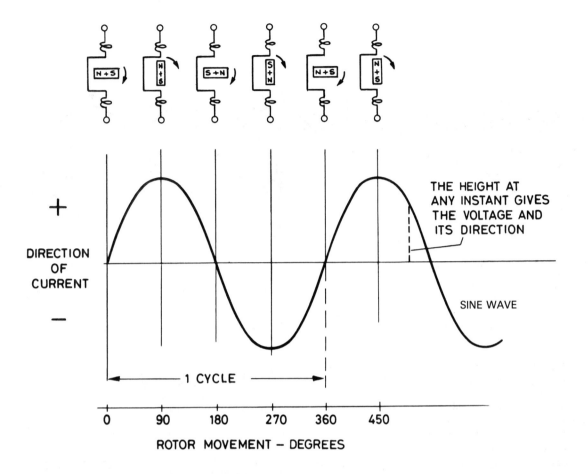

Fig. 12.3 Curve of single-phase alternator voltage (Sec 2)

3   The alternator can be run faster than the dynamo because there is no problem with the commutator. This means that charging can begin at lower engine speeds than is the case with the dynamo (Fig. 12.2).

4   The rectifier used to convert alternating output to direct current will not allow battery current to flow back into the alternator so there is no need for a cut-out.

2   Principles of operation

1   When an electrical conductor crosses a magnetic field a voltage (more properly called an electromotive force – emf) is generated. The same formula that governs dc generation (Chapter 11, Section 2) applies in this case. Generated voltage (emf) depends on the following, all of which are important factors in the design and control of alternators.

*(a)   The **velocity** of the wire(s) passing at right-angles to the magnetic field.*
*(b)   The **length** of the wire exposed to the magnetic field.*
*(c)   The **strength** of the magnetic field.*

2   In order to increase the length of wire exposed to the magnetic field, coils are used; one or more coils is known as a winding. The magnetic field density (flux density) is always enhanced by using laminated iron frames on which the field coils and armature windings are wound.

3   Imagine the simple coil of the alternator (Fig. 12.1, item B) which is cut by the magnetic field of the N and S poles of the rotating magnet. The voltage or electromotive force (emf) generated in the coil sides will change direction as the poles pass close by in cyclic rotation, N S N S etc. Thus if the coil is connected to a complete circuit externally the current flowing will change direction at the same rate, or frequency, at which the poles rotate, hence the name alternating current.

4   The number of revolutions per second of the magnet will also correspond to the number of repetitions, or cycles, per second of the current wave flowing back and forth through the coil. This number was defined originally in cycles per second, but is now called Hertz (Hz); thus 50 revolutions per second of the magnet will give a voltage or current frequency of 50 Hertz. A graph or waveform of the way in which the electric waves change with time is shown in Fig. 12.3.

The sine wave occurs throughout nature – twanging a spring will cause it to oscillate with an amplitude in the form of a sine wave.

3   Single-phase and three-phase generation

1   An alternator which produces a single sine wave of current is a single-phase generator; it is the type of output from cycle dynamos, flywheel alternators, the range of British motorcycle alternators from the 1950's onwards, and other motorcycles where the current demand was moderate.

2   A better way of utilising the winding space round the stator (the stationary part of the alternator on which the output coils are wound) would be to use three pairs of coils, but there has to be a special way of connecting them to bring out the power: this is a three-phase alternator.

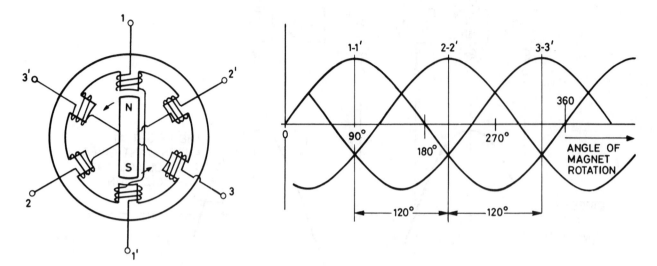

Fig. 12.4 Three-phase alternator and its waveform (Sec 3)

3   If a rotating magnet sweeps past the three sets of coils, then each will produce a sine wave of induced voltage, but in sequence. Since a complete revolution of the magnet corresponds to 360° rotation, then each sine wave of voltage will be 120° apart from the other two (Fig. 12.4). Each coil will have the same voltage generated within it by the rotating magnetic field, but there is a time difference corresponding to the time it takes the magnet to travel from one coil to the next, from 1 to 2, 2 to 3, 3 to 1, etc.

4   It is possible to avoid using six output wires by connecting the coils together in either a 'star' or a 'delta' configuration. Fig. 12.5 shows these connections, both of which are possible for motorcycle alternators.

5   The 'star' connection will result in a higher voltage between any pair of output terminals than is generated by one coil alone, but will not be twice one coil voltage because of the time phase difference between any pair. In fact, the voltage between lines (as the output leads are called) is 1.732 x coil voltage.

In the 'delta' connection, the output voltage will be that of any one coil in value, but the currents generated in each coil will add to give a line current of 1.732 x one coil current. Where heavy current is required the stator windings are preferably connected in delta.

6   Looking again at the waveforms of the three phases (Fig. 12.4); if a vertical line is drawn at any point on the time axis, the nett sum of the waveforms is always zero. This means that there is no need for a return wire from the centre point of the star winding, and additionally that current flowing outwards on any one line is balanced by the inward flow in the other two lines for both star and delta. Under these conditions, the three-phase circuit is said to be balanced.

4   Rectification – converting ac to dc

1   The motorcycle battery acts as a storage unit for electrical energy and is a direct current device. Current flowing out from it is direct current as is the current flowing into it when being charged.

2   It is necessary to convert the alternating current from the alternator into a form of direct current before it is useful. Referring to Fig. 12.3, note that the sine wave shows that alternating current flows first one way round a circuit and then in the opposite direction. If the lower half of the sine wave could be eliminated then current would flow in pulses, but always in the same direction. For battery charging this pulsation of current does not matter, and an ammeter would register the average value of current.

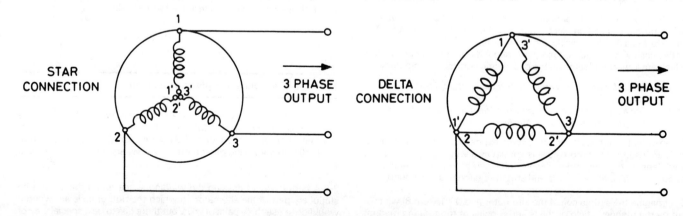

Fig. 12.5 Star and delta connections (Sec 3)

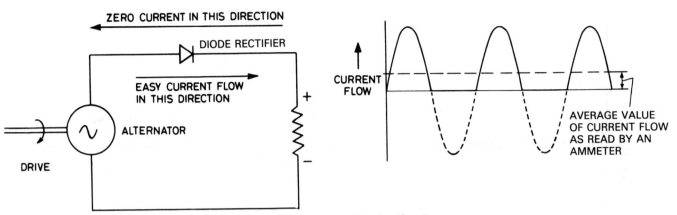

Fig. 12.6 Half-wave rectification (Sec 4)

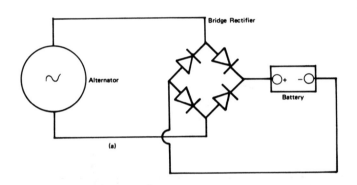

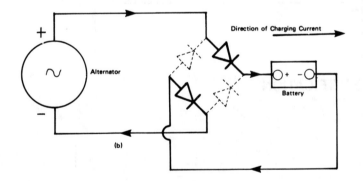

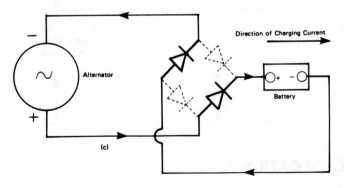

Fig. 12.7 Action of the full-wave rectifier (Sec 4)

Rectifier operation

3   A device which will prevent current flowing in one direction, but allow it to flow in the opposite direction, is called a rectifier. Modern rectifiers are usually made of semiconductor materials and are highly efficient. Fig. 12.6 shows a simple circuit consisting of an alternator connected to a resistive load, via a rectifier. The lower half of the current wave is stopped by the rectifier, allowing pulses to flow through the resistor, but always in the same direction – that is, direct current. For obvious reasons this is known as half-wave rectification: it is inefficient because the lower half of the current wave is wasted.

4   A better method of conversion is to use full-wave rectification. As the name implies the whole of the alternating sine wave is used, and to accomplish this, four rectifiers are used (Fig. 12.7). The alternator will produce an output voltage which changes polarity so that it is, in effect, like a battery which rapidly reverses its leads – and we may give instantaneous + and – signs to the output terminals.

5   Current will flow through a rectifier in the direction of the arrow, but not against it, so if the positive (+) wire at the alternator is traced through, current will flow through the battery and two rectifiers. When the polarity reverses, current flows through the opposite pair of rectifiers, but always in the same direction through the battery. Thus the whole of the ac wave has been routed to the battery.

Fig. 12.8 shows the waveforms from half- and full-wave rectifiers. The physical layout of one type of full-wave rectifier (a bridge rectifier) is shown in Fig. 12.9. The individual rectifier elements are often known as diodes, or sometimes as diode rectifiers.

Note that the diodes 1, 2, 3 and 4, although mounted on a single spindle, can be drawn in a square for easier visualisation. To remember how to draw a full-wave bridge rectifier make the left terminal negative (–), the ac being fed in at top and bottom. Finally, the rectifier shown in Fig. 12.9 could have positive (+) earth (ground) to the fixing bolt if all the rectifiers were reversed. (The fixing nuts must never be disturbed as this would entail buying another rectifier!)

6   Three-phase rectification is along the same lines as the full-wave rectifier shown. Fig. 12.11 shows a three-phase alternator connected to a three-phase full-wave rectifier.

The effect of reversing each negative half cycle is to give an output voltage or current which has a high average value and a much lower ripple than in the single-phase case. In fact there will be six 'half-waves' per 360° (Fig. 12.10) and the average value of direct current or voltage is higher than for a single-phase full-wave rectifier.

The current arrowheads in Fig. 12.11 show the path of currents in the three lines at the instant when the top coil of the alternator is a positive (+) max and the other two will be negative (–) at half max value. Note that this is not a diagram of a complete charging circuit since some form of regulating the alternator output is needed.

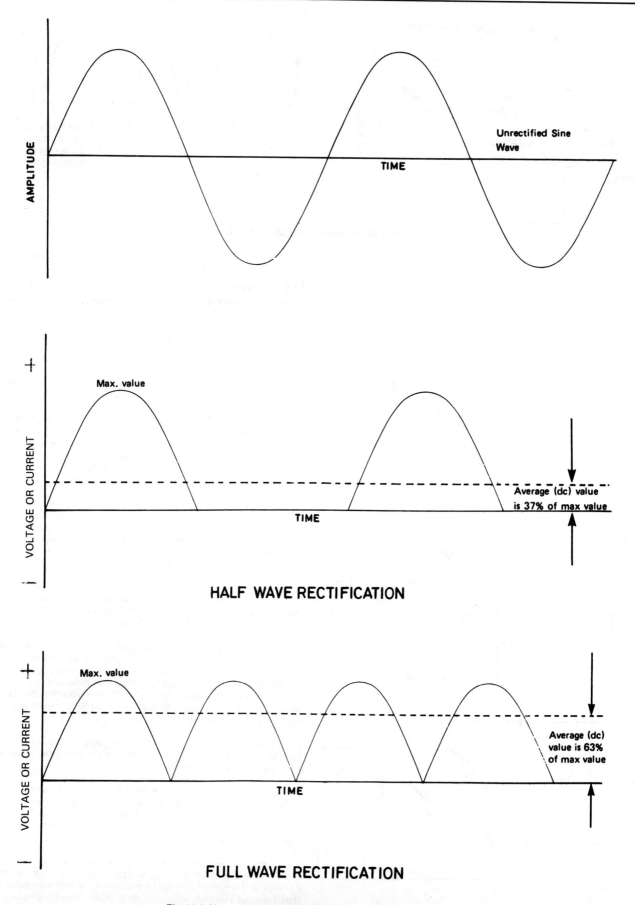

Fig. 12.8 Alternating current and rectified waveforms (Sec 4)

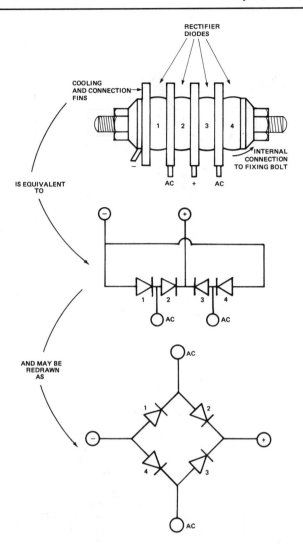

Fig. 12.9 Layout of full-wave (bridge) rectifer (Sec 4)

Rectifier testing

7   If the battery is found to be discharged even after a prolonged run, or after the machine has been standing for only a short while, then the rectifier may be at fault.

Each element of the bridge should pass current in one direction but not in the other. (In practice a small 'back leakage' can be tolerated.) To check that all is in order an ordinary multimeter on the ohms range may be used since this has a built-in battery. Switch to the ohms range ($\Omega \times 1$) and set the pointer to zero, with the test prods shorted together. Then by applying the test prods to each element and swapping the prods over, the readings should be about 10 ohms in one direction and very high (full scale) in the other. Do not worry if the forward resistance is not 10 ohms since the exact value will depend on the make of rectifier and also on the internal voltage of the meter – what is important is that each rectifier element reads the same. If the forward resistances are not the same, or there is a low reverse resistance, the rectifier must be renewed.

If no ohmmeter is available, it is possible to test the rectifier with the aid of a battery and a low wattage bulb. Both battery and bulb could well be those used in a flashlamp. With the leads connected one way round to a rectifier element, the bulb should light, but not with the leads the other way round.

8   The principle of testing the elements is clearly that current will flow through easily when the applied voltage is in the correct direction; this voltage is derived from the internal battery of the tester or the flashlamp battery. Note from Fig. 12.12 the direction of the rectifier arrowhead and the battery/tester polarity.

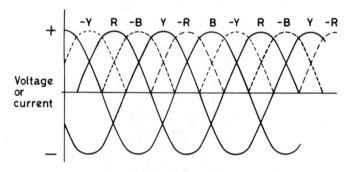

Fig. 12.10 Waveforms of the full-wave three-phase rectifier (Sec 4)

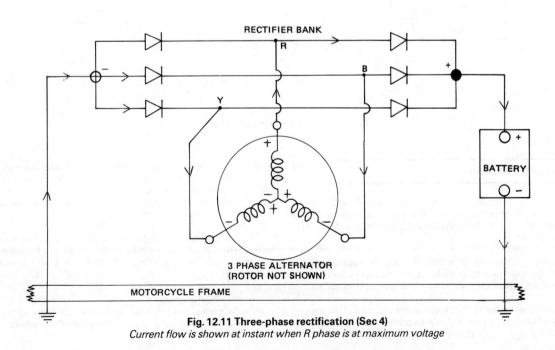

Fig. 12.11 Three-phase rectification (Sec 4)
Current flow is shown at instant when R phase is at maximum voltage

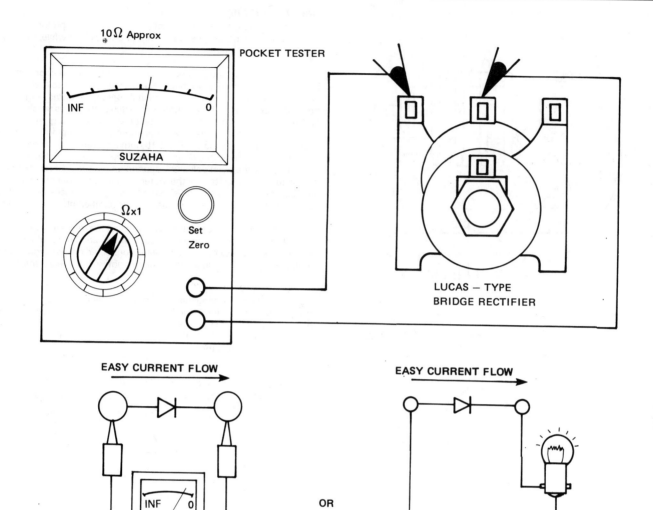

Fig. 12.12 Rectifier testing (Sec 4)

5   Development of the alternator

1   Alternators really entered the motorcycle scene with the development of the flywheel magneto. This found application with smaller machines only, due to the limitation on coil sizes in order to fit inside the rotating flywheel.

2   The early Lucas alternators generated 6 volts dc (approx) after rectification and consisted of a rotating permanent magnet system with a stationary armature (called a stator) on which was wound six coils.

There are difficulties in regulating the charge with machines of this type since the magnetic strength is fixed but coarse control was achieved by switching in some of the coils for daylight riding and all of them at night.

Later this alternator was produced for 12 volt working and was fitted with a Zener diode to achieve charge regulation. Present day designs now include electromagnets in place of the permanent magnets, thus giving far better charge control. In addition, more power is available by the use of three-phase windings.

3   The categories of alternator discussed are as follows, together with the regulators associated with types (b) and (c), the flywheel alternator being essentially self-regulating. Refer to Part A, B or C of this chapter as appropriate.

(a)   Flywheel alternators.
(b)   Permanent magnet single-phase inductor alternators.
(c)   Permanent magnet or electromagnetic three-phase alternators.

Part A: Flywheel alternators

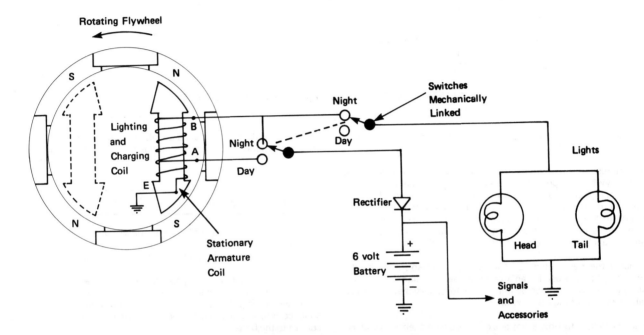

Fig. 12.13 Lighting and charging by flywheel alternator (Sec 7)

6 The Flywheel alternator

1   Generally trouble-free, this set has been touched upon in Chapter 5 where Figs. 5.14 and 5.15 show the details of construction. The flywheel has magnets cast into the rim and these pass over laminated pole shoes on which the lighting and ignition feed coils are wound. As the magnets pass in sequence N S N S, the direction of the magnetic flux changes through the coils and so an alternating voltage is generated.

7 Lighting and charging

1   The lighting/charging coil of the flywheel assembly has a generated voltage of approximately 6 volts ac.

2   One end of the coil is earthed (grounded) to the motorcycle frame at point E (Fig. 12.13) and the electrical output comes from either terminal A or B. The higher output comes when the whole of the coil is used and this is switched in when the lights are on. For daytime use without lights, it is sufficient to pick off only part of the output at tap A.

3   The voltage coming from taps A and B is practically the same when on their respective loads; it is to be expected that the total **generated voltage** at tap B is greater than that at point A, but so also is the load current, since the lights must be supplied. The effect of the heavier current flowing through the whole coil from E to B is to produce a

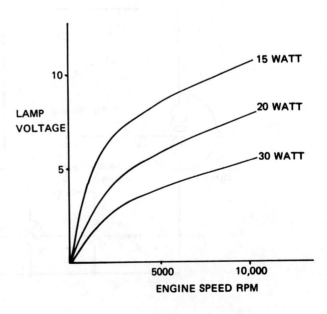

Fig. 12.14 Lighting curves (Sec 7)

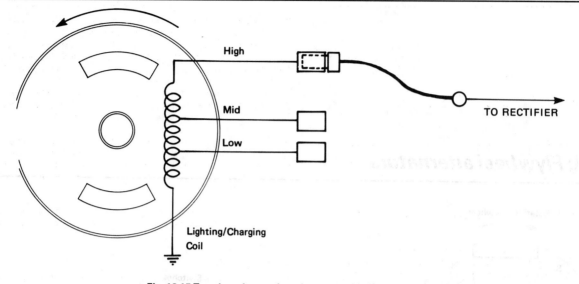

Fig. 12.15 Tap changing to alter charge rate (early models) (Sec 8)

voltage loss so that in fact the voltage that is left is still 6 volts approximately.

4   It is interesting to see what happens when the engine speed rises. Since the flywheel magnets are passing over the armature coil at a faster rate (or higher frequency) one might expect the generated voltage to rise. There are, however, losses in the coil which increase in proportion to the frequency of the current and the rise in voltage is offset by these losses, so that what finally emerges (known as the terminal voltage) is nearly constant after the first 2000 rpm.

Reference to the graph of Fig. 12.14 shows this, and also shows that if a higher wattage bulb is used in an attempt to raise the illumination level this simply results in a further lowering of the terminal voltage, and so a probable lowering of the illumination.

5   Use of a bulb of too low a wattage gives too high a terminal voltage

and the bulb then runs at such a high temperature that its life is very short. It is important, therefore, that the correct wattage bulb is always used.

---

8   Charge rate adjustment

1   Some flywheel assemblies make provision for different rates of charge depending on the use to which the machine is put. Up to 3 tappings are made on the lighting/charging coil in Fig. 12.15.

2   The simple lighting/charging assembly has been used for many years, but modern versions now have electronic regulation. One version is shown in Fig. 12.16. The charging output of the alternator is connected to a regulator/rectifier unit in which diode D1 rectifies the current to the battery.

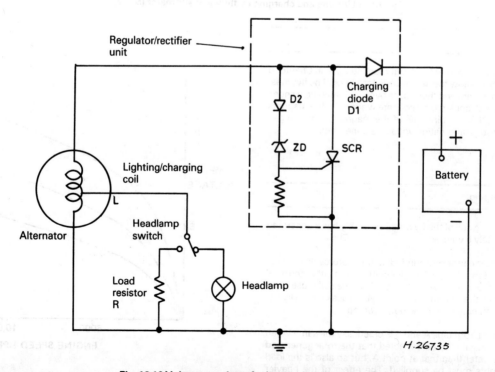

Fig. 12.16 Voltage regulator for low power alternator (Sec 8)

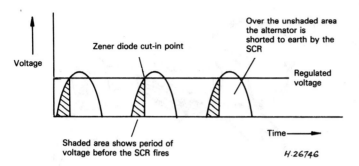

Fig. 12.17 Regulator circuit output waveform (Sec 8)

As the engine speed increases, the alternator voltage rises. Diode D2 conducts on the positive half cycles and at a certain voltage, the Zener diode ZD abruptly conducts, feeding current to the gate of the Silicon Controlled Rectifier SCR (or thyristor). The SCR turns on, short circuiting the output of the alternator to earth (ground). This happens on each positive half cycle of the alternator output and so regulates the voltage to the battery (Fig. 12.17).

3   If the alternator has a combined lighting and charging coil, the charging will be affected by whether the headlamp is on or off.

Referring again to Fig. 12.16, the headlamp switch connects the load resistor (R) to the alternator lighting tap (L) when the headlamp is off, creating a load equivalent to that of the headlamp bulb. This stabilises the output voltage to the battery. This type of regulator is also used on three-phase alternators.

9   Flywheel alternators – troubleshooting

1   The majority of faults occurring in motorcycle electrical systems are simple, but finding them may not be so easy. However, a systematic approach will pay dividends, there being no need for the replacement of every item until 'it works'.

Charging output check

2   An examination of the basic circuit of the flywheel assembly charging system shown in Fig. 12.18 will provide a good example of how to conduct a test routine.

If the battery runs down even though the motorcycle is used regularly, the first thing to check is the charging rate. To do this the circuit between the rectifier and the battery must be broken and an ammeter connected in. *Remember the ammeter is connected always in series with the circuit components as shown.* Note also that if the charging system is working correctly, current will flow through the rectifier in the direction of the arrowhead and down through the battery when the engine is run; thus the ammeter terminals should be connected as indicated in Fig. 12.18.

3   The ammeter should read zero when the engine is not running; if the needle shows a small reverse current, this indicates a leaking rectifier since it should only pass current from left to right in the diagram. If engine speed is increased to 5000 rev/min the charge rate should be about 1 ampere.

If there is no charging current, the next thing is to check the circuit and its components for continuity, ie to see whether there is an electrical path.

Continuity check

4   Use an ohmmeter or a pocket multimeter (a combination instrument which will read volts, amperes and ohms) for this check. If using a multimeter, the 'ohms' or resistance range is required.

The two leads from the tester should be applied to the part under test. The meter scale should, of course, read zero for a continuous path and full scale (or infinity) for a component with no electrical conduction (very high resistance). Lighting/charging coils should show a very low resistance of a few ohms only. Some meters have no scale for continuity checks, but instead a built-in buzzer sounds when there is continuity.

10   Flywheel removal

1   In order to inspect the coils it will be necessary to remove the flywheel with its built-in magnets. To do this correctly, the flywheel must be prevented from rotating, preferably using a special holding tool, whilst its central mounting nut or bolt is removed (Fig. 12.19). Note that the flywheel is mounted on a taper, which usually houses a Woodruff key.

2   A typical flywheel puller is shown, the outer thread of which screws into the flywheel boss once the retaining nut/bolt has been slackened and removed. The puller centre bolt is tightened down on the crankshaft

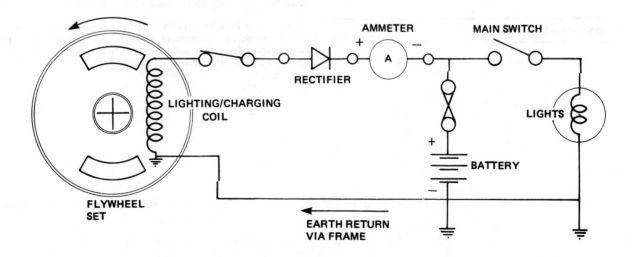

Fig. 12.18 Measurement of charge current (Sec 9)

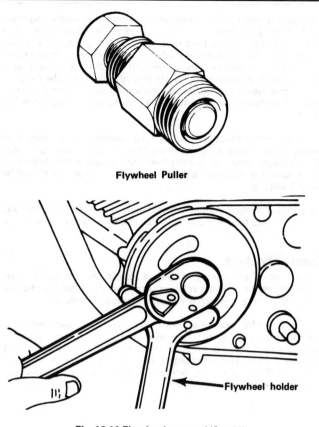

Fig. 12.19 Flywheel removal (Sec 10)

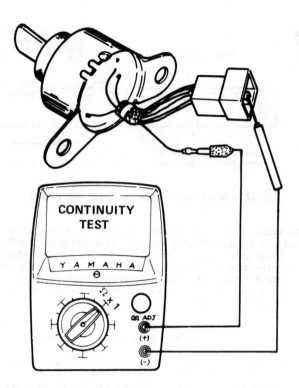

Fig. 12.20 Testing a main/ignition switch for continuity (Sec 11)

end to dislodge the flywheel from its taper. Note the following precautions.

(a) Never hammer the flywheel on or off, otherwise the magnets may be damaged.

(b) Avoid the use of a legged-puller to withdraw the flywheel; this may cause distortion.

(c) Check for wear of the Woodruff key in its crankshaft slot and corresponding flywheel slot.

(d) Check that no foreign objects adhere to the flywheel magnets on re-assembly, eg nails, washers, swarf, etc. The poles must be thoroughly clean before refitting.

(e) Tighten the flywheel nut/bolt to the torque setting specified by the machine manufacturer on refitting.

11   Main/ignition switch faults

1   Switches are made down to a price and are by no means

trouble-free. Sometimes there is simply a mechanical failure but there is the possibility that poor contacts will develop due to corrosion if the motorcycle has been subjected to damp. The fault may then result in imperfect operation of lights or accessories, and usually the only cure is to fit a new switch.

2   To check contacts between any two terminals on the switch, the tester should be switched to the ohms range or continuity test position. The machine's wiring diagram will show which contacts should join at each switch position; the resultant resistance should be zero. Check also for intermittent contact by 'wiggling' the key or knob to the switch, Fig. 12.20.

3   Note that bullet or prong connectors can sometimes come apart underneath their plastic weatherproof covers, without it being apparent; check each one by direct inspection.

Wires can occasionally break internally, even though the outer insulation looks sound, especially where the wire passes close to frame components. Breaks can usually be located by lightly stretching the wire until the insulation 'gives' at the fault point.

Part B: Single-phase alternators

12 The Internal permanent magnet single-phase alternator

1 Alternators of this type are usually mounted on the end of the crankshaft, with the rotor running inside a set of stator coils. The principle of operation is thus the same as for the flywheel alternator. One difference, due to the smaller mass and working radius of the rotor magnets, however, is that there is now no significant flywheel effect.

2 Fig. 12.21 shows one of the Lucas RM series alternators. Troubles were experienced with earlier types because of vibration effects on the coils, often causing the entire stator to work loose. The much improved 47204 encapsulated stator shown cured the loose coil trouble, but it is recommended that whenever a primary chaincase is removed, the stator bolts or studs are fixed with Loctite.

3 The stator consists of six coils set on circular laminations which have six projections or poles. Later models had encapsulated coils to protect them from vibration and also from metallic swarf created by the chain and sprockets in the primary chaincase. It is good practice to drain and change the chaincase oil regularly to prevent swarf attaching itself to the magnetised rotor and to protect stator coils if they are of the older unencapsulated type.

4 Two types of stator are likely to be found, those with 3 wires (early types 1953 to 66) and those with 2 wires (later 12 volt version). The 2-wire version is electrically similar to the early type but the coils are internally connected, and hence give maximum output at all times when running. Early Lucas alternators were designed for 6 volt systems but 12 volt assemblies were supplied for the Triumph Thunderbird in 1965.

5 The rotor has a steel centre which is hexagon shaped like the head of a bolt. A powerful permanent magnet is mounted on each hexagon, the outer face of which is keyed to a laminated pole tip. The whole is then cast into aluminium (which will not affect the magnetism) and lathe-turned to give a smooth external finish. Thus there are six magnetic poles which pass simultaneously under the six stator windings, and the current from the stator will alternate at a frequency dependent on the crankshaft speed. It is important to maintain a gap between rotor and stator of 0.2 mm (0.008 inch). Note also that early rotors suffered from the centre of the rotor separating from the rest of the casting with disastrous results.

13 Early Lucas alternators – 1953 to 1966

1 The main switch has 3 positions, OFF, PILOT and HEAD, and the six coils are switched so as to give 3 levels of output as shown in Fig. 12.22. This shows the lighting switch at HEAD (Headlight) position and all three pairs of coils are in parallel to give maximum output.

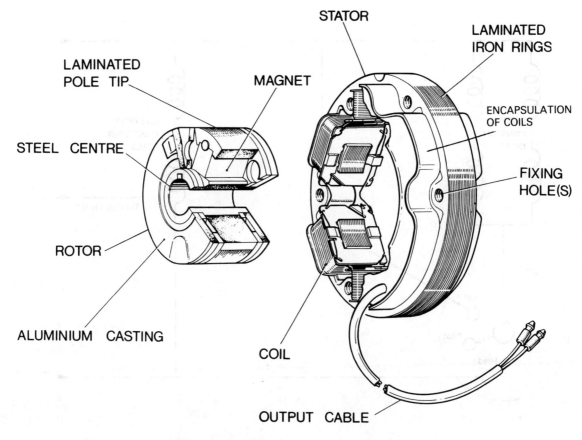

Fig. 12.21 Lucas RM series alternator (RM21) (Sec 12)

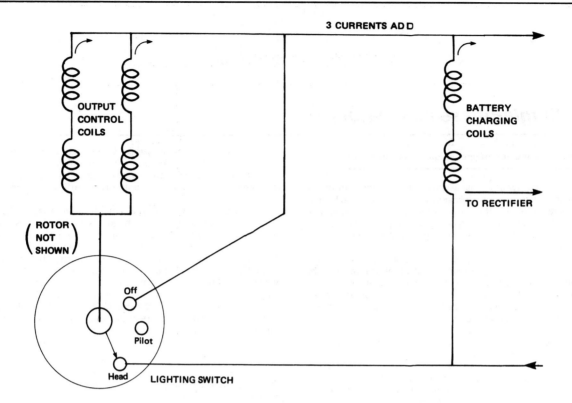

Fig. 12.22 HEAD switch position – early Lucas alternator (Sec 13)

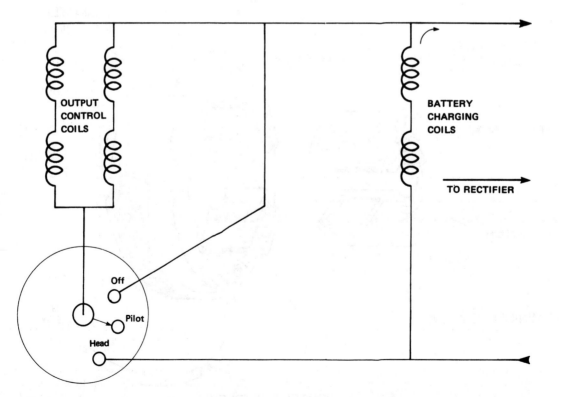

Fig. 12.23 PILOT switch position – early Lucas alternator (Sec 13)

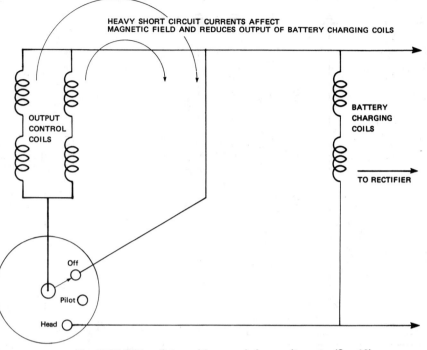

Fig. 12.24 OFF switch position – early Lucas alternator (Sec 13)

2   In Fig. 12.23 with the lighting switch at PILOT position, the output control coils are inoperative and the rectifier receives the current from the battery charging coils only. This is enough to power the pilot and rear lights.

3   When the main switch is OFF (Fig. 12.24) only a trickle charge is required by the battery. Now the output control coils are working into a short circuit and as a result a heavy current will flow through them. This current will create a magnetic field which tends to offset the magnetic field of the permanent magnet rotor so that the net field strength linking with the battery charging coils is reduced and the electrical output is low.

4   Lucas made variations so that in some models two sets of coils are connected permanently for battery charging and only one set for output control. The principle of operation, however, remains the same for all cases.

14   Lucas alternator colour-coding

1   Wiring codes for the three-wire alternators started out using three shades of green but with ageing they became difficult to identify.

A change was made to dark green, green and yellow, and light green, but eventually the colours of green and black, green and yellow, and white and green were chosen for easy identification (Fig. 12.25). For a table of Lucas cable colour codes see Fig. 12.26.

15   Emergency start (EMG)

1   One of the many possible wiring options is the Lucas emergency start connection, for use when a battery is flat. With the switch in the EMG position, the output of four coils is taken to the ignition coil via the two coil wire connected to the lighting switch.

2   The engine may be started and run temporarily in the EMG mode

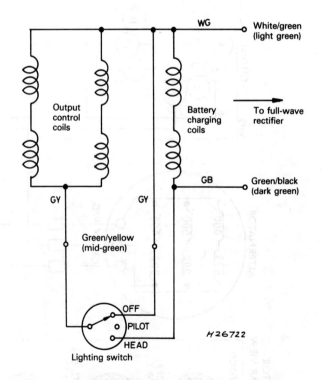

Fig. 12.25 Lucas alternator colour-coding (Sec 14)
Colours in parentheses relate to old Lucas colour-coding

provided the ignition has been accurately timed. Misfiring may soon occur, however, and the switch should be returned to the ignition IGN position. In the EMG connection, the ignition system is converted to Energy Transfer (ET) (see Chapter 5). A connection is still made to the battery, however, and, as its voltage rises, will cause misfiring (Fig. 12.26).

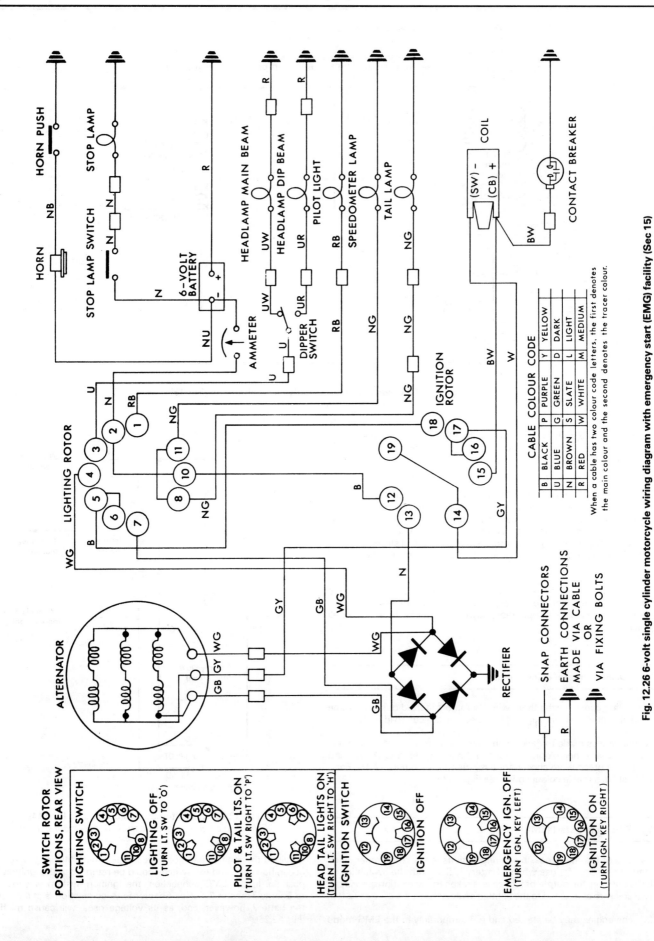

Fig. 12.26 6-volt single cylinder motorcycle wiring diagram with emergency start (EMG) facility (Sec 15)

CAUTION   DO NOT OVERTIGHTEN
STUD NUT
MAXIMUM TORQUE 2 lbf ft

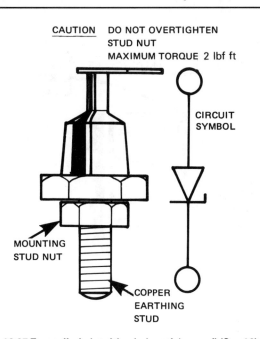

CIRCUIT
SYMBOL

MOUNTING
STUD NUT

COPPER
EARTHING
STUD

Fig. 12.27 Zener diode (positive (+) earth/ground) (Sec 16)

16   Later Lucas alternators

1   Some degree of battery charging control was achieved by switching coils in early circuits but the method was by no means perfect. Motorcycle electrical designers had long wished to use 12 volt circuits and the opportunity came in 1963 with the arrival of the power Zener diode (Fig. 12.27).

Using the standard Lucas RM alternator, which has the ability to run a 12 volt circuit, the solution was a vast improvement over earlier arrangements and was quickly adopted in new motorcycles and by owners who wanted to convert their machines from 6 volt to 12 volt.

2   Basically, the Zener diode behaves like a pressure relief valve. Until

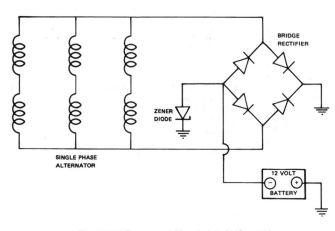

Fig. 12.28 Zener stabilised circuit (Sec 16)

the pressure on it reaches about 14 volts it will not pass current, but at this voltage it becomes partially conductive and drains off to earth (ground) some charging current. As the voltage rises to 15V the Zener passes a large current and virtually none reaches the battery.

If an electrical load, such as the head and tail bulbs is now switched on, this will lower the system voltage and the Zener diode becomes less conductive and more rectified current flows to the battery. It is thus a highly efficient regulator which has no moving parts and requires no maintenance. Connections for later Zener diode 12 volt systems are shown in Fig. 12.28 and for this arrangement it is necessary to use a heat sink (a cooling fin or fins on which the Zener diode is bolted) of at least 36 in^2 and mounted in a good airstream for cooling. Note that all six coils are connected to give maximum power output.

The change to full power output with six coils permanently connected did not occur straightaway with the introduction of the Zener diode and some machines may be found with switched coils. In these cases four coils are used for charging in coil ignition machines, the remaining two being switched in for headlamp loads. Magneto ignition machines used two coils for charging and switched in the remaining four coils for headlamp work. Smaller heat sinks are also used for the Zener diode.

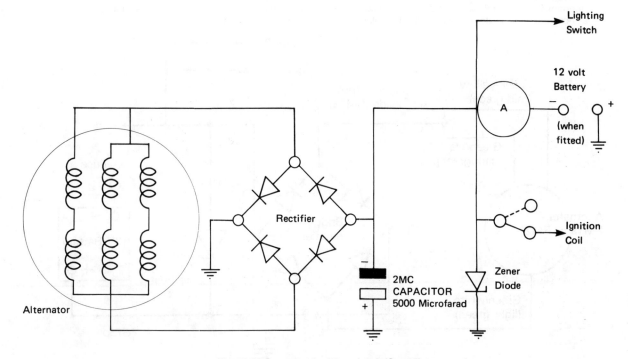

Fig. 12.29 Capacitor ignition circuit (Sec 17)

3   Lucas improved the power rating of alternators and the RM15 and RM18 machines of only 80 watt output were superseded by the RM19 110 watt and the RM21 (two-wire 110 watt) alternators. Inevitably the advantages of using three-phase led to the availability of the RM24 alternator (180 watt). A table of alternators presently available from one source is given below.

Model	Power	Phases	Comment
RM19	110 watt	Single-phase	6 volt 3-wire (can be converted to 12 volt 2-wire
RM21	110 watt	Single-phase	12 volt 2-wire
RM23	180 watt	Single-phase	Needs extra Zener
RM24	180 watt	Three-phase	Zener control

The increase of power, even at kickstart speeds, means that with a flat battery, starting is possible at the third or fourth kick if the ignition system is in good order. Emergency start (EMG) was rendered obsolete by these later designs.

17   Capacitor ignition circuit

1   A capacitor will store electrical charge and allow it to discharge again when a suitable circuit is connected to it. If a large capacitor is connected on the dc side of the rectifier then each alternator pulse will charge up the capacitor; it is then possible to use this stored charge to supply an ignition coil when the battery is disconnected.

Sufficient energy is stored to ensure adequate plug sparking for starting and running at all speeds throughout the engine speed range. The main use of this ignition capacitor is for competition work where the battery is removed, or in cases of a flat battery. It is wise to check that the capacitor is working correctly from time to time by disconnecting the battery and starting the engine.

2   The Lucas 2MC capacitor of 5000 μF capacity is of the electrolytic type, meaning that it must be connected with the correct polarity or it will be quickly destroyed. Fig. 12.29 shows the basic circuit employing both a 2MC capacitor and a Zener diode; the physical mounting of the capacitor is important for the terminals must point downwards. The aluminium case housing the capacitor is pushed into the coiled spring

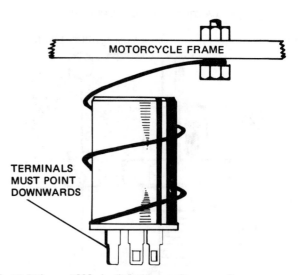

Fig. 12.30 Lucas 2MC electrolytic capacitor mounting arrangement (Sec 17)

until it locates on the groove and the spring is then bolted securely to the frame (Fig. 12.30).

Check the connections carefully, noting that the positive (+) terminal (the small Lucar connector) is taken to earth (ground). The capacitor negative (–) terminal and the Zener diode must both be connected to the negative output terminal of the rectifier or any other convenient point on that line.

Note that the 2MC capacitor is for positive (+) earth (ground) wiring only. Do not run the engine without the Zener diode or the rise in voltage will destroy the capacitor. Also ensure that the negative (–) lead from the battery is insulated from the frame by taping up the terminal.

18   6 volt to 12 volt alternator conversion

1   Alternators designed for a 6 volt system can easily run up to 12 volts without modification.

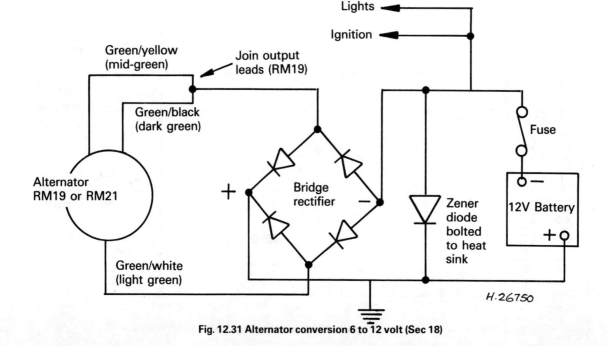

Fig. 12.31 Alternator conversion 6 to 12 volt (Sec 18)

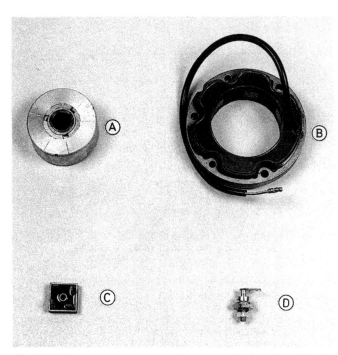

Fig. 12.32 Components necessary for conversion from 6 to 12 volt (Sec 18)

A Rotor   C Rectifier
B Stator   D Zener diode

Components shown were supplied by AO Services

In the case of Lucas RM series alternators the full six coil output may be obtained by joining the green/yellow to the green/black lead. This effectively converts the three-wire alternator to a two-wire type RM21.

2   Figs. 12.31 and 12.32 illustrate the conversion, which involves fitting a Zener diode, new 12 volt bulbs, a 12 volt battery, a 12 volt ignition coil and for good insurance a new capacitor across the ignition points. It is strongly recommended to fit a fuse in the battery output cable (it can be an in-line type) because of the higher system power. The horn may be left in place but it may need adjusting if it gives a peculiar note on its new 12 volt supply!

3   Before undertaking this conversion it is worth thinking about the condition of the alternator. If of the older type, RM15 or RM18 (which give low output), it might be better to fit an RM21 alternator. One other reason is that the rotor may have lost some of its magnetic strength; it is not cost-effective to have it re-magnetised, although it can be done. Similarly, if the rectifier is of the old selenium type it should be replaced with a modern silicon rectifier. Semiconductor developments have resulted in high performance, compact size and low cost, making the retention of a suspect rectifier pointless.

4   An alternative to the Zener diode method is to use the Boyer-Bransden Power Box shown in Fig. 12.33. This unit contains a back-to-back SCR (thyristor) circuit which limits the amplitude of the incoming alternating voltage wave from the alternator. The clipped wave is then passed through a bridge rectifier and is terminated with a 10,000 μF capacitor so that the motorcycle can be run without a battery if required.

The maximum power handling capacity is 180 watts with positive or negative earth (ground) and if fed with a three-wire Lucas alternator, the green/yellow and green/black wires must be joined and connected to one of the yellow input wires to the box. The alternator white/green wire goes to the other yellow input wire. The version shown in Fig. 12.33 has an optional feature which delays power to the lights until the engine is running, allowing all the available energy to go to the ignition while kickstarting. A three-phase version is also available.

Fig. 12.33 'Power box' giving regulated 12 volt dc supply from a single-phase alternator (Sec 18)

19   Testing Lucas alternators

1   The most straightforward way of checking an alternator is to measure the output current under load.

Charging output check

2   Take off the dc output lead from the rectifier and make up a pair of leads which will take current from the rectifier dc output terminal through an ammeter and back to the disconnected output lead. There should be no discernible reverse current from the battery to the rectifier as measured on a low ampere range of the ammeter when the engine is off.

Switch to a high range (at least 10A), start the engine and switch on all the lights. RM19 or RM21 alternators should read about 9 amperes at 3000 rev/min. For the higher power RM23 and 24 types, the current delivery should be 10 amperes or higher at 2,300 rev/min. If the results are significantly lower, this points to trouble with the stator windings or a weak rotor magnet.

Rectifer check

3   Check each element of the rectifier as shown in Section 4 of this chapter.

Stator windings check

4   Measure the resistance between any pair of the 3 stator wires – the ohmmeter should read virtually zero. Measure the insulation resistance between the stator windings and the laminations. It should be very high on the high ohms range. Alternatively, use an ac supply from an isolating transformer not exceeding 40 volts ac in series with a 25 watt bulb. If the bulb lights when the prods are connected between any stator wire and the laminations there is a winding fault.

20   Single-phase alternator control

1   A method of electronic regulation has been used by Suzuki which has some common features with the circuit described in Section 8. The principle is that of bypassing to earth (ground) excess generated current on the ac side of the bridge rectifier.

2   The semiconductor at the heart of this unit is the thyristor (or Silicon Controlled Rectifier, SCR). The thyristor acts very much like a pressure relief valve in hydraulics in that it will not pass current at all until a certain point and then it opens fully (the name thyristor comes from the Greek, meaning 'a door'). In particular, when the gate terminal is supplied with a

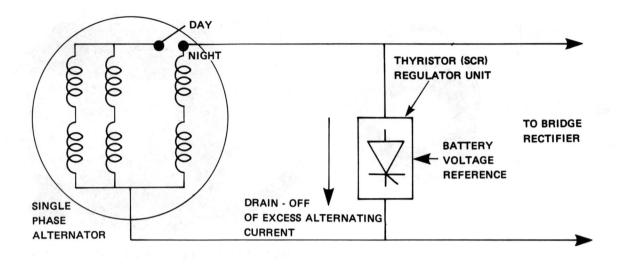

Fig. 12.34 Single-phase alternator and regulator – schematic diagram (Sec 20)

minute current, this is sufficient to switch on the thyristor fully, so connecting anode to cathode.

3   The circuit in Fig. 12.35 has the advantage that the operation of the regulator depends on the state of charge of the motorcycle battery. As the battery voltage eventually rises with charge, the voltage at point A will eventually reach a value at which the Zener diode begins to conduct. Current through the Zener diode will flow into the thyristor gate, thus turning the thyristor ON.

This has the effect of shorting out a portion of one half cycle from the alternator but will not affect the following negative half cycle since the thyristor can only conduct in one direction. By effectively throwing away positive half cycles of energy from the alternator, the regulator has achieved battery-voltage-dependent control. Note that the capacitors serve only to protect the thyristor against transient voltages.

4   Resistance checks can be made from the orange to black/white

leads when, from the diagram it will be seen that the resistance should be about 1.1 kΩ. Measure the resistance in both directions with the ohmmeter between the red/green and the black/white wires. No continuity indicates that the thyristor is likely to be in good condition.

It is important not to alter connections with the ignition switch on or with the engine running since this may give rise to transient voltages which can destroy the thyristor or the Zener diode. Little can be done with a faulty unit since the components are encapsulated in epoxy resin – renewal is essential.

5   Another type of single-phase alternator regulator used in smaller Kawasaki motorcycles is shown in Fig. 12.36. The bridge rectifier incorporates two thyristors (SCR) in place of normal diodes. An integrated circuit (IC) measures the alternating voltage and when the required voltage is reached the IC cuts off the gate signals, so blocking both halves of the ac cycle. The rectifier comes complete with the IC and cannot be repaired.

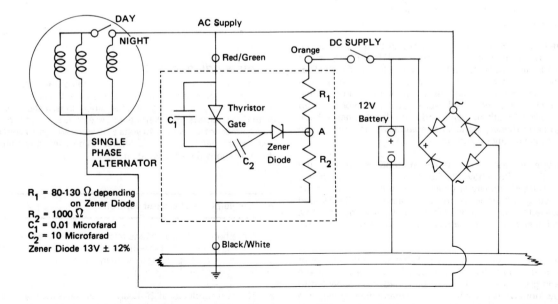

Fig. 12.35 Single-phase alternator with electronic regulator – Suzuki (Sec 20)

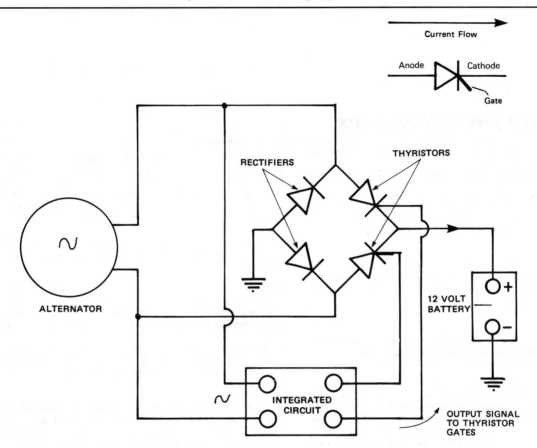

Fig. 12.36 Single-phase alternator with electronic regulator – Kawasaki (Sec 20)

Part C: Three-phase alternators

21 The Three-phase alternator

1   We have already touched upon the principles of three-phase alternators and rectifiers in Sections 3 and 4. An important feature is the production of a rotating magnetic field in the rotor which so far has been produced by permanent magnets for the single-phase generators described earlier.

2   Three-phase alternators may be fitted with permanent magnet rotors or electromagnetic rotors, the advantage of the latter being the ability to control three-phase output voltage by varying the direct current in the rotor winding.

22 Three-phase alternators with permanent magnet rotors

1   A simple two-pole permanent magnet has been shown so far to illustrate the principle of the three-phase alternator. In practice more pairs of poles are used, as shown in the example in Fig. 12.37. Here an outboard set of magnets are cast into the rotor (outboard meaning that the rotor spins outside the stator windings). Inboard rotors are also to be found, but the essential requirement is that a magnetic field should pass through the stator windings in sequence.

2   Control of a three-phase alternator with a permanent magnet rotor always comes down to load 'dumping' when the correct voltage for battery charging has been reached. The Honda circuit shown in Fig. 12.38 shows the principle: 6 rectifiers form a three-phase full-wave bridge and connected to the centre point of each pair is a thyristor (SCR).

When the dc voltage at the battery reaches the required level the voltage sensor's integrated circuit (IC) sends a gate signal to all three thyristor gates. The thyristors conduct and effectively short-circuit the stator output until the dc voltage drops to an accepted level. Note that the stator windings are connected in delta form, the current output being greater than when connected in star form.

3   A similar load dump circuit has been used by Kawasaki. The circuit diagram in Fig. 12.39 and the following text shows one way in which a sensor might work.

One side of the Zener diode ZD is connected to the positive (+) side of the battery via a resistor, to keep a check on charging voltage. The other side goes to the gate terminal of thyristor No 1 (Th_1); it will be seen that each phase has a thyristor and that they are all interconnected.

When the battery terminal voltage is low, say at low engine speed or when heavily loaded, the voltage across the Zener is too low for it to pass current and so all the charge goes from the three-phase rectifier straight to the battery.

When the voltage reaches a predetermined value, somewhere between 14 and 15 volts, the Zener diode conducts and switches on thyristor No 1 (Th_1). The flow of current through R_1 creates a voltage difference between the gate and cathode of thyristor Th_2 which promptly switches on and this acts in the same way to trigger thyristor Th_3. All thyristors bleed off current from the alternator until the battery voltage falls to the required level.

The regulator cannot be repaired and, if faulty, renewal is essential. To test the regulator, check the resistance between the brown wire and earth/ground (black); the reading will be about 300 ohms with the meter

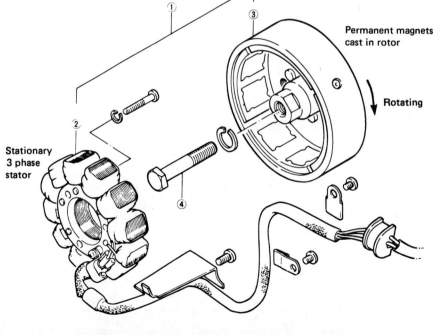

Permanent magnets
cast in rotor

Rotating

Stationary
3 phase
stator

1   Alternator assembly
2   Stator
3   Rotor
4   Centre bolt

Fig. 12.37 Permanent-magnet three-phase alternator – Suzuki (Sec 22)

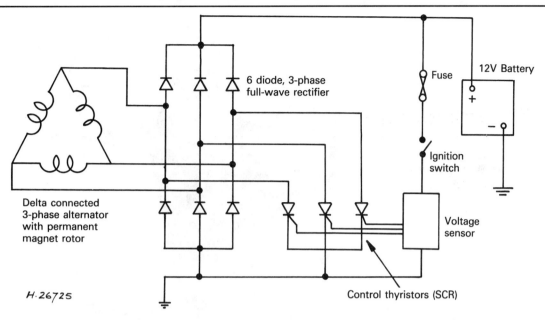

Fig. 12.38 Permanent-magnet three-phase alternator with load dumping regulation (Sec 22)

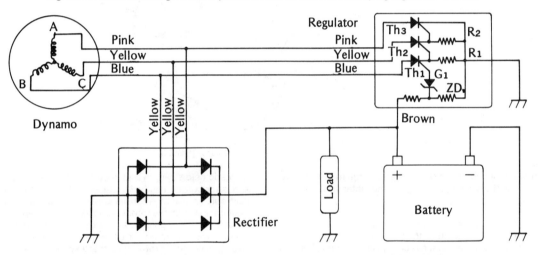

Fig. 12.39 Kawasaki three-phase alternator with load dumping regulator (Sec 22)

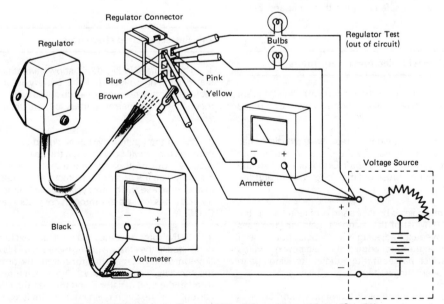

Fig. 12.40 Testing the Kawasaki load dumping regulator (Sec 22)

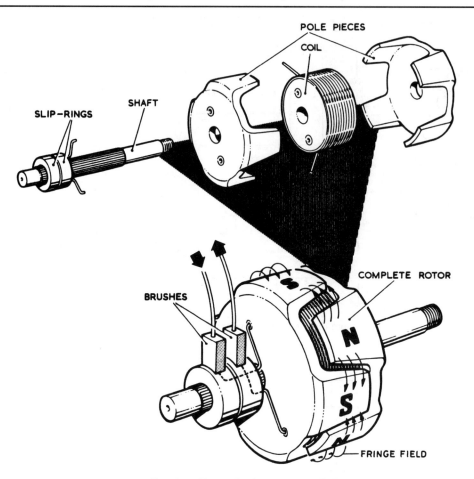

Fig. 12.41 Claw-pole alternator rotor (Sec 23)

positive (+) prod connected to the brown lead and the meter negative
(–) prod connected to the black lead. Reversing the meter prods will give
a reading of about 1050 ohms.

Beyond this it is possible to test the thyristors by gradually increasing
the dc applied voltage (Fig. 12.40) until the bulbs light; this should occur
between 14 and 15 volts. The bulbs act as current limiters and should be
low wattage, eg 12V 5W or similar. If all this is in order the current will be
about 40 mA on the blue lead. Note that it is important to keep the
supply voltage below 18 volts to safeguard the thyristors and Zener
diode.

23   Three-phase alternators with electromagnetic rotors

1   A coil wound around the iron of a rotor and fed with direct current
will produce a suitable field for an alternator. Such an alternator is of the
wound rotor type.

Its advantage over the permanent magnet three-phase alternator has
already been outlined in Section 21, namely the fine control of output
voltage by varying the direct current in the rotor. Disadvantages are the
need for maintenance of slip ring brushes (after long service) and the
extra cost of manufacture.

2   The form of the magnetic poles is usually a series of teeth; this is the
claw pole rotor (Fig. 12.41). Most of the magnetic field (or flux) goes
straight across the gap between the adjacent N and S poles but some of
the magnetic lines of force on the outer edge of the field bow outwards
and it is this fringe field which passes through the stator windings to
generate the three-phase alternating voltage.

3   Direct current is supplied to the rotor coil through carbon brushes
and brass slip rings. Variation of the direct current will control the

magnetic field strength and, therefore, the generated voltage. Control
over rotor current can be by either a vibrating contact regulator, or an
electronic regulator. A further possible variation is the battery-excited
regulator in which the rotor is supplied with current from the battery, or
the self-excited regulator. In the case of the latter, an extra set of 3
diodes takes generated current from the stator, rectifies it and passes it
via a regulator to the rotor. Note that 'excited' is a term used by electrical
engineers to mean the provision of a magnetic field.

24   Battery-excited alternators

1   The diagram in Fig. 12.42 shows a rectifier unit supplied from the
stator windings. Note that the battery is connected straight to the
rectifier; there is no need for a cut-out as with dc generators because the
rectifier will not permit battery current to flow back into the stator
windings.

2   When the ignition switch is closed and the motorcycle is started,
battery current will flow through the coil of the regulator which exerts a
magnetic pull on the regulator armature (Fig. 12.43). Until the voltage
generated on the dc side of the rectifier reaches 15.5 – 16.5 volts (for the
exact figure see the motorcycle workshop manual), the current flow to
the rotor passes straight through contacts A and B which are normally
CLOSED.

3   As the rotor becomes magnetically excited the alternating voltage
generated in the stator winding increases. This means that more current
flows into the voltage regulator coil and the armature is attracted so that
the contacts A and B separate. Now the current to the rotor must pass
through the field resistor R and this has the effect of reducing the rotor
current and hence regulating the direct voltage emerging from the
rectifiers.

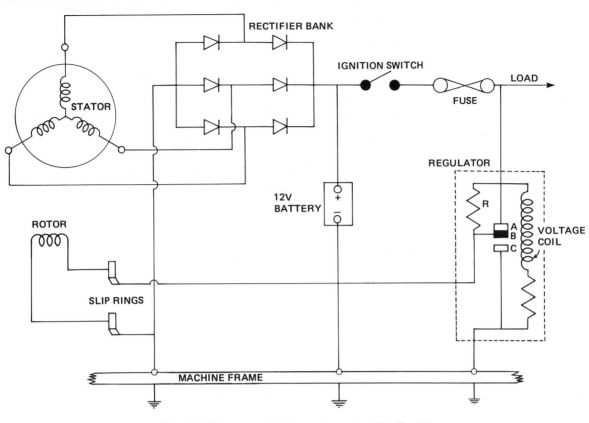

Fig. 12.42 Battery-excited alternator and rectifier (Sec 24)

4 If the alternator speeds up, the armature is pulled down further, to close contacts B and C, thus the rotor is short circuited, the alternator voltage falls rapidly and the contacts separate.

5 The result is that the movable contact B vibrates between A and C, depending on the alternator speed and the load on the battery. Remembering that copper wire increases in resistance with temperature, it will be seen that the current flowing through the voltage coil will decrease as the coil heats up in use. This would affect the output voltage of the alternator since the magnetic field strength would also decrease.

6 To minimise this, a temperature compensating resistor is added in series with the voltage coil. This resistor is made of material which does not change in resistance with temperature and swamps out any

changes in the coil itself. For this reason such resistors are sometimes known as swamp resistors.

25 Self-excited alternators

1 These may be immediately recognised by the rectifier unit, which contains 9 diodes (Fig. 12.44) compared with the 6 diode pack for the battery-excited type of alternator.

2 The regulator works in much the same way as the 6 diode type but the magnetic field of the rotor is derived from current rectified by the energising diodes. Start up is due to the residual magnetism in the rotor

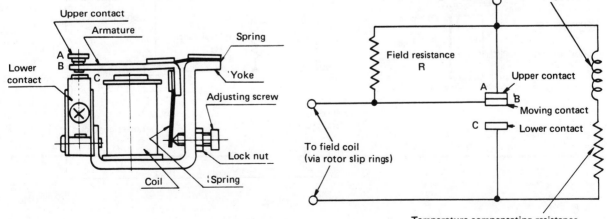

Fig. 12.43 Regulator construction (Sec 24)

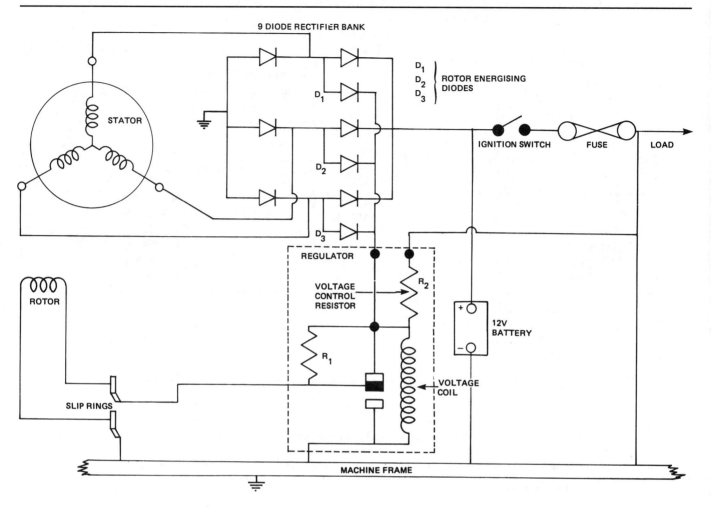

Fig. 12.44 Self-excited alternator and regulator (Sec 25)

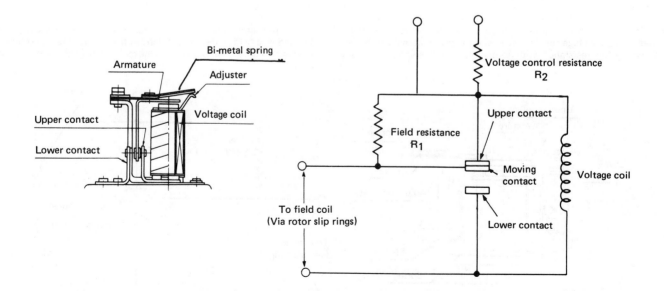

Fig. 12.45 Regulator with bimetal spring temperature compensation (Sec 25)

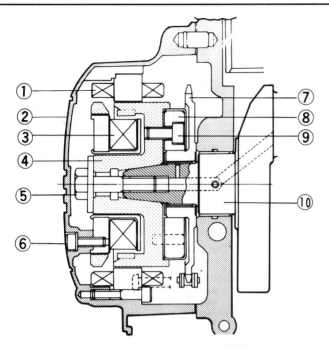

Fig. 12.46 Kawasaki brushless alternator on KZ/Z750 (Sec 26)

1 Stator windings	6 Allen bolt
2 Alternator cover	7 Starter motor sprocket
3 Rotor windings	8 Starter motor clutch
4 Rotor	9 Allen bolt
5 Rotor bolt	10 Crankshaft

iron aided by battery current via the voltage control resistor; when the alternator is driven, a small alternating voltage is generated in the stator winding. This is rectified by the energising diodes and so rapid build-up occurs. In certain cases it is possible to fire up the engine by bump starting even if the battery is flat.

3   The battery is not totally independent however for it is linked to the regulator coil by a resistor R_2 so that the operation is to some extent determined by the state of battery charge.

4   Additionally, the flow of current through R_2 from the battery when ignition is switched on helps to strengthen the residual magnetism in the rotor and ensures a rapid build-up of alternator voltage.

Fig. 12.47 Brushless alternator on Yamaha XS1100 (Sec 26)
See text for details

5   In the regulator shown in Fig. 12.45 the spring is a bimetal strip to take temperature variation into account. If the temperature rises, then the copper voltage regulator coil would take less current because the resistance has increased. This would mean less magnetic pull on the armature but this is compensated by the bimetal spring, which bends so as to reduce the spring force on the regulator armature.

---

26   Brushless alternator with electronic control

---

1   This type is the most powerful of the three-phase alternators and is usually mounted externally to the engine – the so called 'piggyback' fixing. It is used for high capacity motorcycles and is run at a speed higher than the engine by gearing or chain drive.

2   Technically this alternator is an advanced design because both the stator and the rotor windings are stationary. The absence of moving parts should lead to long life and little or no maintenance.

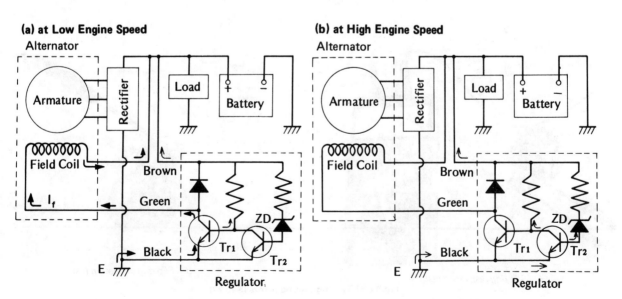

Fig. 12.48 Electronic regulation of wound rotor alternator on Kawasaki KZ/Z750 (Sec 26)

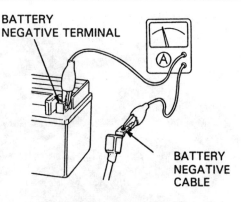

Fig. 12.49 Leakage test (Sec 27)

Study of Fig. 12.46 shows that both stator (1) and the rotor windings (3) are bolted to the cover; the magnetic field created by the rotor windings is picked up by the iron of the rotor (4) to reach the stator windings (1). The magnetic flux must jump airgaps to complete its path but nevertheless can be made sufficiently strong to generate the voltage required in the stator windings (1).

A Yamaha alternator of similar design is shown in Fig. 12.47. The inner coil (A) is the provider of magnetic flux which magnetises the inner part of the rotor. Flux then passes round to the claw poles (B) which have been marked N S for the purpose of identification. The fringe field cuts the stator windings (C) to generate three-phase in them when the rotor iron is running.

3   The electronic control unit switches rotor current on or off to maintain the dc output voltage at the required level.

Operation

4   At low battery voltage the Zener diode does not conduct and so transistor Tr_2 is cut off (Fig. 12.48). Absence of collector current means that the volt drop in the centre resistor will be low, thus the base/emitter voltage difference of transistor Tr_1 will be sufficient to switch on and the current flows down through the field coil into the collector of Tr_1.

The rectifier is to absorb shock transients such as occur when voltages are suddenly changed. At high engine speeds the Zener conducts, Tr_2 conducts and the collector load voltage drop switches off Tr_1 and also the field coil current.

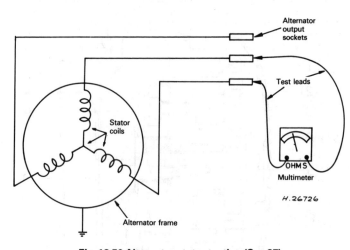

Fig. 12.50 Alternator stator testing (Sec 27)
Stator continuity: check between each pair of stator coils as shown – low ohms should be shown
Stator insulation: check between any stator and alternator frame using the high (x 100 ohms) range for insulation testing – infinity should be shown

27   Testing three-phase alternators

1   If the battery goes flat without any obvious reason, check circuits as follows.

2   Switch on the lights, then start the engine, if possible. Increase engine speed to about 3000 rev/min and note if the lights brighten up. If they do, the alternator is charging. However it is possible that current is leaking away out of the battery. The usual problem in this case is a rectifier with back leakage.

Rectifier

3   To check if leakage is occurring, stop the engine and switch off all loads. Use a multimeter on the amperes range to measure current from the battery to the rectifier. A simple way to do this is to disconnect the battery negative terminal and connect the ammeter as shown in Fig. 12.49.

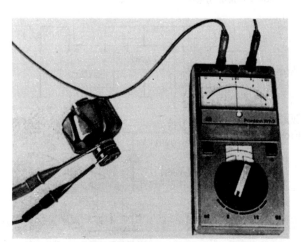

A   Slip ring resistance test

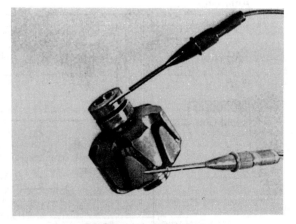

B   Slip ring insulation test

Fig. 12.51 Testing wound rotors (Sec 27)

Always start on the highest range of the ammeter and switch down ranges until the leakage current (if any) can be measured. It should be less than 0.1 ampere according to one manufacturer but a personal view is that even this is too high to be acceptable. A new rectifier is required if leakage is shown. If the motorcycle is used infrequently the rider can defer the replacement by disconnecting the earth (ground) lead after use: but do not delay too long!

To check individual diodes, test each one separately as explained in Section 4, paragraph 7 of this chapter.

Stator

4   The 3 stator wires can usually be reached at a block connector joint. Separate the connector and make the test on the alternator side. Testing between any pair should show the same resistance (Fig. 12.50).

For a typical three-phase 180 watt permanent magnet alternator the resistance between any pair should be in the range 0.1 – 1.0 ohm. For a three-phase 350 watt wound rotor alternator this figure might typically be 0.4 – 0.6 ohm. Whatever the value of resistance the important thing is that all three results should be the same. If there is a significant difference it points to a stator winding fault.

Next check the insulation between any stator wire and the alternator frame. It should be infinite or very high, at the top of the x 100 ohms range.

Rotor – wound rotor design only

5   Check the resistance between the slip rings as shown in Fig. 12.51 (A). If the alternator is in situ, make the connections to the appropriate terminals of the block connector socket. A low ohms figure should be read, for example the Honda CBR1000F is 2.0 – 2.6 ohms and the BMW rotor shown reads 6.9 ohms.

Finally, check the insulation resistance to earth (ground) as shown in Fig. 12.51 (B). This can be done with the multimeter on the high ohms range or a 40 volt ac test with a 25 watt mains lamp in series. This ac voltage should be derived from an isolating transformer and not directly from the mains.

Chapter 13 Batteries

Contents

1 The Lead-acid battery

1   Motorcycles invariably use the lead-acid battery for the storage of electrical energy.

A battery is made up of several cells connected in series packed together in one container. Each cell contributes a nominal 2 volts; a 12 volt battery has six 2 volt cells (Fig. 13.1). The principal features of the lead-acid cell are as follows.

(a)   *It may be recharged after giving up its stored electrical energy.*
(b)   *The internal resistance is low, so that heavy currents may be drawn without great loss of terminal voltage.*

2   Until 1983, motorcycles always used batteries with free liquid acid and a filler plug/gas vent for each cell. Periodically the acid must be topped up with distilled water due to evaporation. These batteries are still in widespread use, but in that year Yuasa introduced the maintenance-free (MF) battery for motorcycles.

The maintenance-free battery is still of the lead-acid type but with some important differences in construction. For these reasons we will consider the **conventional** and **maintenance-free (MF)** types separately.

2 Conventional lead-acid batteries

1   The battery used for energy storage in motorcycles is a secondary type, that is, it may be recharged when exhausted. This is in contrast to primary cells or batteries such as those in hand-held flashlights, which are expendable and cannot be recharged.

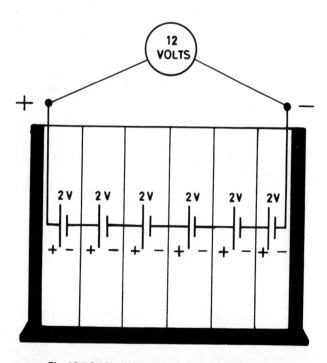

Fig. 13.1 A 12 volt battery of six 2 volt cells (Sec 1)

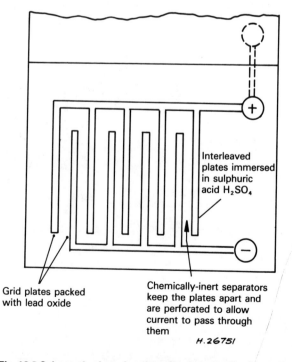

Fig. 13.2 Schematic view showing plate interleaving in one 2 volt cell (Sec 2)

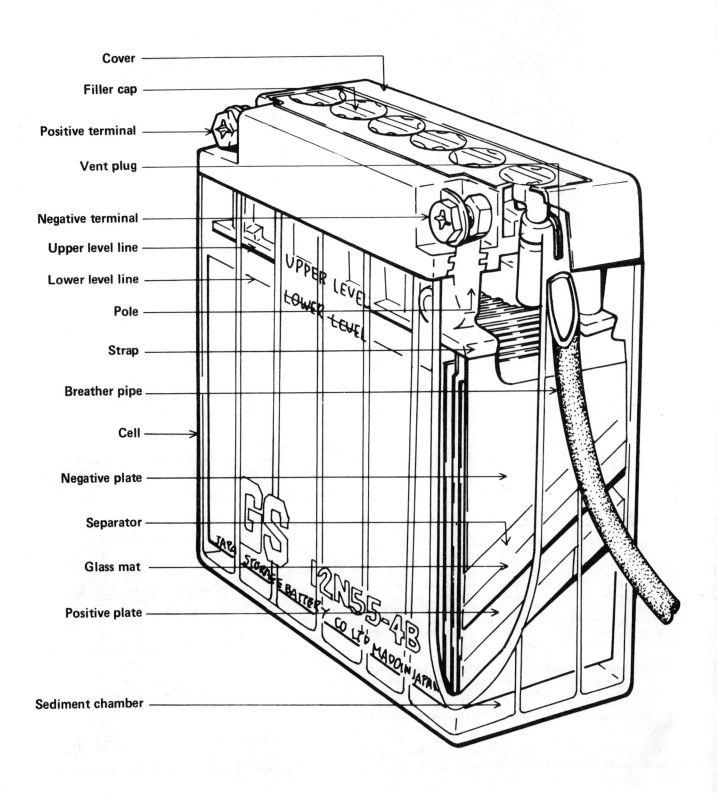

Cover
Filler cap
Positive terminal
Vent plug
Negative terminal
Upper level line
Lower level line
Pole
Strap
Breather pipe
Cell
Negative plate
Separator
Glass mat
Positive plate
Sediment chamber

Fig. 13.3 Cutaway view of a 12 volt motorcycle battery (Sec 2)

Fig. 13.4 Construction of 12 volt motorcycle battery with two cells sectioned (Sec 2)

2   For storing electrical energy it is necessary to have two suitable dissimilar conducting materials immersed in close proximity in a conducting liquid (or compound) called the electrolyte.

The lead-acid battery uses lead-antimony grid plates (several per cell) and the grid holes are filled with lead oxide pastes. These grid plates are interleaved, one set being connected to one battery terminal and the other set to the other battery terminal (Fig. 13.2). Glass matting helps to retain the grid paste in place and the plates are kept apart by separators. Figs 13.3 and 13.4 show the components and construction.

3   When current is passed through the battery, chemical reactions take place which convert the pastes into the required dissimilar conducting materials.

3   Charging, overcharging and discharging

Charging

1   When a battery is charged, current is forced through it in the opposite direction to normal, in much the same way as filling a tank via its outlet tap (Fig. 13.5). The battery gives a direct current (dc) and so it follows that a direct current is required to recharge it. Clearly, if the battery has a terminal voltage of, say, 12 volts, then in order to force current into it, it will require a battery charging voltage somewhat in excess of this, say, 14 to 16 volts depending upon the charge rate required and the internal resistance of the battery.

2   Looking now inside the battery (Fig. 13.6), while under charge conditions we see that the flow of current breaks up the electrolyte and that the electrolyte oxygen moves to combine with the lead of the positive (+) plate to form lead peroxide. Both plates give sulphate to form sulphuric acid in the electrolyte, and the negative plate turns to spongy lead.

3   Thus the two plates are altered chemically and the concentration of sulphuric acid increases, ie the density or specific gravity, of the electrolyte goes up as charging continues.

4   Near the end of the charge, oxygen and hydrogen gases are given off (Fig. 13.7) and the cells are said to be gassing; this occurs when the voltage reaches 2.4 volts per cell. The combination is an explosive mixture and care must be taken to avoid having sparks, cigarettes or naked flames near the battery vents. Remember that battery acid will

attack eyes, skin, clothing and motorcycle paintwork. Affected parts should be washed with cold water in case of accidents.

5   Water is lost from the electrolyte during charging especially near the end. This loss has the following two effects.

   (a)   *The level of electrolyte goes down and, if the plates are partially uncovered, the battery capacity decreases.*

   (b)   *The lost water must be replaced with distilled water. This process is 'topping up' and must be to the level mark and no more. Tap water must not be used or the battery will be ruined.*

Overcharging

6   Overcharging occurs when the positive and negative plates have been fully converted to lead peroxide (+) and spongy lead (–) respectively. It is at this stage when gassing increases, and if left on charge, the battery will lose water rapidly. The charging current now

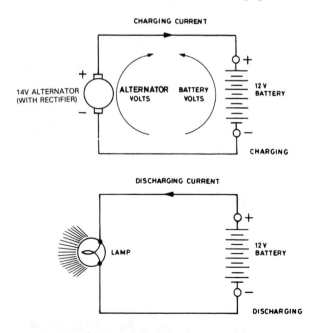

Fig. 13.5 Charging and discharging action (Sec 3)

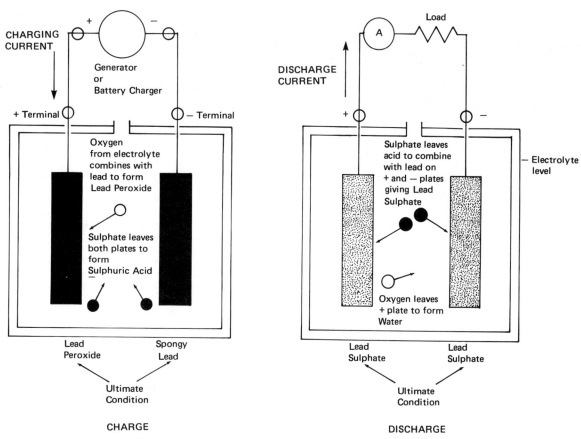

Fig. 13.6 Charging and discharging a lead-acid battery (Sec 3)

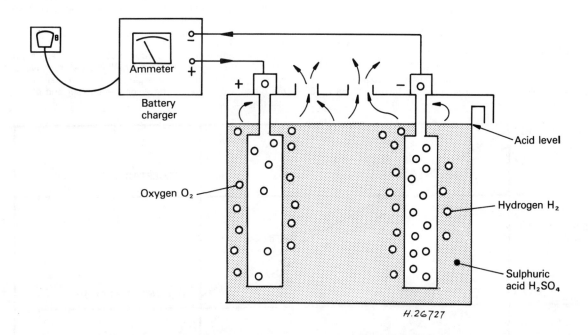

Fig. 13.7 Gas emissions from a battery on charge (Sec 3)

Gases are given off a battery when being charged, but mostly at the end of charge period. Unscrew the battery filler caps when bench charging and do not allow sparks, cigarettes or flame near.

Hydrogen with Oxygen is an EXPLOSIVE combination

serves only to split water into oxygen and hydrogen, which escape as a potentially explosive combination.

Discharging

7   When discharging, the battery sends current out from the positive (+) terminal, around the external circuit and back in again at the negative (–) terminal. (It is useful to think of the battery as a pump which sets electricity in motion round a circuit, like a pump pushes fluid round a liquid cooling system.) The reverse chemical action now takes place in the battery; sulphate leaves the acid to combine with lead on both the positive (+) and negative (–) plates to form lead sulphate. Oxygen leaves the positive plate to form water. Two things have happened at this stage.

(a)   *The positive and negative plates are converted to both be lead sulphate. Because they gradually become identical chemically, there is no difference between them and the voltage between them drops, but should never be allowed to fall below 1.8 volts per cell (10.8 volts for a 12 volt battery).*

(b)   *Water dilutes the sulphuric acid and lowers the specific gravity.*

Battery condition table

Battery condition	Positive (+) plates	Negative (–) plates	Acid	Voltage
Charged	Lead peroxide	Spongy lead	High specific gravity	2.2 volts (approx) per cell*
Discharged	Lead sulphate	Lead sulphate	Lower specific gravity	1.8 volts per cell

*After a rest period

8   The state of charge can be measured by the specific gravity of the battery acid using an hydrometer or by the terminal voltage. In practice, specific gravity measurement is more reliable and is widely used.

4   Battery capacity

1   This is a measure of the total quantity of electricity which a fully charged battery can pump round a circuit. It is measured in ampere-hours (Ah).

2   The rated current is the steady load current which would completely discharge the battery in 10 hours; it is known as the 10-hour-rate current. If the actual discharge rate is higher, then the output capacity is reduced. For example, the 10-hour-rate of a 15 Ah battery is 1.5 amperes. If the battery were actually loaded at 3 amperes it is unlikely that the battery would last as long as 5 hours (3A x 5h = 15 Ah) but would probably be exhausted in, say, 4.5 hours.

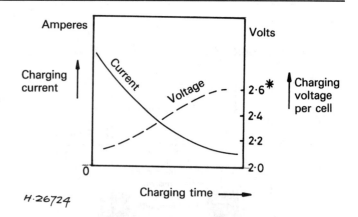

Fig. 13.8 Charging characteristic of a lead-acid battery on an unregulated battery charger (Sec 5)
Cell voltage falls after disconnection from charger

3   As a rough guide, the charging Ah should be about 1.3 x the rated ampere-hour figure; for example, if the above 15 Ah battery were in a state of complete discharge it could safely be given about 15 x 1.3 = 19.5, say, 20 Ah of charge.

5   Charging rate

1   The battery manufacturer sometimes displays the charge rate on the case, but if no figure is available, use between $\frac{1}{10}$ and $\frac{3}{10}$ of the battery capacity. Using the Kawasaki GPZ900R as an example, which has a 14 Ah battery, the charge at the $\frac{1}{10}$ rate is determined as follows.

$$\text{Charging current} = \frac{1}{10} \times 14$$
$$= 1.4 \; amperes$$
$$\text{Charging time} = \frac{18}{1\cdot4}$$
$$= 12 \; hours, \; 50 \; minutes$$

2   Quick-charging is sudden death to motorcycle batteries and should be strictly avoided. The main trouble is overheating, causing the plate paste to swell and severe distortion of the grid structure to occur. Paste drops to the bottom of the battery, reducing the Ah capacity and eventually shorts out the plates.

3   In practice, the charge rate is not constant (but see MF batteries) since the battery charger is often a constant voltage supply. With an unregulated charger of this type the battery voltage will rise over the charging period and the charging current will fall. This is because the difference in voltage between the charger and battery becomes less (Fig. 13.8).

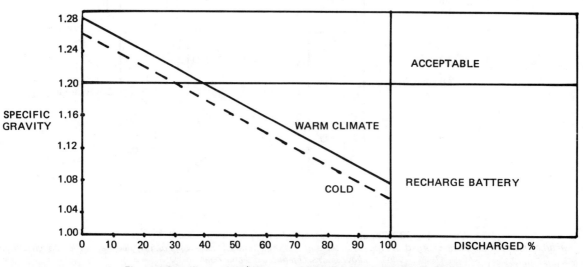

Fig. 13.9 Specific gravity of battery acid during charge/discharge (Sec 6)

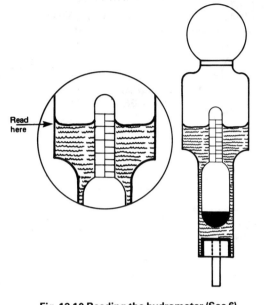

Fig. 13.10 Reading the hydrometer (Sec 6)

SPECIFIC GRAVITY REQUIRED	PARTS OF DISTILLED WATER TO 1 OF CONC. SULPHURIC ACID
1.25	3.4
1.26	3.2
1.27	3.0
1.28	2.8
1.29	2.7
1.30	2.6

Fig. 13.11 Distilled water/concentrated sulphuric acid ratio by volume (Sec 7)

6 Specific gravity

1 Battery acid varies in specific gravity throughout the charging period (Fig. 13.9) and the state of charge may be accurately assessed by using an hydrometer. Since the graduations are often closely spaced, read off as indicated at the bottom of the curved surface of the liquid (the meniscus).

2 Fig. 13.10 shows an hydrometer which consists of a float inside a suction vessel. The nozzle is inserted into a battery cell and enough acid is withdrawn to read the float. The reading gives a good indication as to the battery charge state, assuming that the correct specific gravity of acid was used for the initial filling.

3 Electrolyte specific gravity temperature correction is necessary because the volume varies with temperature. The volume rises with temperature so the weight per unit volume will decrease, ie the specific gravity will decrease. The standard temperature at which makers' figures are quoted is 15°C (60°F), so if an hydrometer reading is taken at any other temperature it should be corrected for best accuracy. A rule of thumb is:

Specific gravity falls by 0.007 per 10°C (18°F) rise above 15°C (60°F)

Specific gravity rises by 0.007 per 10°C (18°F) fall below 15°C (60°F)

So, for example, if the reading of specific gravity of a battery were taken at 25°C (77°F) and was measured as 1.22 then:

Specific gravity at 15°C (60°F) = 1.22 + (1 x 0.007)
= 1.227

7 Battery filling

1 If battery acid is to be prepared from the concentrate, great care should be taken and the wearing of goggles gives essential protection for the eyes.

2 To mix electrolyte first work out roughly how much distilled water and concentrated acid is required. The table (Fig. 13.11) gives the proportions (by volume) of distilled water required to 1 part of concentrated sulphuric acid (specific gravity 1.835). **It is important always to add the acid to the water never the other way round because of the heat generation.** Add slowly and stir until the required specific gravity is obtained (Fig. 13.12).

8 Open circuit voltage

1 Battery terminal voltage on no-load is the open circuit voltage and it is related to the state of charge (specific gravity).

2 If the battery has recently been on charge a false reading (high) will be obtained. It is necessary to let the battery rest for an hour before connecting the voltmeter which should be a large scale accurate instrument. The approximate relationship between open circuit voltage and specific gravity is as follows.

Open circuit voltage = Specific gravity + 0.84 volts per cell

If, for example, the specific gravity was known to be 1.25 in a 12 volt battery then the following would apply.

Cell voltage .... 1.25 + 0.84 = 2.09 volts
Battery voltage .... 6 x 2.09 = 12.54 volts

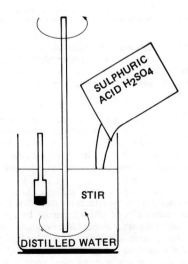

Fig. 13.12 Mixing acid and distilled water (Sec 7)

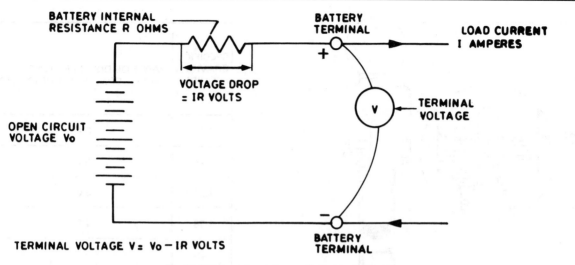

Fig. 13.13 Internal resistance of a battery (Sec 9)

9   Internal resistance

1   All batteries have an internal resistance, but this is very low in the case of a lead-acid battery in good condition. In fact, it is because of the inherent low internal resistance that this type of battery is favoured for vehicle work where starting current demand can be very high.

2   Fig. 13.13 shows a battery with its equivalent internal resistance. Calculation will show that if, for example, the internal resistance were 0.05 ohms and the open circuit voltage 12.0 volts, then, with a lighting load of 10 amperes the terminal voltage would be as follows.

$$
\begin{aligned}
\textit{Battery terminal voltage} &= \textit{12 – internal volt drop} \\
&= \textit{12 – (10 x 0.05)} \\
&= \textit{11.5 volts}
\end{aligned}
$$

The table below shows terminal voltages for this battery under various loads. It does not represent a good battery or any particular size, but serves to show the importance of even a small internal resistance.

Open circuit voltage	Load current (A)	Internal drop	Terminal voltage
12 volts	10 amperes	0.5 volt	11.5 volts
12 volts	20 amperes	1.0 volt	11.0 volts
12 volts	50 amperes	2.5 volts	9.5 volts
12 volts	100 amperes	5.0 volts	7.0 volts

3   The internal resistance is made up of various individual resistances, namely between electrodes and the electrolyte, the plate resistances, internal connectors and resistance of the electrolyte to ion flow (ions are particles moving through the electrolyte and carrying a positive (+) or negative (–) charge).

Additionally, the internal resistance depends upon the state of discharge and cell temperature, the value being higher as the battery is discharged. The designer controls one factor of the internal resistance by the surface area of the plates. Batteries with a larger number of plates (and therefore larger ampere-hour capacity) will have a lower internal resistance.

4   As batteries age, one of the effects is a rise in the internal resistance. Clearly there will come a point where there will be insufficient terminal voltage left to turn the starter motor fast enough for the engine to fire. For a cold morning start, extra torque will be required to free the crankshaft and the minimum engine turnover speed for firing will be about 100 rev/min. It is under these conditions that the end of the battery life is determined.

10   Cold cranking

1   All motorcyclists know that the battery has a tough time in cranking the engine on a cold morning. Where a battery is intended for starter motor work (not all are), the manufacturer gives a figure for cold cranking. Yuasa give the following specification which complies with that stated by the Society of Automotive Engineers (SAE) standard and Japanese JASO Automotive Battery Standard.

Cold cranking = Current in amperes at which the voltage is 7.2 volts at –18°C after 30 seconds

There are other standards in use by European battery manufacturers and more details are given in the Author's *Automobile Electrical and Electronic Systems Manual* (Haynes).

11   Self discharge

1   Over a period of time a battery which is not used will gradually lose its charge due to several factors.

(a)   Internal chemical processes.
(b)   Leakage currents.
(c)   Self discharge.

Internal chemical processes

2   Batteries which have been in service for some time suffer from the effect of antimony deposits on the negative plates. These set up miniature batteries, in effect, which are short circuited upon themselves and use up the charge of the negative plate. In addition, impurities in added water, particularly traces of iron, will result in the self discharge of both positive and negative plates.

Leakage currents

3   Dirt and the effects of acid fumes on the top surface of the battery can result in conducting film paths between the positive (+) and negative (–) battery terminals. This trouble can be minimised by periodic cleaning of the battery top (throw the rag away afterwards).

Sediment paths at the bottom of the battery case can also lead to leakage paths.

Self discharge

4   Self discharge takes place at the rate of 0.2% to 1% of the battery ampere-hour capacity per day, depending on the age of the battery. The rate of discharge goes up with temperature and also with the specific

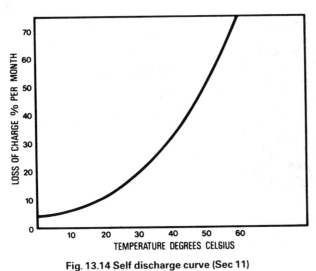

Fig. 13.14 Self discharge curve (Sec 11)

gravity value. Batteries of quality use lead of highest purity in the active plate area with the antimony proportion kept small (Fig. 13.14).

The remedy for self discharge is to charge the battery periodically or to maintain a trickle charge approximately equal to the self discharge rate, this being found by trial and error; a rule of thumb to calculate the trickle charge rate is as follows.

$$\frac{1}{1000} \times \text{ampere-hour rating}$$

Thus, a 14 Ah battery would be trickle charged at 14 mA.

5   If a simple battery charger with no rate control is used for this purpose, a good way of reducing the charge rate is to run the battery on charge with a bulb in series. Again the bulb is chosen by trial and error with an ammeter in circuit to check the charge rate.

12   Sulphation

1   Under normal discharging, fine crystals of lead sulphate are formed on the plates and, by recharging, these are convertible. If the battery is left discharged for a long period, however, these crystals turn into coarse lead sulphate crystals which are not easily converted back to the fine state and may ruin the battery.

2   Sulphation will reduce the battery Ah capacity and impede the charging process, causing the battery to become very hot. In minor sulphation cases, extended periods of charging at low currents will improve the situation, but in serious cases the battery becomes unusable because of the internal short circuits which result.

3   When a sulphated battery is first put on charge the terminal voltage rises rapidly, whereas that of a healthy battery rises slowly. As the sulphation breaks down, the battery voltage falls and slowly rises again as normal chemical changes associated with charging take place.

13   Battery maintenance and troubleshooting

1   If a battery is suspected of being defective this can usually be determined by its performance on the motorcycle. A dramatic change in headlight illumination between tickover and high revs, or poor starter motor turnover, are both indications of a battery with high internal resistance. Before condemning the battery, however, check that good connections are being made to earth (ground) and that the battery terminals are not corroded (if so, clean off with a solution of baking soda and water).

2   Measure charging current with an ammeter, remembering **not** to use a starter motor with an ammeter in circuit! If all appears to be in order, remove the battery for inspection and refer to the following table to assess its condition.

Battery troubleshooting guide

Component	Good battery	Suspect battery	Action if suspect
Plates	+ chocolate brown colour, – grey colour	White sulphation on plates, plates buckled	Scrap
Sediment	Little or none	Deep sediment up to plate level	Scrap
Voltage	Above 12 volts	Below 12 volts	Test charge
Electrolyte	Normal level	Low, especially if one cell is low	Fill and test charge
Specific gravity	Above 1.200 in all cells, with no more than 0.020 difference	Below 1.100 or wide difference between cells	Test charge
Case	Sound and leak proof	Leaking case	Scrap. Wash down affected bike parts in baking soda solution

3   Test charging often reveals troubles; firstly charge at the ordinary rate and if the voltage and specific gravity come up to normal the battery may be returned to service.

4   Check the voltage of the battery by switching off the charge shortly after starting. A good battery will rise to 12 volts and then gradually rise to 12.5 – 13 volts within an hour after charging has started; fully charged it could reach even higher for a short period.

5   A battery which exhibits a rise to 13 volts plus, just after the start of charging probably has a high resistance due to sulphation of the plates. Look for even bubbling of all the cells as the battery charge rises – no gassing in one cell indicates an internal short, especially if the cell specific gravity is low.

14   Rules to extend battery life

1   Use only distilled water – do not believe stories that the tap water in your district is safe for batteries.

2   Never leave a discharged battery to stand a long time.

3   Recharge a stored battery every 30 days.

4   Never add sulphuric acid to battery electrolyte – only distilled water.

5   Never quick-charge a battery.

6   In cold weather keep a battery charged. Discharged batteries freeze more easily.

7   Check that the battery vent pipe is in order; it can get blocked by bending, pinched between frame components or even melted shut if in contact with a hot surface.

8   Never get the battery leads reversed. This is an expensive accident that need not happen.

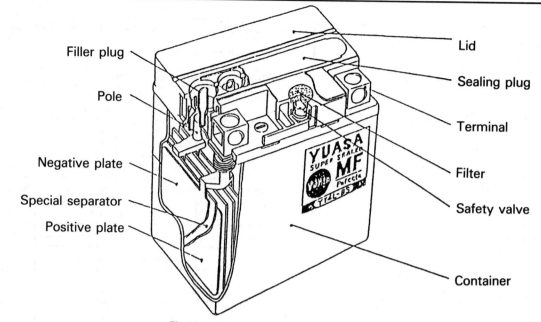

Filler plug

Pole

Negative plate

Special separator

Positive plate

Lid

Sealing plug

Terminal

Filter

Safety valve

Container

Fig. 13.15 Maintenance-free (MF) battery (Sec 15)

15   Maintenance-free (MF) batteries

1   In 1983 Yuasa introduced the maintenance-free (MF) battery for motorcycles (Fig. 13.15). With proper use the MF battery will last for some years, but does require somewhat different care from the conventional battery. Its main properties are as follows.

2   The battery is sealed after the initial filling of sulphuric acid; it is neither possible nor necessary to top up the acid during its lifetime. There can be no spillage, even if the motorcycle falls over because the battery is sealed and there is no free liquid acid. When filled, the fibre expanded-foam separators absorb all the acid.

3   Under charging, the 'Oxygen Cycle' will recombine gases generated at the plates to return as water to the electrolyte. It is not necessary to top up with distilled water because under normal conditions there is no water loss.

4   In the event of severe overcharging, gas pressure may build up inside the sealed case. The MF battery has safety valves which release the pressure but close again when the internal pressure reduces. No breather tubes are fitted as with conventional batteries and because also there is no need for gas space above the plates, the MF battery is more compact and has no breather protrusions.

5   The plates are constructed of a lead-calcium alloy which gives much less self discharge than lead-antimony. Because the expanded-foam separators fill the space between the plates completely, the MF battery can stand vibration better than the conventional type. In addition, if accidental electrical overload occurs, the active pastes in the plates are held firmly in place by the separators.

6   On the debit side, the MF battery becomes heavily sulphated when it is completely flat. It is sometimes thought that the battery is scrap because it will not accept a charge with an unregulated constant voltage battery charger. What is required is recharging from a constant-current battery charger which may initially produce 25 – 30 volts to break down the sulphate. Honda recommend the BATTERYMATE charger which costs somewhat more than the conventional home charger.

7   See Section 18 for details of charging.

16   Why no topping up of the MF battery? – The OXYGEN CYCLE

1   When the conventional battery is fully charged the negative plate is

converted to spongy lead. The MF battery has a larger negative plate (pole) design, such that it is never fully converted to lead by the time the positive plate has been changed to lead peroxide.

2   When the overcharging point is reached, oxygen is given off from the positive plate but since the negative plate never reaches the overcharge condition, **no hydrogen is given up from it.**

3   Oxygen migrates through the separators from the positive to negative plate and reacts with the lead of the negative plate to give a layer of lead oxide on it. The lead oxide reacts with the sulphuric acid to give water. This is the **Oxygen cycle.** The battery suffers no water loss because of this process and may therefore be sealed for life.

A summary of the chemical reactions is shown in Fig. 13.16. The process is explained but for those familiar with chemistry the reaction equations are also given.

THE MAINTENANCE FREE BATTERY OXYGEN CYCLE

Two reactions occur simultaneously when the battery is overcharging:-

(1) $O_2 + 2Pb \Rightarrow 2PbO$
Oxygen (O_2) reacts with lead (2Pb) on the negative plate to produce a layer of lead oxide (2PbO)

(2) $PbO + H_2SO_4 \Rightarrow PbSO_4 + H_2O$
Lead oxide (PbO) reacts with the sulphuric acid (H_2SO_4) to give lead sulphate ($PbSO_4$) and WATER (H_2O)

This means no loss of water under normal conditions, therefore the battery may be sealed

Fig. 13.16 Oxygen cycle of the MF battery (Sec 16)

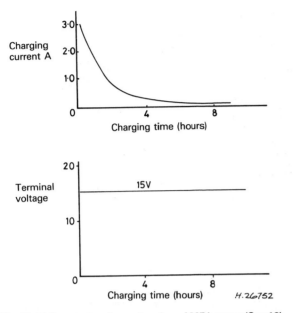

Fig. 13.17 Constant-voltage charging of MF battery (Sec 18)

17 Filling the MF battery

1 New MF batteries come supplied with a special acid container. This is pushed into the filler apertures in one movement to provide the correct amount and specific gravity of acid, and the battery is then sealed.

2 Because of the need to absorb all the acid in the separators, a highly concentrated filler acid of specific gravity 1.310 kg/litre is used instead of 1.280 as in conventional batteries. Additionally, to prevent sulphation, a quantity of sodium sulphate ($Na_2 SO_4$) is added to the battery acid.

18 Charging MF batteries

Constant-voltage charging

1 On the motorcycle the alternator electronic regulator will hold the charging voltage steady at between 14 – 16 volts (or less according to the motorcycle specification). This is the constant-voltage charge characteristic (Fig. 13.17).

Assuming the battery is not completely flat then:

(a) A high initial current flows, decreasing rapidly as the battery voltage rises.
(b) A small current (say about 0.1A) will continue to flow after the battery reaches full charge.

If the battery starts off completely flat, it takes a long time to break through the lead sulphate crystals and may not be possible at all with this type of charging. This is why many batteries are thought to be scrap after being deeply discharged.

Constant-current charging

2 With this type of charger, the charge current is set according to the battery label information.

3 For conditions where the battery is not completely flat, refer to Fig. 13.18 in conjunction with the following.

(a) The battery voltage rises steadily up to about 15 volts.
(b) The oxygen cycle starts and the voltage rises to about 18 volts – bubbling may be heard.
(c) This is the fully-charged condition. Stop charge at this point.
(d) The negative plate acquires lead sulphate as part of the oxygen cycle and this causes the voltage to fall again.

4 Where the battery is completely flat, refer to Fig. 13.19 in conjunction with the following.

(1) Sulphation on the plate needs to be broken down and setting the current (say 3A according to battery spec) will raise the charger voltage to the maximum level.
(2) The lead sulphate layer is broken through. The voltage decreases and the current rises to the pre-set level.
(3) From this point onwards the charging is the same as for the case above.

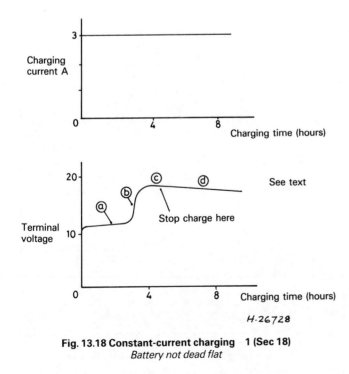

Fig. 13.18 Constant-current charging 1 (Sec 18)
Battery not dead flat

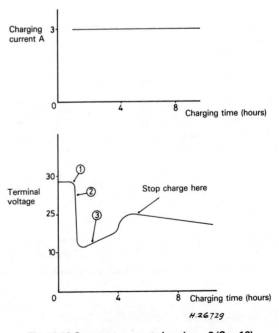

Fig. 13.19 Constant-current charging – 2 (Sec 18)
Battery competely flat

Summary

5   Constant-voltage chargers are good to keep the battery in charged condition. The motorcycle alternator is a constant voltage charger and constant voltage bench chargers are available.

6   Constant-current chargers are ideal for bench charging. They will 'recover' sulphated batteries quickly but must be used with a timer or voltage sensor to avoid overcharging. The battery must not be charged in situ on the bike or damage to the electrical system will occur using a constant-current charger.

7   Unregulated chargers should not be used with MF batteries, for they will destroy them by overcharging.

19   Testing MF batteries

1   As hydrometer testing is not possible, the simplest test is to measure the open circuit voltage (ie with no electrical load). The method is, however, not very accurate since variations occur between batteries and the result will not indicate starting performance.

The open circuit voltage should be measured with a good quality voltmeter allowing first a rest period of 30 minutes after charging. Fig. 13.20 shows the approximate relationship between terminal voltage and remaining charge.

2   If the battery will turn the starter motor then this is the definitive

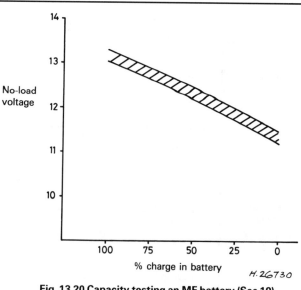

Fig. 13.20 Capacity testing an MF battery (Sec 19)

test. An alternative is to test the battery using a high current discharge tester. This should be arranged to take a current equal to starter current load and consists of a resistance load clipped across the battery terminals with a voltmeter in parallel.

Chapter 14 Lighting and signalling

Contents

1 Introduction

1   The lights fitted to a motorcycle are all in parallel (see Chapter 2), which means that each is connected across the battery supply and that the total current is the sum of the separate bulb currents.

2   A simple lighting circuit is shown in Figs. 14.1 and 14.2. Many large capacity motorcycles may have more facilities, but still work on the same principle that each lamp is switched in circuit and all are in parallel with the battery and alternator/dynamo. Lighting circuits are generally uncomplicated, but when shown as part of the whole electrical wiring diagram can look more involved than they really are.

3   Referring to Fig. 14.1 or 14.2, note that protection is by a 20A fuse and all lights can be operated only after the ignition switch is on.

In the ON position, the headlight switch will illuminate all lights, the dip (or dimmer) switch controlling the high and low beam of the headlight. The lighting switch also has a mid position which only illuminates the position light, tail and instrument lights. For main beam flashing a wire is taken from the main supply before the headlight switch, and then to the passing button.

4   The lighting circuits on US and Canadian models have no lighting switch, all lights come on when the ignition is on. The front turn signals double as running lights and also come on with the ignition; twin filament bulbs are used for this purpose. Sealed beam headlight units may be encountered on certain models; which means that the complete unit must be renewed if bulb failure occurs.

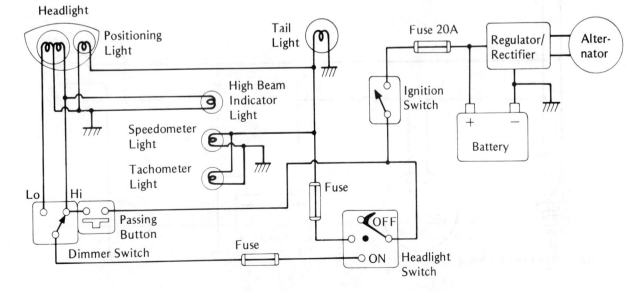

Fig. 14.1 Typical lighting circuit for European models (Sec 1)

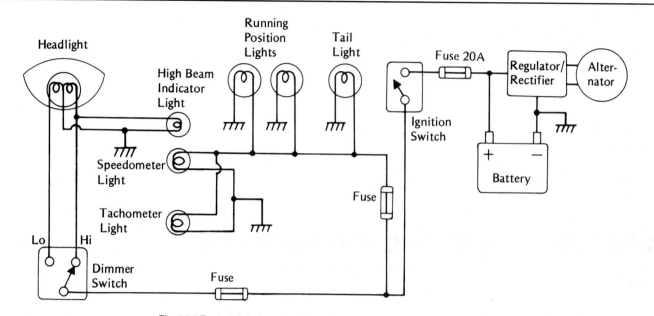

Fig. 14.2 Typical lighting circuit for US and Canadian models (Sec 1)

2   Brake lights

1   Brake light switches are normally fitted to both front and rear brakes. Older British motorcycles generally have only a rear brake light switch. The switches are usually operated mechanically being of the plunger type, but may be operated hydraulically on some hydraulic disc brake systems.

2   When the brake lever or pedal is operated, the switch contacts are brought in contact, completing the electrical circuit. Such switches are normally very reliable, corrosion due to road dirt and water normally being the only problem; water dispersant aerosol works well here. Fig. 14.3 shows how either or both front and rear brake switches will operate the brake light.

3   Lighting faults

1   Vibration failure is the most common fault for motorcycle bulbs but as sophistication of engine design proceeds this may not always be the case. In any event, if a lamp does not light check that the filament has not burned out. Usually a burned out filament is obvious by inspection; there is frequently staining of the glass and tungsten debris in the envelope. If in doubt, check using an ohmmeter between the bulb pins and the metal case.

2   Blown bulbs frequently take a circuit fuse with them, so after checking and possibly renewing the bulb, look next at the fuse if there is still no light.

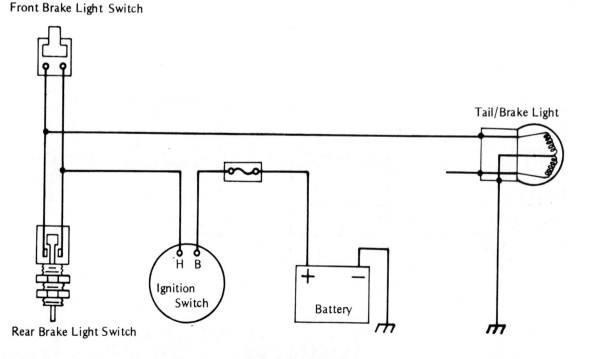

Fig. 14.3 Brake light circuit (Sec 2)

If all is well here and supply voltage is getting to the bulb pins, then earthing (grounding) should be checked. Corrosion sets in all too easily at the frame or lamp shell connection points on road vehicles, so make sure that the earth (ground) leads are really making good contact. If necessary, unscrew the tag and scrape both tag and frame point clean before screwing/bolting up tight again. A light touch of grease or a spray of water dispersant fluid in the bulbholder and on the bulb metal body will be good protection.

3   Switches may be checked with an ohmmeter in conjunction with the machine's wiring diagram. The switch leads usually terminate in a multi-pin connector, making checking possible without dismantling. Most switch faults are due to internal corrosion of contacts or water contamination, and these can usually be cured by cleaning and the application of a water dispersant fluid. Switches which are particularly susceptible to water contamination should be packed with silicone-based grease.

4   Certain US motorcycles use a reserve lighting system which automatically switches in the remaining bulb filament in the event of a headlamp beam failure. If the dip beam fails, then the main beam is switched on as a get-you-home facility, although the light intensity may be reduced (vice versa if the main beam fails).

This is achieved by a detector which senses a lack of current in the alternative filament and operates a blown filament warning light in the instrument cluster. To test, switch to the dip beam and then pull off the dip beam connector to the bulb in the headlamp. The main beam and the warning light should come on. Check for broken wires and if necessary replace the reserve lighting unit.

4   Light units

1   A headlight needs a concentrated source of white light at the focal point of a reflector to project the light forward. This source can be a bulb, which is plugged in place in a reflector or, alternatively, an integral system called a sealed beam unit in which the light-emitting filaments are built into a lens and reflector assembly which is sealed against ingress of air and, of course, dust.

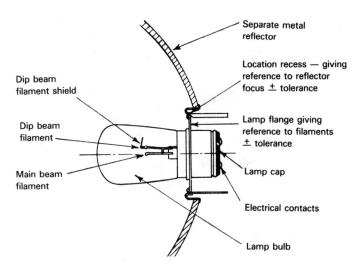

Fig. 14.4 Prefocus bulb located in reflector (Sec 5)

5   Bulbs – conventional tungsten filament types

1   Pre-focus bulbs are made with accurately located tungsten filaments and have a metal flange with some form of location tab to give precise positioning of the bulb inside the reflector (Fig. 14.4).

The main beam filament is located at the focal point of the reflector and the dipped beam filament situated above and to one side of the main beam filament so that its light is projected downwards and to one side of the road (Fig. 14.5).

Sometimes a small metal shield welded to the filament supports is used to give a good dipped beam since light is allowed to the upper half of the reflector only (Fig. 14.6). Ideally the filaments should be a white light spot of infinitely small size, but practically, this cannot be.

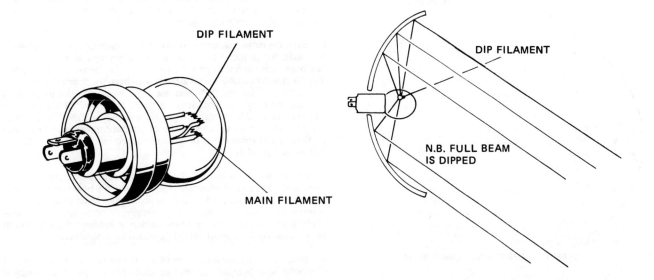

Fig. 14.5 Headlamp bulb with offset dip filament (Sec 5)

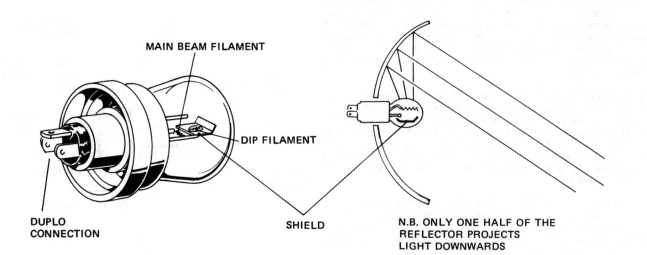

MAIN BEAM FILAMENT

DIP FILAMENT

DUPLO
CONNECTION

SHIELD

N.B. ONLY ONE HALF OF THE
REFLECTOR PROJECTS
LIGHT DOWNWARDS

Fig. 14.6 Headlamp bulb with shield dip filament (Sec 5)

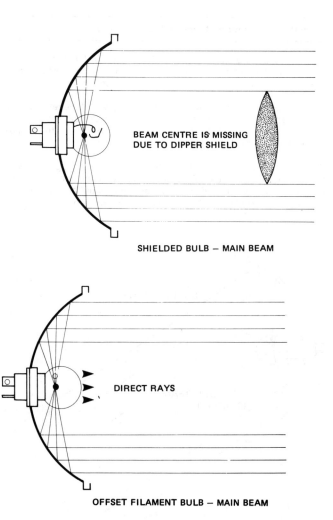

BEAM CENTRE IS MISSING
DUE TO DIPPER SHIELD

SHIELDED BULB – MAIN BEAM

DIRECT RAYS

OFFSET FILAMENT BULB – MAIN BEAM

**Fig. 14.7 Main beam patterns for shielded and offset filament bulbs
(Sec 5)**

2   The coil of the filament is wound horizontally so that any stray light will illuminate the road edges and not the sky. This is important since upward rays will be reflected by fog back to the rider and may cause dazzle.

One final point on the pros and cons of shield dip and offset filament dip bulbs – the shield does have an effect on the main beam in that the 'centre' of the parallel rays is missing and also on dip only the top half of the reflector is projecting light downwards (Fig. 14.7).

6   Disadvantages of separate bulb and reflector

1   The makeup of the main and dipped beams is primarily dependent upon the filament position relative to the focal point of the reflector, and for many years road vehicles used the prefocus bulb in which the filaments were welded in place with precision.

2   Even the close tolerances to which this design could be made were too wide for proper beam control. To them should be added the tolerances between the lamp seating in the reflector and the focal point (Fig. 14.8). Additionally, about 20% of light from the filament is lost due to obscuration by the bulb and cap; also in service the evaporated tungsten from the filament settles on the upper surface of the bulb, and although the total light from the lamp is reduced by 10% – 15% only at half life (about two years say) the obscuration presented to a large section of the reflector is of serious consequence and the beam is disturbed (Fig. 14.9).

3   Finally, due to oxidation and the effects of dust and dirt, the reflector loses efficiency so that after four years' service the beam intensity may be reduced to about 60% of the original value. Most of the troubles mentioned occur because in the design, reflector and bulb were considered as separate entities. When combined into a single sealed-beam unit a considerable improvement is obtained.

4   Despite the possible troubles of a separate bulb and reflector, the European specifications of motorcycles mostly use a semi-sealed system in which the front glass and reflector are in one piece and the bulb clipped accurately in place. With the arrival of the tungsten halogen bulb the combination is proving successful. US specification machines tend to use sealed beam headlamps more than in Europe.

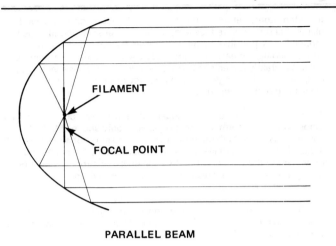

PARALLEL BEAM

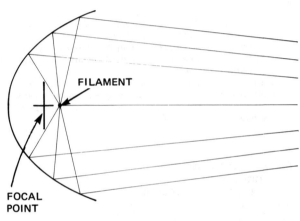

CONVERGENT BEAM

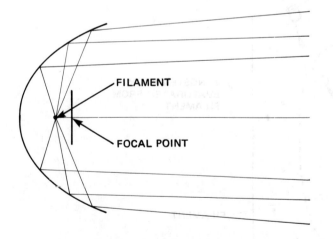

DIVERGENT BEAM

Fig. 14.8 Filament location should be at focal point of reflector (Sec 6)

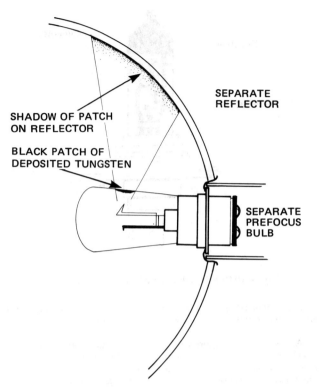

Fig. 14.9 Obscuration due to lamp blackening (Sec 6)

7 Bulbs – service life (tungsten types)

1   Bosch give figures for the life and light intensity of vehicle bulbs against applied voltage, but although the information relates to automobiles the same general pattern should apply to the motorcycle.

2   Assuming that the standard life of a bulb in hours of working is attained at 6.75 volts for a 6 volt system and 13.5 volts for a 12 volt system, then the relationship between applied voltage, light intensity and life is as shown below.

Applied voltage	85%	90%	95%	100%	105%	110%	120%
Light intensity	53%	67%	83%	100%	120%	145%	200%
Life	1000%	440%	210%	100%	50%	28%	6%

It will be seen that the light and life of a vehicle bulb depend upon a correct working voltage; it is therefore important that the voltage regulator is working correctly.

8 Bulbs – quartz halogen types

1   The quartz-halogen bulb is in now in common use on all but the smallest motorcycles. It is known by various other names: quartz-iodine, tungsten-halogen or tungsten-iodine, but all are really the same thing, namely a bulb giving a much higher illumination and longer life than a conventional type. Several considerations determine the high efficiency, shape and life of quartz-halogen bulbs.

2   The normal wearing-out of a conventional filament bulb is due to the evaporation of tungsten from the filament surface (for a mental picture of evaporation think of steam coming from the surface of water). As the filament temperature is raised then evaporation increases rapidly and not only does the filament become thinner but the tungsten vapour blackens the inside of the bulb and illumination decreases.

3   It is found that if one of a group of chemical elements known as halogens (elements that compound themselves to form salts) is added in precise quantity to the normal inert gas filling of a bulb, great improvements are possible in terms of life and illumination.

4   When tungsten vapour leaves the filament surface it works its way towards the glass envelope. Between the filament and the glass there exists a temperature gradient; when the tungsten atoms reach the zone of about 1450°C (2640°F) the halogen combines with tungsten to form

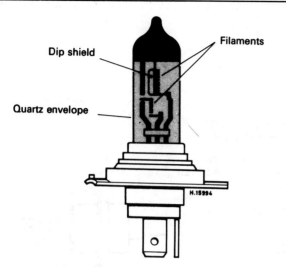

Fig. 14.10 Quartz-halogen bulb construction (Sec 8)

tungsten halides (Fig. 14.11) and these diffuse back to the region of the filament without the glass-blackening effect taking place.

5   As the filament is approached the temperature rises again towards 2000°C/3630°F (the surface temperature) and the tungsten halides break up again into tungsten and halogen at the 1450°C/2640°F boundary. The halogen goes back to the gaseous area whilst the tungsten atoms return to the filament, although some surround the filament and tend to reduce evaporation. Because evaporation is thus reduced it is possible to have a hotter filament and so there is a corresponding increase in illumination. Also because the filament is being constantly replenished with tungsten atoms it has a very long life and, because the tungsten atoms do not reach the glass there is no blackening of the inner surface.

6   Note that the usual halogen is presently iodine and the tungsten-halogen formed with it is gaseous only above 250°C (480°F). For this reason the bulb must be small so as to stay hot and so not only are the bulbs much smaller in volume but also they are made of quartz to withstand the temperature. Because quartz is stronger than normal bulb glass, designers increase the gas pressure which in turn reduces the amount of evaporation.

7   The increase in gas pressure and the halogen cycle of returning tungsten to the filament produces a lamp of high luminous power which is almost constant throughout the life of the lamp.

8   There are two factors (in fact disadvantages) relating to the life of the bulb.

(a)   *The bulb should not be handled with the fingers because the salt from body perspiration will stain the quartz: should the bulb be accidentally touched it may be wiped carefully, whilst cold, with methylated spirit (stoddard solvent) and allowed to dry before use again.*

(b)   *Life is reduced rapidly if the quartz bulb and the gas filling are not maintained at the correct working temperature. A low supply voltage results in not only a drop in luminous power but a serious fall in service life.*

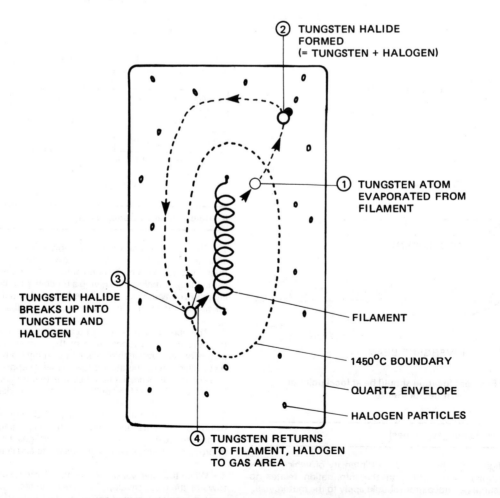

Fig. 14.11 Regenerative cycle in quartz-halogen bulb (Sec 8)

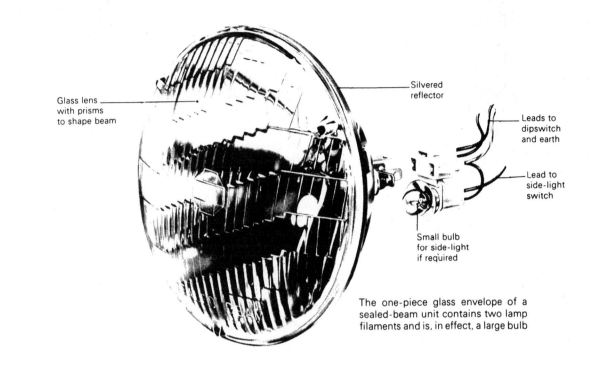

Glass lens
with prisms
to shape beam

Silvered
reflector

Leads to
dipswitch
and earth

Lead to
side-light
switch

Small bulb
for side-light
if required

The one-piece glass envelope of a
sealed-beam unit contains two lamp
filaments and is, in effect, a large bulb

Fig. 14.12 Sealed beam unit (Sec 9)
(From the 'AA Book of the Car', reproduced by kind permission of the Publishers, Drive Publications Limited, London)

9 Sealed beam unit

1 Lighting engineers, conscious that separate bulb and reflector headlights had serious disadvantages, eventually combined these two elements, the result being the sealed beam unit. This consists of an all-glass sealed unit containing two filaments but without a bulb; the back of the unit is 'silvered' to form a reflector and the front glass is moulded in the shape of a lens (Fig. 14.12).

In effect the unit is a large bulb which is sealed for life against the entry of dirt or damp.

10 Design aspects

1 Lenses are cast into the front glass of headlamps to produce correct lighting patterns on the road for both main and meeting (dip) beams. The complex block lens shown in Fig. 14.13 is an excellent example of applied optical principles.

2 For a single, central, filament the beam emerging from the parabolic reflector is approximately circular. However, this gives no side spread to kerb and road centre line and the upper part of the beam is largely wasted in illuminating objects above the rider's eye level.

The refracting (light bending) prisms shown in Fig. 14.13 can give any desired configuration of the light beam and because the borosilicate glass is so thick (3 – 5 mm) it is ideally suited to moulding into prisms during manufacture. Reflector surfaces are evaporated aluminium and are protected through the life of the lamp by the inert gas filling.

3 The sealed beam unit suffers little from tungsten evaporation because it is so thinly spread on the large reflector surface, and light intensity remains higher than 98% at the end of the estimated five year life, compared with up to 58% for a separate light bulb headlamp. Internal construction is shown in Fig. 14.14.

Quartz halogen lamp designs were soon incorporated into sealed beam units, originally with one filament only, but in 1966 a means was found of incorporating both main and meeting (dip) beam filaments. They are now standard original equipment on many motorcycles.

4 A comparison of conventional and tungsten halogen bulb units is seen in Fig. 14.15.

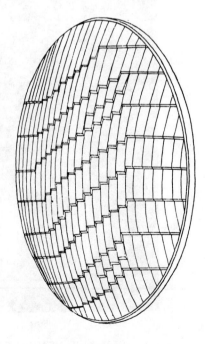

Fig. 14.13 Complex block lens for twin filament headlamp (Sec 10)

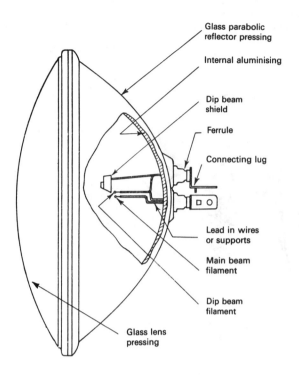

Glass parabolic reflector pressing

Internal aluminising

Dip beam shield

Ferrule

Connecting lug

Lead in wires or supports

Main beam filament

Dip beam filament

Glass lens pressing

Fig. 14.14 Internal construction of sealed beam unit (Sec 10)

11   Lighting loads

1   As an example of electrical loading for lighting purposes the specification for a Honda NX500 is given below.

Headlight......................................	*12V 60/55W*
Stop/taillight	*12V 21/5W*
Turn signal light (front/rear)......	*12V 21W x 4*
Instrument light...........................	*12V 1.7W x 4*
Parking light	*12V 4W*
Indicator lights:	
High beam...........................	*12V 1.7W*
Neutral	*12V 3.4W*
Turn signal	*12V 3.4W x 2*
Side stand warning	*12V 3.4W*

2   The manufacturer will determine the maximum possible lighting load from the above table in order to specify the wattage rating of the alternator.

12   Turn signal circuits

1   The turn signal circuit consists of two pairs of lamps, a turn signal relay (flasher unit), and a three position switch to give LEFT, OFF and RIGHT. Additionally, most circuits also incorporate either a shared or handed warning light in the instruments, and mid to large capacity models often have a hazard facility.

Several types of flasher units exist (see Section 13), the essential principle with all being the ability to switch turn signal lamps on and off at a repetition rate between 60 – 120 times per minute.

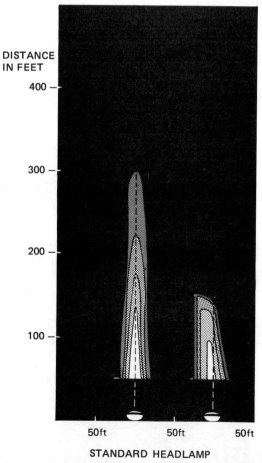

DISTANCE IN FEET

400 —

300 —

200 —

100 —

50ft   50ft   50ft

STANDARD HEADLAMP

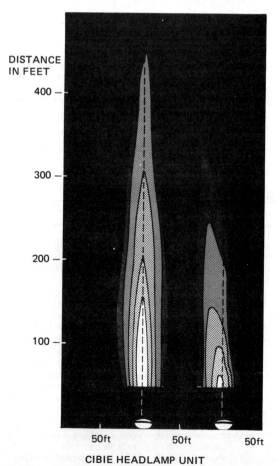

DISTANCE IN FEET

400 —

300 —

200 —

100 —

50ft   50ft   50ft

CIBIE HEADLAMP UNIT

Fig. 14.15 Comparison of standard and quartz-halogen headlamp units (Sec 10)

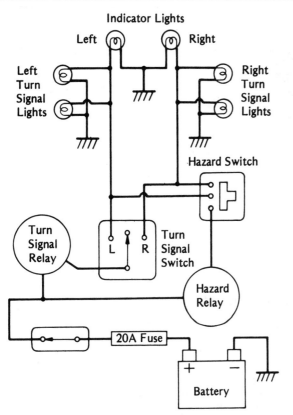

Fig. 14.16 Turn signal circuit (Sec 12)
In this example a second relay is used to operate the hazard function

2   The circuit shown in Fig. 14.16 shows a turn signal circuit, complete with indicator lamps mounted in the instrument cluster. A separate heavy duty hazard relay connects to all four lamps by the hazard switch.

3   Local regulations govern the bulb wattage requirements; in the UK this is 21 watts, and 23 watts in the US.

---

13   Turn signal relays (flasher units)

1   There are several types of flasher units. All have the same purpose of making and breaking the circuit to the turn signal lamps at the legal flashing rate of 60 – 120 operations per minute.

The two main types are the capacitor relay and bi-metal relay, and these are discussed under the relevant sub-heading below. Several other types of relay exist, for example, those that depend upon the expansion of a hot wire which allows lamp contacts to close but these are not very common on motorcycles.

The capacitor relay

2   Fig. 14.17 shows this unit which comprises a relay solenoid with a current coil A and a voltage coil B.

Current coil A is a few hundred turns of wire and is connected in series with the supply, the contacts and then the flasher switch. Voltage coil B has several thousand turns of fine wire and is connected to the upper stationary relay contact and to a capacitor C.

3   When the ignition is ON and the turn signal switch is OFF, capacitor C will charge up to the battery voltage with the polarity shown.

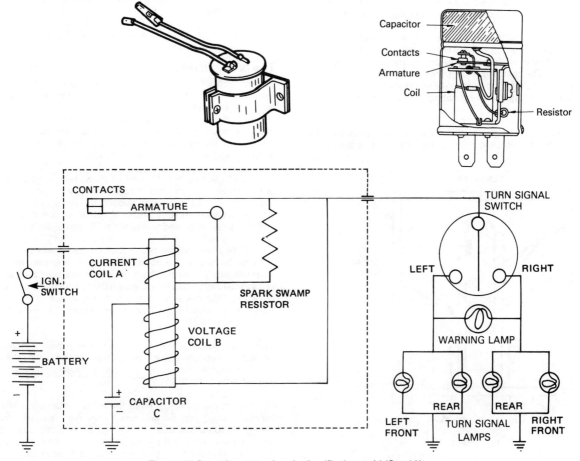

Fig. 14.17 Capacitor turn signal relay (flasher unit) (Sec 13)

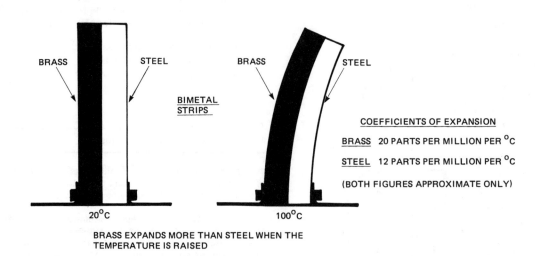

BRASS   STEEL   BRASS   STEEL

BIMETAL
STRIPS

COEFFICIENTS OF EXPANSION

BRASS 20 PARTS PER MILLION PER °C

STEEL 12 PARTS PER MILLION PER °C

(BOTH FIGURES APPROXIMATE ONLY)

20°C   100°C

BRASS EXPANDS MORE THAN STEEL WHEN THE
TEMPERATURE IS RAISED

Fig. 14.18 Principle of the bi-metal strip (Sec 13)

When the turn signal switch is moved to the left position, current flows from the battery through current coil A and the left turn signal lamps. The warning lamp will also light because it is connected to earth (ground) through the right turn signal lamps. The right turn signal lamps will not light because the warning lamp current is too small.

The current through coil A pulls in the relay which opens the contacts, switching off the turn signal lamps. With a simple relay, spring pull on the armature would close the contacts again, but in the flasher relay, the capacitor C discharges through the voltage coil B to earth (ground) via the left turn signal lamps. The discharge current, flowing through the voltage coil, holds the contacts open until the capacitor is discharged.

When the contacts close, the left turn signals will light again and current will flow through the current coil A. This will not immediately open the contacts again, however, because now the empty capacitor C starts to charge up again. The charging current flowing through the voltage coil produces a magnetic flux **opposite** to that produced by the current coil A so the nett magnetic pull on the armature is zero and the contacts (and left turn signals) stay on.

When the capacitor C charges up, the voltage across equals that of the supply and so (by Ohms Law) no more current will flow through the

voltage coil. The current in coil A now pulls in the armature, the turn signals go out and the cycle repeats.

4   Important features of the capacitor-type relay are as follows.

 (a)   The capacitor is always ready charged and the contacts closed so that lamp flash is given as the turn signal switch is operated, with no delay.
 (b)   The flashing rate is fairly accurate and does not vary greatly with changes in battery voltage.
 (c)   The relay unit is rugged and not susceptible to vibration from the engine.
 (d)   Failure of any of the lamps causes the relay to stop and also the warning lamp ceases flashing. Thus the rider has definite warning of failure.

The bi-metal relay

5   The principle of the bi-metal strip is based on the fact that metals expand at different rates when heated. If two such dissimilar metal strips are riveted or spot welded together then a rise in temperature will cause the bi-metal strip to bend (Fig. 14.18). Such movement is used in many ways to switch current or operate hydraulic valves in various branches of engineering, and in this case is used to switch turn signal lamps on and off at a pre-determined rate.

6   The physical layout of Fig. 14.19 shows two bi-metal strips clamped at the lower ends and with a contact on each, normally apart, at the upper tips. Of the two coils, wound in heating resistance wire, the voltage coil has more turns and so higher resistance than the current coil which has few turns and carries the full lamp currents.

7   Fig. 14.20 shows the circuit with the turn signal switch in the OFF position. Note that the contacts are apart and that the voltage coil connects straight to the battery. When the switch is operated, the voltage coil carries a current through the turn signal lamps which do not, however, light because of the high resistance of the voltage coil. However, enough current flows to bend the left bi-metal strip towards the right (Fig. 14.21).

At the point when the contacts close, the lamp current increases sharply because the voltage coil is now almost shorted out by the current coil which, remember, is of much lower resistance: the left lamps light (Fig. 14.22).

The voltage coil no longer heats the left bi-metal strip which cools and begins to straighten. Simultaneously the right bi-metal strip bends to the right and so the contacts part rapidly and the lamps go out. The sequence continues as the left strip begins to bend to the right again and the right strip now having no current coil heating returns to the upright position (Fig. 14.23).

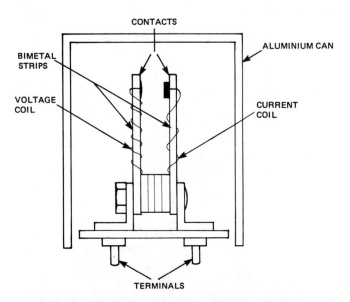

CONTACTS

ALUMINIUM CAN

BIMETAL
STRIPS

VOLTAGE
COIL

CURRENT
COIL

TERMINALS

Fig. 14.19 Bi-metal turn signal relay (flasher unit) (Sec 13)

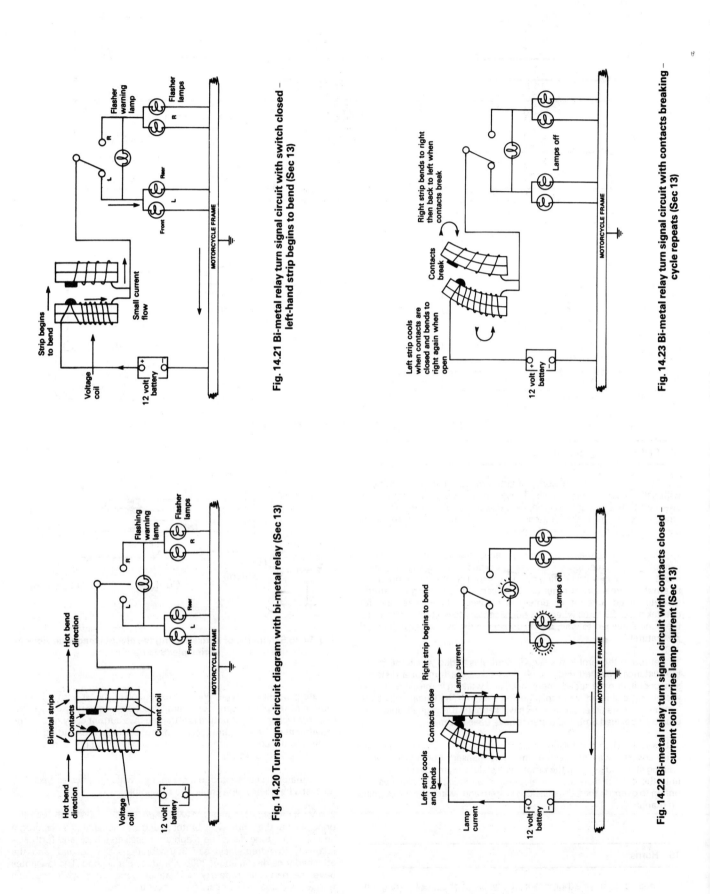

Fig. 14.21 Bi-metal relay turn signal circuit with switch closed – left-hand strip begins to bend (Sec 13)

Fig. 14.23 Bi-metal relay turn signal circuit with contacts breaking – cycle repeats (Sec 13)

Fig. 14.20 Turn signal circuit diagram with bi-metal relay (Sec 13)

Fig. 14.22 Bi-metal relay turn signal circuit with contacts closed – current coil carries lamp current (Sec 13)

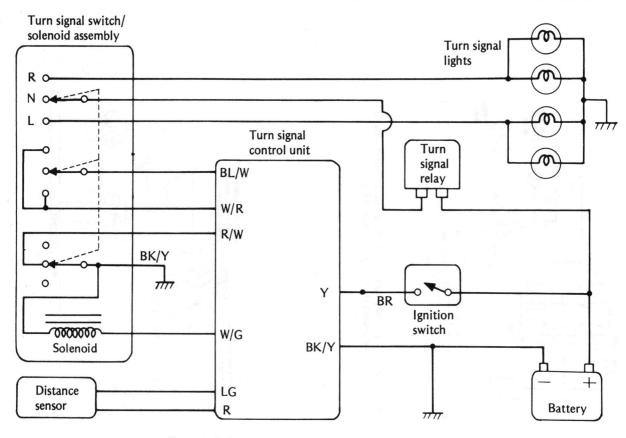

Fig. 14.24 Self-cancelling turn signal circuit diagram (Sec 14)

14   Self-cancelling turn signals

1   For many years the majority of automobiles have been equipped with self-cancelling turn signals. These are controlled by a small cam attached to the steering column; as the steering wheel returns to the straightahead position after negotiating the turning, the turn signal control is tripped back to the OFF position.

2   Unfortunately, the simple cam-operated arrangement used on cars cannot be implemented on a motorcycle because the steering stem moves surprisingly little during normal riding. The obvious approach is to employ some sort of timer circuit to cancel the turn signals after a predetermined amount of time has elapsed. This works fine for overtaking, or for turns where it is not necessary to wait for traffic, but if the rider is obliged to wait, it would result in the system switching off prematurely.

To get round this problem a second control is added which measures the distance travelled (Fig. 14.24). This takes the form of a distance sensor built into the speedometer head and working in the same way as the pickup coil in an electronic ignition system. The signal pulses are 'counted' by the timer circuit, which will keep the turn signals operating until the specified time and distance have been covered.

In this way, when overtaking on a straight road, the distance will have been covered way before the timer has elapsed. Conversely, when waiting at a road junction the timer will rest, leaving the system running until the correct distance has elapsed. In addition, the rider has the option to override the self-cancelling system and switch the turn signals off manually.

15   Horns

1   Today motorcycle horns are nearly all of the electro-magnetic

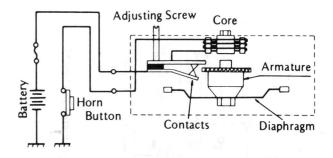

Fig. 14.25 Schematic of horn showing the electro-magnetic vibrator principle (Sec 15)

vibrating diaphragm type. With the exception of the air horn, vibratory motion of the diaphragm is on a similar principle to that of the electric bell, in which an iron armature is attracted by a current carrying coil; the movement of the armature breaks a pair of contacts thus cutting off the current to the coil, the armature returns under spring pressure and the cycle repeats (Fig. 14.25).

The armature is connected to a diaphragm which pushes air back and forth at a frequency high enough to be audible.

2   Most motorcycles are fitted with a horn which works on the vibrator principle, but there are two vibrator sound sources due to a diaphragm and also to a tone disc. The diaphragm oscillates back and forth at a relatively low frequency, say 300 vibrations per second, and the attached tone disc at about 2000 vibrations per second. The low notes have the particular property of distance penetration while the high frequency notes will be heard easily over traffic roar.

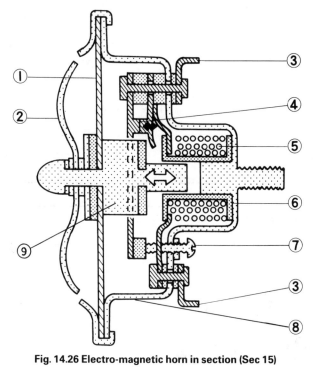

Fig. 14.26 Electro-magnetic horn in section (Sec 15)

1 Diaphragm	6 Insulator
2 Tone disc	7 Sound adjuster
3 Wire terminal	8 Horn body
4 Contacts	9 Armature
5 Coil	

Fig. 14.26 illustrates the principle of operation; when the horn button is pressed the coil energises the electromagnet and the armature is attracted to it and hits it. The movement breaks the contacts and so the armature releases, the contacts close, and the process repeats so long as the button is pressed. The mechanical shock of armature/magnet impact makes the tone disc 'ring'. The tone disc vibrates at an overtone frequency of the diaphragm (ie at an exact multiple) and the resulting combined tone produces an effective penetrating sound which is (hopefully) not too harsh.

3 Wind tone horns are sometimes fitted to motorcycles and operate on the same principle, except that a sea-shell-shaped horn produces an acceptable note, but in order to obtain both distance and penetration they should work ideally in pairs. The current drain is high and would be a very heavy battery load. Where they are used, a relay will avoid the need for thick wires to the horn button.

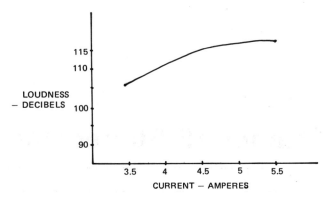

Fig. 14.27 Horn current and loudness graph (Sec 15)

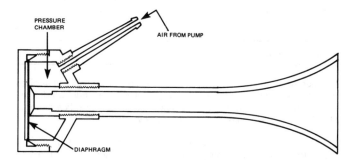

Fig. 14.28 Simple air horn construction (Sec 15)

4 Although horns are frequently subjected to engine heat and the weather, they are remarkably reliable, but after long use the contact points may roughen with the effects of quality and volume loss. In this case adjustment may be made via the adjuster on the rear of the unit until satisfactory performance is restored. After adjustment lock the adjuster with lacquer. Little else can be done to horns and the only other likely cause of trouble is corrosion in the horn button which should be taken apart and cleaned or replaced. Fig. 14.27 shows the typical loudness and current consumption of a simple horn of the electro-magnetic vibrating diaphragm type.

5 Air horns are simple in principle. Air or gas is pumped in under pressure to a chamber which is closed one end by a diaphragm; against the diaphragm pressure the annular end of the horn prevents escape of air/gas. When the pressure is high enough the diaphragm is pushed to the left (Fig. 14.28) and the air/gas is released up the horn mouth. The diaphragm closes and the cycle repeats. Electric pumps are connected to the motorcycle supply and activated by a normal horn button.

Chapter 15 Starter motors

Contents

1 Introduction

1 Electric starter motors are commonplace on motorcycles of all sizes from the smallest machines up to superbikes, and undoubtedly the attraction of push-button starting is now so great that it has become standard specification on almost all motorcycles.

2 The principle of operation of the starter motor is closely related to that of the generator. Basically, the only real difference is that in the case of the generator the input is mechanical torque to turn the rotor, the output being electrical energy, whereas in the starter motor electrical energy is put in and mechanical torque taken out at the shaft. Indeed, all dc generators can be made to run as motors simply by supplying direct current, and conversely all dc motors can be made to act as generators.

3 For the production of torque at the drive shaft it is necessary to supply direct current to an armature situated in a magnetic field. The simple motor of Fig. 15.1 shows the main field from N to S, an armature loop and a commutator which ensures that the armature current switches so that it always flows in the same direction as it passes under a particular pole. (See also Chapter 2 for electric motor principles).

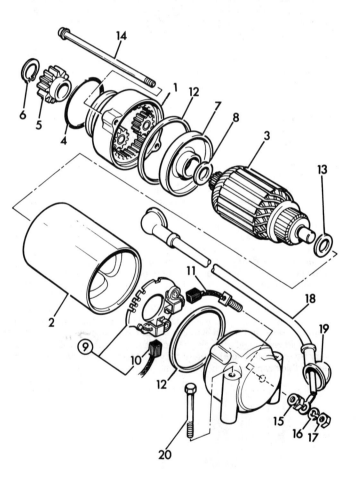

Fig. 15.2 Exploded view of a typical 2-brush starter motor (Sec 1)

1	Reduction gear unit	11	Brush
2	Stator	12	Sealing ring
3	Armature	13	Washer
4	O-ring	14	Bolt
5	Pinion	15	Nut
6	Circlip	16	Spring washer
7	End plate	17	Nut
8	Washer	18	Cable
9	Brush holder plate	19	Boot
10	Brush	20	Bolt

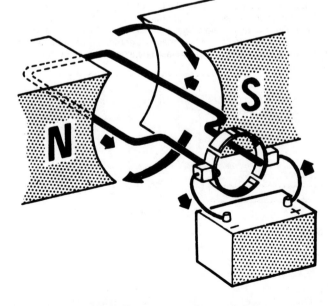

Fig. 15.1 An elementary dc motor (Sec 1)

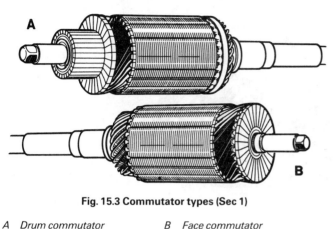

Fig. 15.3 Commutator types (Sec 1)

A   Drum commutator   *B   Face commutator*

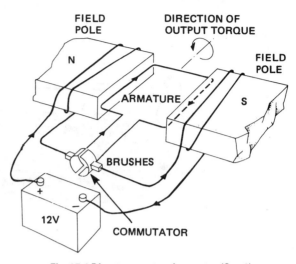

Fig. 15.4 Direct current series motor (Sec 1)

4   The practical armature has a series of coils which are connected to a multi-segment commutator giving a practically uniform torque over a complete armature rotation (Fig. 15.2). Armature coils are embedded in slots of the iron frame used to make the iron path for the magnetic flux of the main field.

The commutator is supplied with current by two or four copper/carbon brushes which are small shaped blocks in contact with the commutator bars under light spring pressure. Contact with the brushes is made by a drum or face type commutator (Fig. 15.3).

The armature frame is made up of laminations pressed tightly together but insulated one from another, the reason being to prevent the flow of induced eddy currents in the iron, which would cause heating losses.

5   The magnetic field may be produced by permanent magnets attached to the starter motor frame (stator); this is the PERMANENT MAGNET MOTOR. Alternatively the magnetic field may be obtained by

winding field coils round the pole pieces. The field coils are wound in heavy gauge wire and connected in series with the armature; for this reason, this type is called a SERIES MOTOR (Fig. 15.4). The series motor has an ideal characteristic for turning over an engine from standstill. At switch-on, the armature is stationary and has no back emf to limit the current which is, therefore, high. This current flows through the series field winding also and the high magnetic field it produces reacts with the high current in the armature conductors giving maximum torque at standstill. This is just what is required to turn over a cold engine.

6   Note that a characteristic of the series motor is that it will race up to high speeds on no-load. Do not leave a series motor running light for long or the armature may be damaged due to windings flying out of place due to centrifugal force. A sectioned series motor is shown in Fig. 15.5.

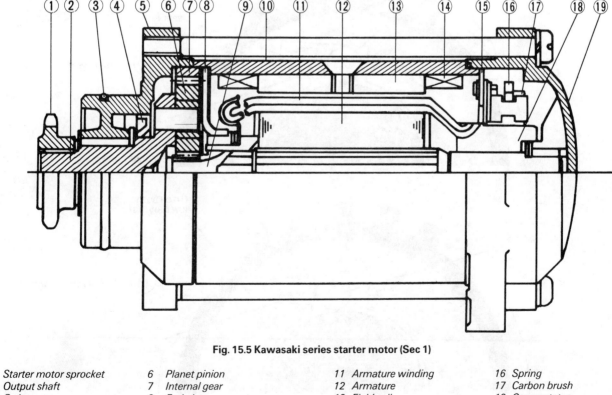

Fig. 15.5 Kawasaki series starter motor (Sec 1)

1 Starter motor sprocket	6 Planet pinion	11 Armature winding	16 Spring
2 Output shaft	7 Internal gear	12 Armature	17 Carbon brush
3 O-ring	8 End plate	13 Field coil	18 Commutator
4 Oil seal	9 Sun gear	14 Core	19 End cover
5 End cover	10 Yoke assembly	15 Brushplate	

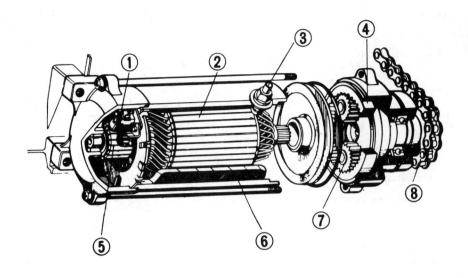

Fig. 15.6 Honda starter motor showing gear reduction (Sec 2)

1	Carbon brush
2	Armature
3	Terminal
4	Inner gear
5	Commutator
6	Field coil
7	Planetary gear
8	Starting chain

2   Starter motor – operation

1   Considerable gearing down is necessary for a starter motor (series type) to turn over a motorcycle engine, a ratio of about 14:1 being average. Reference to Fig. 15.6 shows a Honda motor; at the end of the armature, the pinion drives two planet gears which drive an inner gear and the chain sprocket.

2   When the engine fires it is necessary to disconnect the mechanical drive between starter and crankshaft. In most motorcycles this is by means of a roller-type clutch. Fig. 15.7 illustrates starter motor clutch operation. The clutch body is driven by the crankshaft. When the starter clutch sprocket rotates in the direction of the arrow (Part A) the roller is in the narrow space between the sprocket hub and the clutch body and so drive is transmitted.

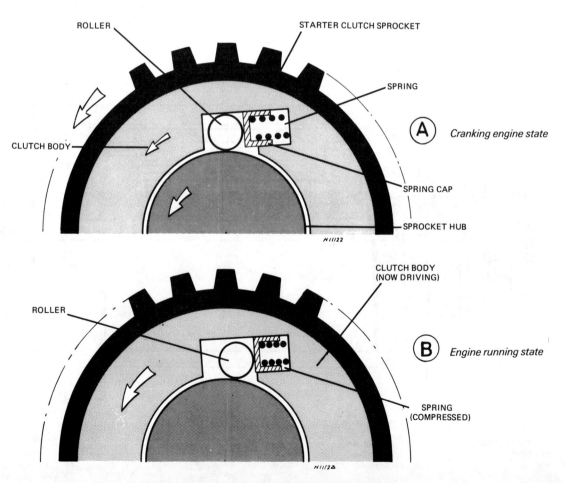

Fig. 15.7 Roller-type starter clutch operation (Sec 2)

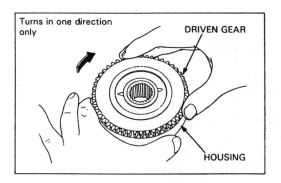

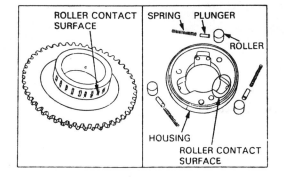

Fig. 15.8 Honda roller-type starter clutch assembly (Sec 2)

As soon as the engine fires, the clutch body runs faster than the clutch sprocket, so the roller drops back against spring pressure to the right (Fig. 15.7, part B) and drive between starter motor and engine is broken. Clearly wear is bound to take place eventually with a system of this type and the symptoms are either that the starter motor stays locked to the engine or that it will not engage at all. Another view of this type of clutch is shown in Fig. 15.8.

3   Sometimes a sprag clutch is used as an alternative to the roller type described above. Sprags are pivoted eccentrics that release transmission in one direction but lock up in the opposite direction (Fig. 15.9).

4   The pre-engaged starter has been used by BMW and Moto-Guzzi and in this type the starter drive pinion is meshed in place before the motor windings are supplied with current (Fig. 15.10). The solenoid (relay) is mounted on top of the starter frame (Fig. 15.11) and when the starter button is pressed a laminated iron plunger is pulled into the solenoid centre. By a fork arrangement the starter pinion is driven into mesh with the engine flywheel; as the plunger completes its travel it closes a heavy duty switch which connects the motor windings straight to the battery.

5   For armature protection an over-running clutch is used (Figs. 15.12 and 15.13) and this is usually of the roller type, not dissimilar to the type already described.

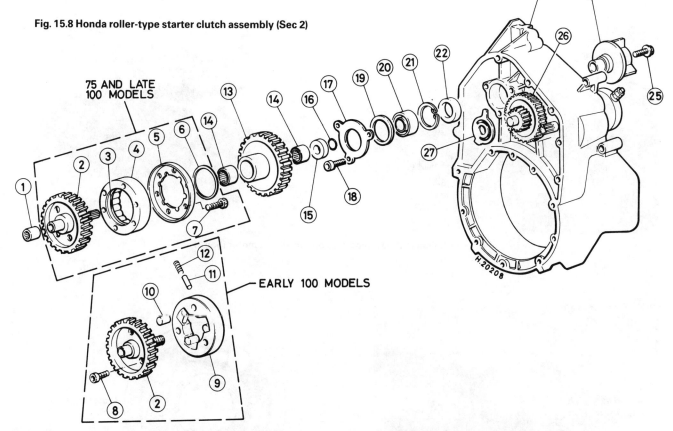

Fig. 15.9 Sprag-type starter clutch fitted to later BMW K-series models (Sec 2)

1	Bearing	8	Screws
2	Auxiliary drive shaft	9	Roller-type starter clutch
3	Cage	10	Rollers
4	Sprag-type starter clutch	11	Plungers
5	End cover	12	Springs
6	Conical spring washer	13	Starter clutch gear pinion
7	Bolts	14	Bearing

15	Thrust washer	22	Oil seal
16	O-ring	23	Bellhousing
17	Retainer plate	24	Alternator drive flange
18	Allen bolts	25	Bolt
19	Conical spring washer	26	Starter idler shaft
20	Bearing	27	Spring (where fitted)
21	Circlip		

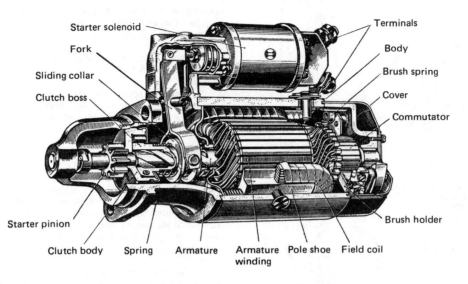

Starter solenoid
Fork
Sliding collar
Clutch boss

Terminals
Body
Brush spring
Cover
Commutator

Starter pinion
Clutch body   Spring   Armature   Armature   Pole shoe   Field coil
                                         winding

Brush holder

Fig. 15.10 Pre-engaged starter motor (Sec 2)

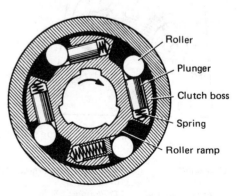

Fig. 15.11 Solenoid (relay) mounted on the starter motor (Sec 2)

Fig. 15.12 Over-running clutch (Sec 2)

Roller
Plunger
Clutch boss
Spring
Roller ramp

Fig. 15.13 Over-running clutch detail (Sec 2)

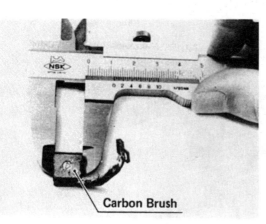

Fig. 15.14 Checking brush length (Sec 3)

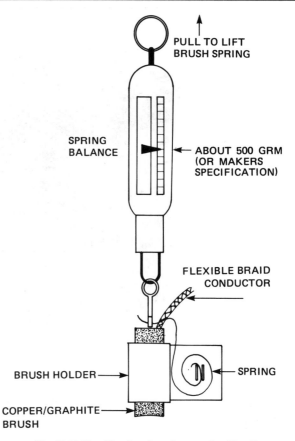

Fig. 15.15 Checking brush spring tension (Sec 3)

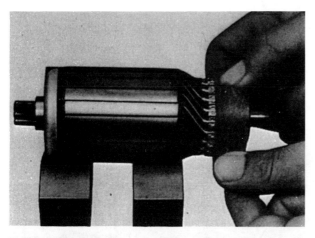

Fig. 15.16 Commutator clean-up using sandpaper strip (Sec 3)

(Fig. 15.16); do not use emery because the hard particles become embedded in the commutator surface.

After using abrasive paper it is important to clean away the last traces of residue or the brushes will be damaged. Some manufacturers do not approve of any abrasive being used and in those cases, clean the commutator with methylated spirits (stoddard solvent) and a clean rag. It is worth trying an ink eraser to burnish the segments so as to remove any surface oxide before installing the brushes.

Commutator

4   Bad burning of the commutator calls for skimming true on a lathe, but note that each manufacturer will specify a minimum diameter – if

---

3   Starter motor – brush gear and commutator

Brushes and springs

1   Brushes must be of low resistance in order to maximise the current through the motor, so they are made of copper and graphite. Care should be taken to replace brushes with genuine types since they vary according to the type of starter motor, rated output and voltage. When worn down to the limit specified by the manufacturer they must be renewed (Fig. 15.14). Regular inspection is advisable.

2   Brush springs sometimes are out of place or faulty with the result that pressure on the brush is insufficient to pass the large operating currents involved; doubts about spring pressure can easily be checked with a spring balance – about 500 grm or 1lb is normal (Fig. 15.15).

3   Starter motors frequently have 4 poles and can have up to 4 brushes, although it is possible to have only 2 brushes which will, in that case, be more heavily loaded. Inspection of the commutator is called for if the motor shows poor performance and bad sparking at the brushes (although most dc motors have a small amount of sparking). It may be possible to clean up the commutator with a fine grade of sandpaper

Fig. 15.17 Checking the commutator diameter (Sec 3)

Fig. 15.18 Undercutting mica insulation (Sec 3)

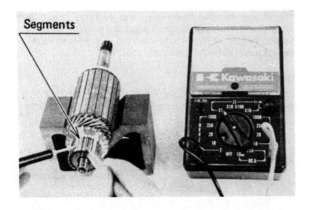

Fig. 15.19 Check for equal resistance between adjacent commutator segments (Sec 3)

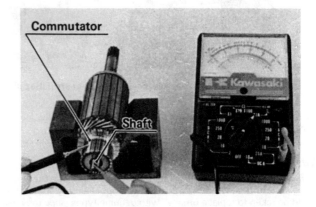

Fig. 15.20 Insulation test between commutator and shaft (Sec 3)

truing up takes the commutator below this limit, the armature must be renewed (Fig. 15.17).

5   Skimming of the commutator will necessite undercutting of the mica insulation between the commutator bar segments. A thin saw blade is required, together with patience and great care; after undercutting to about 0.6 mm (0.02 in) take the burr off the commutator segments or the soft brushes will be quickly ruined (Fig. 15.18).

6   Using an ohmmeter or multimeter, check the following.

   (a)   Check the resistance between adjacent commutator bars on the R x 1 ohms range. All should read the same; if one pair gives a very high reading this indicates an open circuit (Fig. 15.19).

   (b)   Check the insulation between any commutator bar and the shaft (Fig. 15.20). Using the highest ohmmeter range, measure the resistance – any reading below full scale indicates a short circuit or partial short.

In both cases it is unlikely that repairs can be effected. Whilst the starter motor is stripped down, it is worth checking with an ohmmeter that the field coils are continuous and that the insulation to the frame is very high.

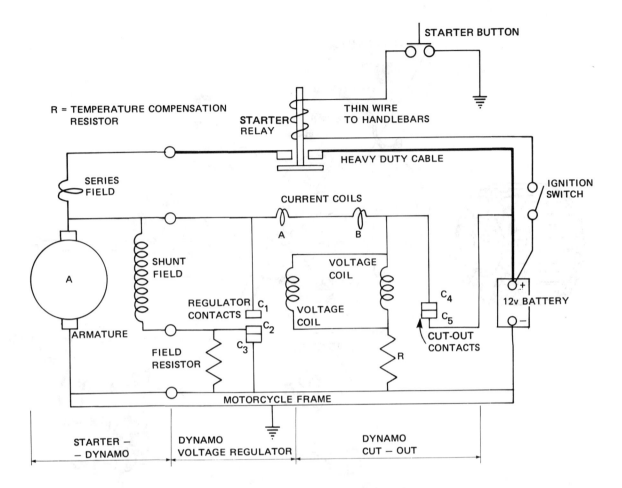

Fig. 15.21 Starter-dynamo and associated circuits (Sec 4)

4 Starter-dynamo

1 As the name implies, the starter dynamo performs the function of starter motor and dc generator. This combined unit is normally coupled to the crankshaft by direct drive with no gear reduction, and for this reason it is confined to smaller motorcycles up to about 200 cc. It is not now popular but enjoyed success on the Yamaha RD200 in the 1970s and 1980s.

2 The starter-dynamo fitted to the RD200 has a stator, an armature, contact breakers and a centrifugal ignition advance unit. The voltage regulator, cut-out and magnetic switch (ie relay) are mounted elsewhere on the motorcycle frame (Figs. 15.21 and 15.22).

5 Starter-dynamo – operation

1 When a direct current machine has both series and shunt field windings it is a **compound** wound type. The starter-dynamo runs as a compound motor when acting as a starter but after the motorcycle engine is running it runs as a shunt dynamo, the series winding being un-used (Fig. 15.23).

2 In the generating mode it is necessary to use a voltage regulator, to keep the charging current correct, and also a cut-out to prevent the battery feeding current back to the dynamo when the motorcycle engine is stopped.

3 As with all starter motors, it is necessary to keep the heavy current leads between the battery and starter as short as possible for minimum volt drop; a starter relay is used for this purpose (imagine a ¼inch thick cable being led up to the handlebars!). This point is illustrated in Fig. 15.21.

6 Starter relay

1 Remembering that the starter takes a heavy current on load, it is essential to use thick cables from the battery and the shortest convenient cable route. For these reasons the starter button switch is always remotely-operated by a relay (or magnetic switch), which is a form of electromagnet.

2 The relay coil (shown in Fig. 15.21) takes a low current which is easily handled by the starter button switch. The relay magnetic field pulls the iron plunger to the centre of the coil, and in so doing closes the heavy duty contacts of the starter switch.

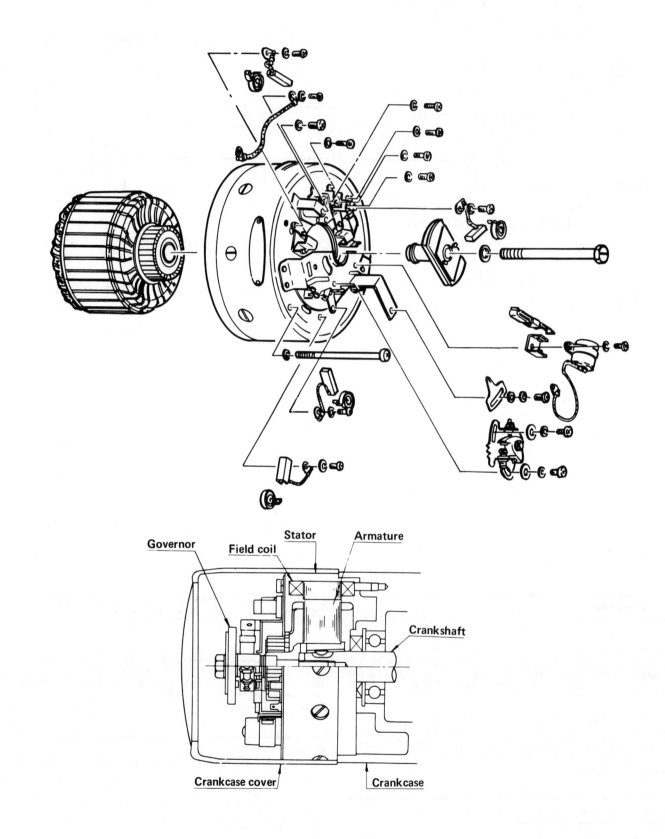

Fig. 15.22 Yamaha RD200 starter-dynamo assembly (Sec 4)

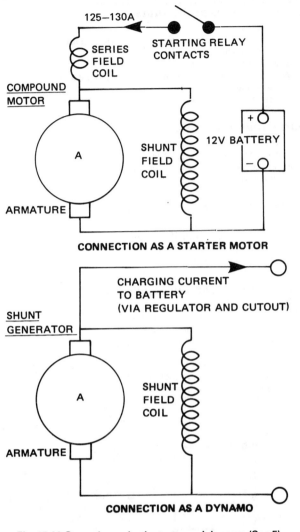

Fig. 15.23 Operation as both starter and dynamo (Sec 5)

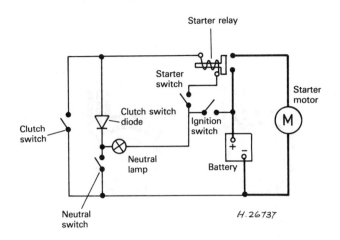

Fig. 15.24 Starter lockout circuit – manual gearbox (Sec 7)

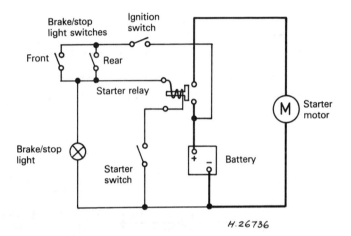

Fig. 15.25 Starter lockout circuit – automatic transmission (Sec 7)

7 Starter lockout circuits

Manual transmission models

1 Fig. 15.24 shows the arrangement of the clutch, neutral and starter button switches in the starter circuit.

If the starter button switch is pressed, battery current will pass through the starter relay coil and reach earth (ground) if either or both the clutch switch or neutral switch are on (closed). The clutch switch closes when the rider pulls the clutch lever in and the neutral switch closes when the gearbox is in the neutral position. Thus if the engine stalls in traffic, it is possible to re-start without returning to neutral.

The purpose of the diode (which lets current through in the direction of the arrow but not the other way) is so that the neutral indicator lamp will not light if the neutral switch is open (ie bike in gear), but the clutch switch is closed (ie the clutch lever has been pulled).

Automatic transmission models

2 On scooters and the few other motorcycles with automatic transmission, provision is made so that the starter motor will operate only when either or both front or rear brakes are applied. This is to prevent the bike running away if the engine surges up in speed when starting, due to the centrifugal clutch engaging. A typical circuit is shown in Fig. 15.25.

Side stand switch

3 A common cause of accidents is the rider forgetting to retract the side stand before starting off. Many motorcycles are now fitted with a safety circuit which will prevent this happening.

The side stand is fitted with a rotary switch or a plunger-operated switch, which, unless the stand is retracted (up) will prevent the starter motor from operating and/or the ignition from working.

Fig. 15.26 shows the rotary side stand switch in the down and up positions. When in the down position, the side stand warning light will illuminate and the starter/ignition circuit will be broken. In the retracted (up) position, the side stand warning light will extinguish and the starter/ignition circuit will be on.

4 Fig. 15.27 shows a motorcycle starter circuit (with manual transmission) incorporating a side stand switch. When the ignition switch is ON and the starter button switch is pushed, battery voltage reaches the starter relay coil.

The coil is not connected to earth (ground) to allow the starter motor to operate unless the neutral switch is ON (transmission actually in neutral), causing the current to flow through the clutch switch diode to earth (ground), or both the clutch switch and side stand switch are ON (lever pulled in and stand retracted).

5 The ignition circuit may also be inhibited by taking a connection from the neutral switch and from the clutch switch to the ignition unit, where the circuit is disabled without a path to earth (ground) through diodes D1 or D2.

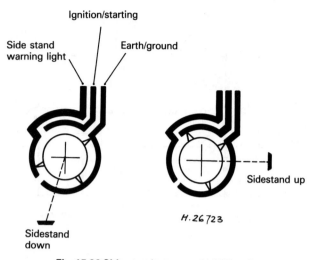

Fig. 15.26 Side stand rotary switch (Sec 7)

Under these circumstances ignition is not possible if the side stand is down or the transmission is in gear. Only when the ignition unit has an electrical path to earth (ground) can ignition firing take place.

8 Starter system – troubleshooting

1   Troubleshooting starts from looking for performance symptoms as follows.

Starter motor does not rotate

Fuse blown.
Faulty starter button switch, clutch switch, neutral switch or side stand switch (where fitted).
Starter relay faulty.
Wiring open- or short-circuit at any point in the system.
Battery dead.
Starter motor defective.

Starter motor turns slowly

Low specific gravity in battery (or dead battery).
Poorly connected battery cables.
Poorly connected starter motor cable.
Faulty starter motor.

Starter motor relay 'clicks', but engine does not turn over

Crankshaft does not turn due to mechanical problem.
Excessive reduction gear friction.
Faulty starter pinion engagement.

Starter motor turns, but engine does not turn

Starter motor is running backwards.
    Brushes assembled improperly.
    Case assembled improperly.
    Terminals connected improperly.
Faulty starter clutch.
Damaged or faulty starter pinion.
Damaged idler gear or reduction gear.
Broken starter motor drive train.
Engine seized.

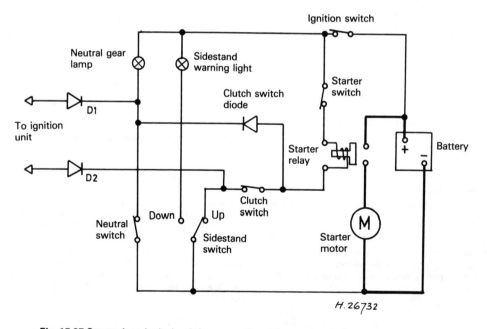

Fig. 15.27 Starter interlock circuit incorporating side stand switch – manual gearbox (Sec 7)

Chapter 16 Wiring, tools and testing

Contents

1 Wiring

1 Electrical equipment is joined by wires gathered together in groups to form the wiring loom. The wires (or cables) may be taped together and sections joined by single- or multi-pin connectors; these are designed to withstand mechanical stress and are usually water resistant. Taping or moulding the separate wires together gives mechanical strength and protection against vibration fracture.

2 Wires emerging from the loom will be cut to the required lengths to reach the component for which current is to be provided. The wires will be terminated or joined with some form of connector – a Lucar-type blade or blade socket, eyelet, bullet connector or self-stripping (Scotchlok) type connector being common (Fig. 16.1).

Bare wires are sometimes terminated by a post connector which may be a moulded-in part of an item of equipment (Fig. 16.2).

3 Multi-pin connectors are used at a major junction of several wires and are moulded in two parts designed to fit one way only (Fig. 16.3). A locking latch is usually provided. It is worth packing the inside of the two halves with silicone-based grease to prevent corrosion between the male and female pins, particularly on off-road motorcycles.

4 The importance of good clean electrical connections on a motorcycle cannot be overstressed, due to their exposure to the weather.

Things to look for are corroded battery terminals, poor earth (ground) connections to the frame and wire insulation that chafes due to the motion of the machine; it is always good practice to clip wiring in place and make use of the cable ties and clamps provided by the manufacturer. Remember that the object of the cable is to convey current to the point where it will be used with minimum voltage drop.

For example, a poor connection between a battery terminal and its cable attachment can result in a loss of voltage, and when a large current is required, such as when the starter button is pressed, the connection may go temporarily open-circuit – every electrician seems to meet this phenomenon at some time!

5 Instrument panel wiring is now frequently in the form of a printed circuit board (PCB). The PCB is a sheet of insulating board which has a

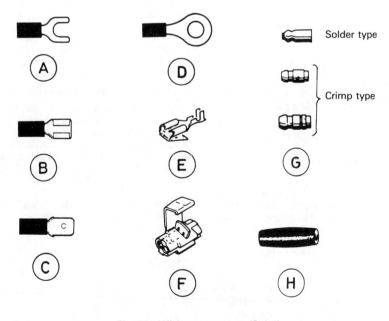

Fig. 16.1 Wiring connectors (Sec 1)

A Fork
B Lucar female
C Lucar male
D Eyelet
E Lucar piggy back
F Self-stripping connector
   (Scotchlok and Lucas)
G Bullet connector male
H Bullet connector female
   (can be single or multiple)

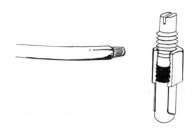

Fig. 16.2 Post connector (Sec 1)

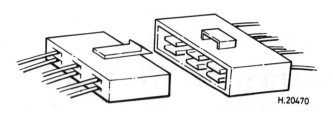

Fig. 16.3 Multi-pin connector with security latch (Sec 1)

thin copper foil sheet bonded to both sides. The 'wire routes' are drawn out by photographic means and the unwanted copper stripped away by etching or other means, leaving only the required conducting paths. It is possible to join points on the back and front of the board by through-pins, which are then soldered. Connectors specially designed to grip and make contact on the board result in a much cheaper method of making the instrument panel connections. Care must be taken to ensure that no current overload occurs on a PCB, because the copper foil quickly blows, like a fuse.

Connections can be troublesome, and it is worth checking the PCB plug and socket if intermittent faults occur. Sometimes capless bulbs are used in the board as indicator lamps, and special attention should be given to ensuring good connections.

Should a copper foil strip be damaged and broken, it is possible to bridge a gap with thin tinned fuse wire using the minimum amount of soldering iron heat.

2 Cable sizes

1   It is important that the cross-sectional area of the copper wire is large enough to carry the current without overheating. Additionally, the volt-drop in the wire must be low enough to ensure correct operation of the equipment to which it is connected. For all this, on the grounds of cost, the manufacturer will use the minimum size of cable which is consistent with the above requirements.

2   Rarely is the cable made of one single copper wire, because it would be difficult to bend round corners and, in any case, might fracture with vibration. Cables are made up of strands of copper wire (often tinned) twisted in a slow spiral and then covered with an insulator which is extruded like toothpaste.

3   Both metric and inch measurements are in use, depending upon the country of origin, but the principles of choosing the correct size are the same. The manufacturer will use a cable which is the minimum size to do the job (a thought to bear in mind when adding accessories), the criteria being as follows.

(a)   The volt-drop on full-load must not be too great (especially in the headlight circuit).
(b)   The cable heating must be within specified limits.

4   In order to carry current to meet condition (a) the copper cross-sectional area must be sufficient; cable heating (b) will also depend on the cross-sectional area, but additionally, the factor of the cable's ability to get rid of the heat is important. A single cable exposed to air can be used to carry a much higher current than if it were bunched up with other cables as a part of a loom. Cables that carry current for only a short time (eg the starter motor) can be worked at a higher current density, but here the permitted volt-drop is the important consideration.

5   Wires are graded by denoting the number of strands and the diameter of a single strand; for example, 14/0.01 (inch) has 14 strands, each of which has a diameter of 0.01 inch. In the case of metric cables the same idea is used so 14/0.3 (metric) indicates 14 strands, each of diameter 0.3 mm. Metric dimensions are now in widespread use and will be referred to in the following sections.

Wires are graded differently in the US, see Section 3.

3 Cable volt-drop and current ratings

1   In the accompanying table, it is assumed that the current density is 8.525 amperes per square millimetre (A/mm^2) of copper for cables up to 44/0.3 metric and 6.975 A/mm^2 for larger sizes.

Metric cable size (mm)	Current rating (amperes)	Volt-drop (volts per metre per ampere)
9/0.3	5.5	0.0271
14/0.3	8.75	0.01742
28/0.3	17.5	0.00871
44/0.3	25.5	0.00554
65/0.3	35.0	0.00375
84/0.3	42.0	0.00290
97/0.3	50.0	0.00251
120/0.3	60.0	0.00203

The current ratings shown may be reduced to 60% for cables run in the interior of a loom.

2   From this table the choice of 14/0.3 cable would be satisfactory for general applications on the motorcycle such as parking and tail lamps, turn signals, etc., and 28/0.3 for headlights, horns and any other added high current loads.

3   A 180 watt alternator on full-load will give 180/12 amperes approximately – that is 15 amperes (remember volts x amperes = watts). For this loading, a 28/0.3 cable would just do, but choosing a larger size would be better, say 44/0.3 or 65/0.3, to keep the volt-drop from the alternator to battery to a minimum.

4   In the United States, cables are rated according to the number of circular mils of cross section in the cable wire. A mil is 0.001 inch and a circular mil is the square of the mil figure. For example, an 18 AWG wire that has a diameter of 0.0403 inch has a circular mil area of:

$$40.3 \times 40.3 = 1624 \text{ circular mils}$$

A rule for equipment design might be to choose a current density of 230 circular mils per ampere according to how the wire is used. From this the 18 AWG wire could run at 7 amperes. In a wiring loom this would be just adequate but it is always better to use a thicker wire if possible, particularly in a 6 volt system where a cable volt drop is more significant than in a 12 volt system. In practice, tables are used to select a wire for a particular current load.

5   The American Wire Gage (AWG) and the British Standard Wire Gauge (SWG) have a near equivalence as shown in the table below:

Metric size (sq.mm)	AWG	SWG (nearest)	Amperes*
0.205	24	25	1.76
0.326	22	23	2.79
0.518	20	21	4.4
0.823	18	19	7.0
1.310	16	18	11.2
2.080	14	16	17.9
3.310	12	14	28.4
5.260	10	12	45.2

*Based on current density of 230 circular mils per ampere

FUSES (Flat Bladed)   FUSES (glass cartridge)

cone end   flat end

Identification	Rating
Purple	3
Pink	4
Orange	5
Brown	7.5
Red	10
Blue	15
Yellow	20
White	25
Green	30

Identification	Lucas Ratings
Length 25.4mm (1")	
Cone end	AMP
Blue	3
Yellow	4.5
Nut Brown	8.0
Red on Green	10.0
White	35.0
Length 29.4mm (1^5/32")	
Flat end	
Red on Blue	2.0
Red	5.0
Blue on Green	8.0
Black on Blue	10.0
Light Brown	15.0
Blue on Yellow	20.0
Pink	25.0
White	35.0
Yellow	50.0

FUSES (ceramic type)

Identification	BSS Ratings
Length 25mm	AMP
Yellow	5
White	8
Red	16
Blue	25

FUSIBLE LINK
(ribbon fuse)

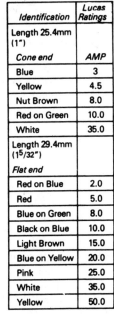

Fig. 16.4 Fuse types and ratings (Sec 4)

---

4 Fuses

1   Many electrical circuits have protective devices so that in the event of a short-circuit, the battery is isolated. The battery is capable of driving a high current into an accidental short-circuit and this may be sufficient to burn the insulation off cables, damage sensitive electronic components, possibly buckle the battery plates, or cause a fire – **a fuse is used for such protection**.

2   A fuse consists of a cartridge with contacts on each end and a strip of soft metal or length of tinned wire connected between them. When an overload occurs the fuse wire or strip will melt, breaking the circuit. The fuse must be renewed but it is first necessary to trace and rectify the fault otherwise the new fuse will also melt.

On small motorcycles and mopeds a single fuse is fitted, often of the 'in- line' type and located near the battery. On larger motorcycles fuses are used for the separate circuits; these may be located in a fusebox either behind a sidepanel, on the steering head or under the seat, or may be part of a central junction box shared by relays.

3   Four types of fuse are presently in use on motorcycles (Fig. 16.4).

   (a)   Flat-bladed fuses.
   (b)   Glass tubular fuses.
   (c)   Ceramic fuses.
   (d)   Fusible links or ribbon fuses.

Note that glass fuses are normally rated at the fusing value, but ceramic fuses are rated at the maximum continuous current that they can carry, being half of the fusing value.

Flat-bladed fuses are now common on motorcycles and consist of a coloured plastic holder with two flat projecting blades which plug into a fuse socket. The fuse wire spans the two blades internally.

Glass tubular fuses come in two types, the flat end and the cone end (note that they have different lengths as shown in Fig. 16.4).

Ceramic fuses have a coloured ceramic body with a one-piece fuse strip and end caps. They do not have a glass shield and are open to the air. This type of fuse appears on motorcycles of European manufacture. The whole fuse is clipped between spring terminals.

Fusible links (or ribbon fuses) are not common but may be found on a few models. The soft fuse element is held at each end by a screw and is designed to protect main circuits.

4   Following automobile practice, the thermal **circuit breaker** may be met on the motorcycle. The advantage is that a circuit breaker may be reset after a fault has been cleared.

Breakers are of the bi-metal strip type in which the heat generated in the strip by the short-circuit current causes it to bend. This opens a pair of contacts which may be closed by push button after the unit has cooled down. A circuit fault must, of course, be found and corrected before re-setting the breaker.

---

5   Wiring diagram symbols

1   An understanding of circuit diagrams is important for troubleshooting in a motorcycle electrical system. In order to follow manufacturers' wiring diagrams it is necessary to know most of the symbols used to indicate components, but these unfortunately have not been standardised throughout the world.

2   Japanese wiring diagrams use symbols which are sometimes pictorial in that they look like what they represent (Fig. 16.5). In addition, the component name is usually printed alongside.

3   On European motorcycles (eg BMW and MZ) the German DIN standards will be met and in these cases the diagrams are not so clear, being less pictorial, but have the advantage that manufacturers stick closely to DIN without introducing many variations of their own (Fig. 16.6). Names are not always printed by the side of the component but instead a number is given which corresponds to the key shown at the end of this section.

Only some of the more common symbols in use on motorcycles are given and it will be seen that, in general, where coils are drawn to look like coils in Japanese diagrams, the DIN standard uses a black solid bar.

For a full treatment of DIN symbols see the Bosch booklet *Graphical Symbols and Circuit Diagrams for Automotive Electrics.*

DIN component and terminal key

Terminal number	Wire leading from	To
1	Ignition coil	Contact breaker or ignition control unit
2	Magneto	Ignition switch (shorting switch)
4	Ignition coil HT	Spark plug
15	Ignition switch	Ignition coil
15a	CDI pulse coil	CDI trigger terminal
15/54	Main switch or ignition switch	Coil, warning light, fuse for daylight current consumers (brake lights, horn, turn signals, etc)
30	Battery +	Starter, ignition switch
31	Battery –	Earth (ground)

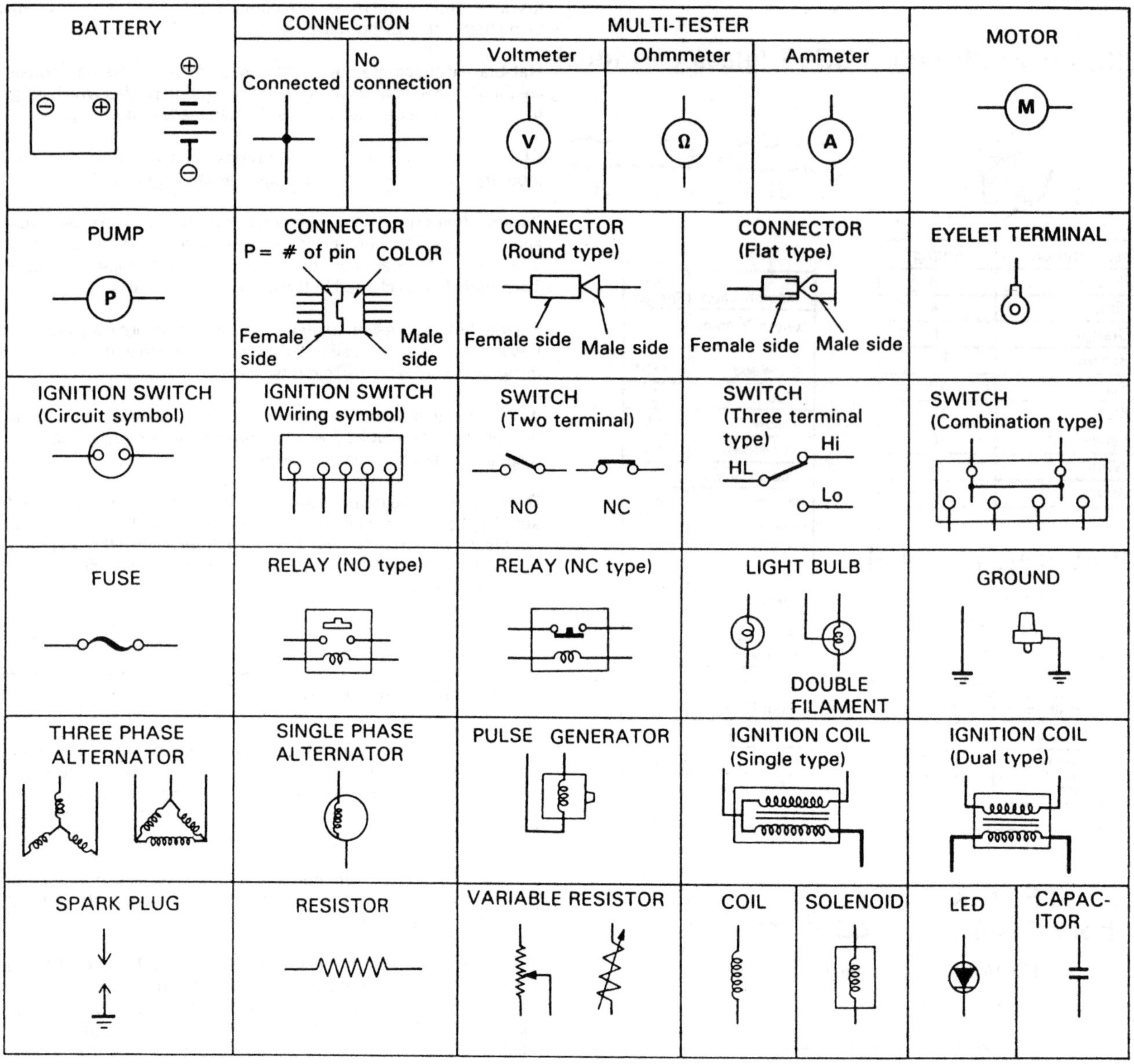

BATTERY	CONNECTION		MULTI-TESTER			MOTOR
	Connected	No connection	Voltmeter	Ohmmeter	Ammeter	
$\ominus$ $\oplus$			V	Ω	A	M

PUMP	CONNECTOR P = # of pin COLOR	CONNECTOR (Round type)	CONNECTOR (Flat type)	EYELET TERMINAL
P	Female side Male side	Female side Male side	Female side Male side	

IGNITION SWITCH (Circuit symbol)	IGNITION SWITCH (Wiring symbol)	SWITCH (Two terminal)	SWITCH (Three terminal type) Hi HL Lo	SWITCH (Combination type)
		NO NC		

FUSE	RELAY (NO type)	RELAY (NC type)	LIGHT BULB DOUBLE FILAMENT	GROUND

THREE PHASE ALTERNATOR	SINGLE PHASE ALTERNATOR	PULSE GENERATOR	IGNITION COIL (Single type)	IGNITION COIL (Dual type)

SPARK PLUG	RESISTOR	VARIABLE RESISTOR	COIL	SOLENOID	LED	CAPAC-ITOR

Fig. 16.5 Range of symbols used by Honda (Sec 5)

Abbreviations used:
NO = Normally open, switch is open at rest
NC = Normally closed, switch is closed at rest
# = Number

DIN component and terminal key (continued)

Terminal number	Wire leading from	To
31b	Switch	Earth (ground)
49	Ignition switch	Flasher unit
49a	Flasher unit	Turn signal switch
50	Starter button switch	Starter relay (solenoid)
51	Alternator or generator regulator	Battery, starter button or main switch
54	See 15/54	–
L54	Turn signal switch	Left turn signal light
R54	Turn signal switch	Right turn signal light
56	Lighting switch	Dip (dimmer) switch
56a	Dip (dimmer) switch	Headlight main beam and warning light
56b	Dip (dimmer) switch	Headlight dipped beam
57	Lighting switch	Parking light

Terminal number	Wire leading from	To
58	Lighting switch	Tail light, licence plate light, side light (side car)
59	Charging coil of flywheel magneto	Rectifier
61	Alternator or generator regulator	Charge warning light
B+	Battery positive	–
B–	Battery negative	–
D+	Generator +	Regulator
DF	Generator exciter winding	Regulator
L	Turn signal switch	Left turn signal light
R	Turn signal switch	Right turn signal light
UVW	Individual phase terminals	3-phase rectifier pack

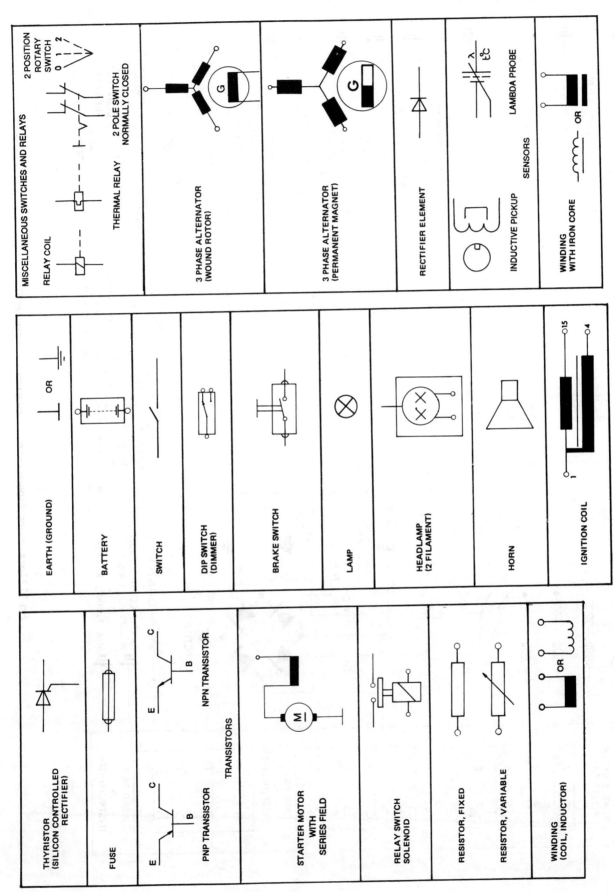

Fig. 16.6 DIN circuit symbols (Sec 5)

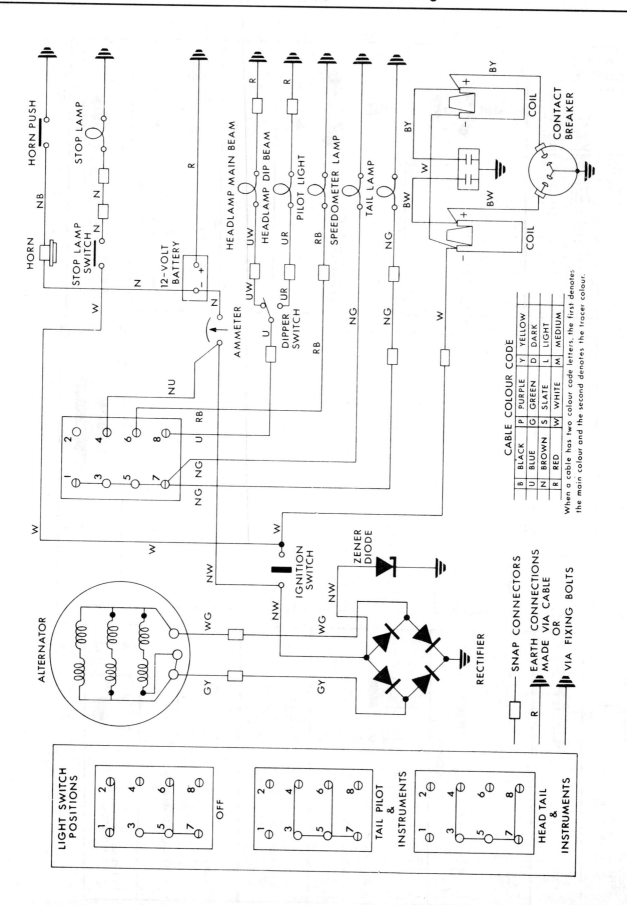

Fig. 16.7 Lucas wiring diagram layout showing colour coding (Sec 7)

CABLE COLOUR CODE

B	BLACK	P	PURPLE	Y	YELLOW
U	BLUE	G	GREEN	D	DARK
N	BROWN	S	SLATE	L	LIGHT
R	RED	W	WHITE	M	MEDIUM

When a cable has two colour code letters, the first denotes the main colour and the second denotes the tracer colour.

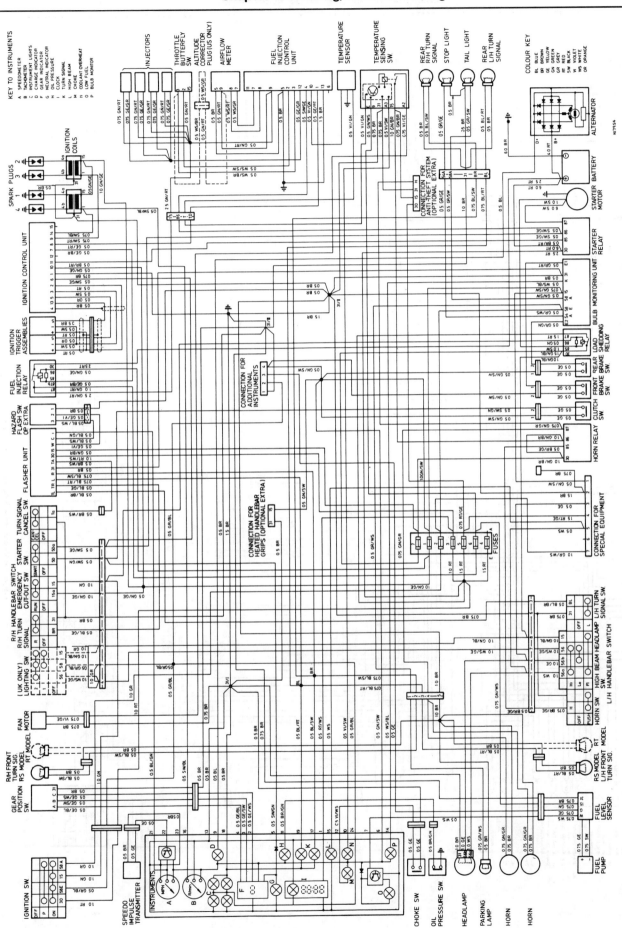

Fig. 16.8 BMW 8-valve K100 wiring diagram (Sec 8)

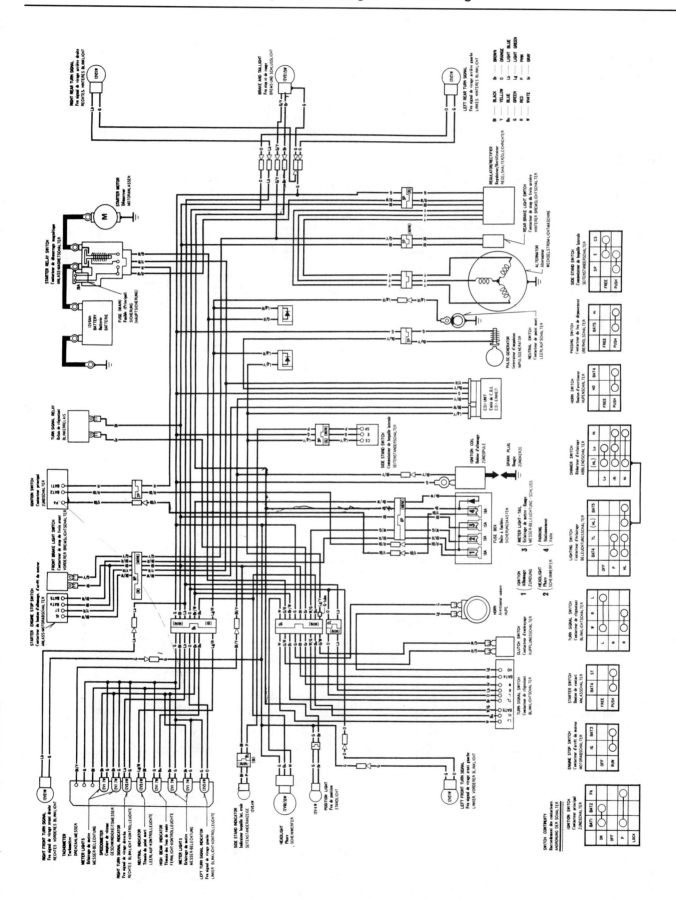

Fig. 16.9 Honda NX500 wiring diagram (Sec 8)

6 Terminal markings

1   When confronted with a component such as a voltage regulator which may have several screw or brass tag terminals, it is helpful if they are marked for identification. Some manufacturers use letters for coding, such as the following.

D	*Dynamo armature*
F (or DF)	*Dynamo field*
E	*Earth (or ground)*
CB	*Ignition coil terminal to be connected to contact breaker*
SW	*Ignition coil terminal to be connected to ignition switch, etc*

2   An advantage of this system is that the letters usually give an indication of what they are intended for, but this cannot be said of the DIN system, which mostly uses numbers. For those working on European motorcycles it pays to learn at least the most common code numbers, some of which are listed at the end of Section 5; it should be noted that, exceptionally, some letters are used.

3   Certain code numbers are most important for it is seen that any terminal marked 30 is always live without a switch being operated (an accessory could be connected here therefore): 31 represents an earth (ground) terminal and 31b is used when an electrical load is operated by a switch in the return circuit to earth (ground).

7 Wire colour coding

1   Colour coding of cables is most helpful in identifying leads on the motorcycle. Unfortunately, standardisation has not fully taken place and reference must be made to the colour key provided by the manufacturer.

2   Lucas label their diagrams (Fig. 16.7) and show the code; the majority of cables are two colour – the main colour shown by a letter followed by another letter for the trace (ie a spiral of colour superimposed). Thus BW indicates a black cable with a white trace.

3   The German DIN standard lays down rules for cable colours, and circuit diagrams show the code which not only gives colour, but the cross sectional area of the cable. Fig. 16.8 shows a wiring diagram of the later 8-valve BMW K100 models to illustrate this.

4   British Standard AU7a Colour Code for Vehicle Wiring should be consulted for those wishing to use UK wiring colours. A suitable extract is to be found in the Lucas booklet *Cable and Cable Products*.

For comparison of styles, the reader should consult ·wiring diagrams issued by various manufacturers from which it may be seen that wide differences in practice occur.

8 Wiring diagram layout

1   Most suffer from poor layout and the unnecessary crossing of wires and are difficult to follow, especially in poor lighting conditions. Long overdue is the simplification which could easily be achieved by adoption of the principles of layout of the Lucas system of Fig. 16.7, at least for small to medium machines.

As circuit complexities increase, complete wiring diagrams will become too tiresome to follow. What may possibly come about is to break the complete diagram into sections, say one for lighting and signalling, and others for charging, ignition, starting and special features such as ABS braking control.

2   As an illustration of complex wiring diagrams, Fig. 16.8 shows the wiring of the later 8-valve BMW K100 models. Note the use of DIN

symbols. The Honda NX500 wiring diagram in Fig. 16.9 shows a contrasting style. Note how the manufacturer has situated the components to give an outline of their physical position on the motorcycle.

3   Although diagrams may look complicated when shown in entirety, do not be daunted by them. Each individual item breaks down to a supply wire coming from, or to, the battery, then to the load item concerned. Usually the motorcycle frame forms the return 'wire' and it is important that good earth (ground) connections are made to the frame. All the separate circuits are in parallel and the currents taken by them add up to the total load current. This should not exceed the wattage rating of the alternator (or dynamo) – the starter motor current is not included because it is a short term load.

9 Switches

1   The term 'switch' covers everything from a simple horn button up to complex multi-switches, and could even include the heavy current starter relay which is an electrically-operated switch.

2   Contact resistance within a switch is very low when it is in good condition, but after long use corrosion or wear may occur. Then trouble can show up as an intermittent contact or a total break.

3   British motorcycles used Miller, Wipac and Lucas switches and some could be dismantled, but with risk of flying apart in the process. Spring-loaded roller switches bridged two connector terminals per roller, while others used wiping contacts. A wiping-contact Miller switch is shown in Fig. 16.10. The brass strip rotor is turned by the switch knob and connects in head and tail lights, pilot and tail, or switches all off.

The seven terminal Lucas switch (Fig. 16.11) distributes current by a moving spring-loaded rotor contact which presses onto the terminals. In this example, the rotor is permanently connected by a brass strip to No. 5 terminal which supplies tail lights and any other auxiliaries required. The rotor contact is shown bridging the headlight and battery terminals. Turning another clickstop clockwise would turn off the headlight and connect the pilot light.

Maintenance is confined to keeping switches clean and making sure that no strands of connecting wire stick out of one terminal and accidentally touch another. If the switch can be taken apart the contacts may be cleaned and treated with an aerosol electrical contact cleaner.

4   Modern machines (with the regrettable exception of some Italian types) have excellent switches which have a long trouble-free life. It is

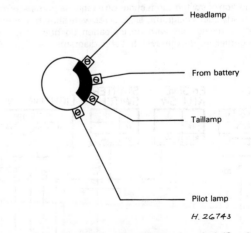

Fig. 16.10 Wiping contact rotary switch (Sec 9)
The central rotor is a three position distributor which links up to three terminals. In the position shown, the head and tail lights are on. Further rotation clockwise gives tail and pilot lights on, then all off

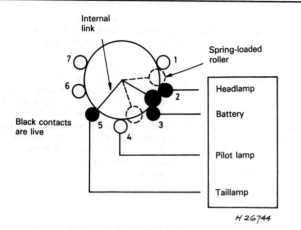

Fig. 16.11 Seven-contact Lucas switch used on many post war British motorcycles (Sec 9)

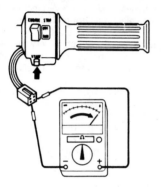

Fig. 16.13 Simple continuity checks can often save unnecessary dismantling of the switch (Sec 9)

not always easy or possible to take them apart and replacement is usually essential, but it is worth trying to revive a switch with a spray of contact cleaner or water dispersant fluid.

Handlebar switches are usually in two halves clamped around the handlebar (Fig. 16.12). Before stripping down to investigate a suspected fault, carry out a continuity check with an ohmmeter or multimeter to confirm this. By disconnecting the wire connectors from the switch, a continuity check can be made in accordance with the switch connections shown on the machine's wiring diagram (Fig. 16.13).

5   Representation of switch connections on circuit diagrams was most frustrating on early Lucas diagrams, since wires were shown connected to numbered terminals, but with no indication on how they were connected together inside the switch. Later diagrams (see Fig. 16.7) corrected this.

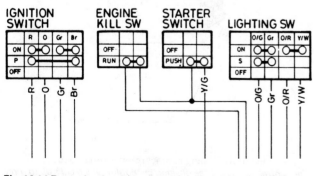

Fig. 16.14 Example of switch grid layout on the Suzuki GSX1100 (Sec 9)

Fig. 16.12 Handlebar switches are usually clamped around the handlebars (Sec 9)

Switch connection diagrams on today's machines are illustrated on a grid diagram (Fig. 16.14). Owners of early motorcycles would be well advised to check their main switches with a multimeter and draw up for themselves a grid diagram.

6   When switching the main-to-dip beam of a direct lighting system, care has to be taken not to break the main contact before connection is made to the dip beam contact. A momentary cutting off of the load will send the generated voltage up so high that the tail light would probably blow. Switches of this type are called make-before-break switches.

7   Switches are often the heart of warning lamp circuits, and appear also on an instrumentation panel in the nacelle.

10   Electrical tool kit

1   It is advantageous to keep a set of special tools just for electrical work, since there must be no possibility of oily tools being used anywhere on vehicle circuitry. Here follows a list to meet most needs.

Pocket knife (for scraping connections clean)
Spark plug spanner with rubber insert for plug tops
Electrician's screwdriver set
Cross-head screwdriver (chubby and 4 inch)
Engineer's combination pliers
HT cable pliers (optional)
Side-cutting pliers
Snipe-nosed pliers
Circlip (snap ring) pliers
Impact driver
Adjustable wire stripper
Crimping tool, with box of assorted connectors
Sets of Allen keys (Metric and Imperial)
Ignition spanners (for magneto adjustment)
Flat file for dressing contact points
Feeler gauges (plastic and steel types)
Jump leads with heavy crocodile clips
Small bulb in holder with prod leads, to act as a test lamp
Rubber grommet kit
Hydrometer
Soldering iron (45 watt for small work, 65 watt upwards for heavy jobs)
De-soldering pump (for printed circuit work)
Test instruments (see Section 14)

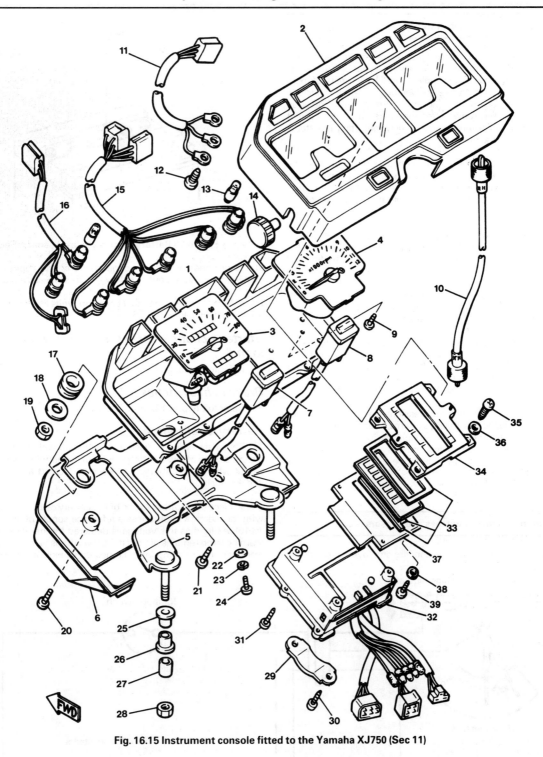

Fig. 16.15 Instrument console fitted to the Yamaha XJ750 (Sec 11)

1	Instrument housing	11	Wiring harness
2	Instrument cover	12	Screw
3	Speedometer	13	Bulb
4	Tachometer	14	Reset knob
5	Mounting bracket	15	Bulbholder assembly
6	Instrument lower cover	16	Bulbholder assembly
7	Control switch	17	Grommet
8	Control switch	18	Washer
9	Screw and washer	19	Nut
10	Speedometer drive cable	20	Screw

21	Screw	31	Screw
22	Washer	32	Computer monitor unit
23	Spring washer	33	Computer monitor panel
24	Screw	34	Panel cover
25	Damping rubber	35	Screw
26	Damping rubber	36	Washer
27	Spacer	37	Backing plate
28	Nut	38	Washer
29	Bracket	39	Screw
30	Screw		

Note the row of warning lamps across the top of the panel, and also the LCD monitor panel between the speedometer and tachometer

11   Instrumentation and warning systems

1   Like almost every aspect of motorcycle design, instruments have become increasingly sophisticated in recent years. The basic mechanical speedometer has been supplemented by a variety of extra instruments, usually electronically-operated. These include tachometers, voltmeters, ammeters, clocks and fuel gauges. The array of warning lamps has also grown over the years and most current models are fitted with a comprehensive display indicating the status and general condition of the machine.

2   The level of sophistication is, naturally enough, dependent on the type of machine. At one extreme there are simple mopeds with only a speedometer and one or two warning lamps, whilst some of the larger capacity machines are equipped with complicated microprocessor-based instrument systems.

3   In some of the latter arrangements, the instruments are interconnected via a central 'black box' which monitors all aspects of the engine and electrical functions while the machine is being ridden, and carries out a comprehensive self-checking sequence each time the engine is started. Information is gathered from a variety of switches and sensors and any fault is displayed by warning lamps or, in some cases, on a Liquid Crystal Display (LCD) panel and/or a meter built into the instrument console.

4   As might be expected, the more complex systems use a number of sealed units, which are difficult to deal with in the event of a fault. The usual approach in these cases is to substitute new components for those that are suspect until the fault is isolated, though the construction of the control circuits is invariably such that repair is impracticable.

5   Another problem that besets the professional and home mechanic alike is the wide variation in monitoring systems, even between similar models from one manufacturer. As an example, the Yamaha XJ650 and 750 range features a wide variety of instruments and warning systems on the various models; Fig. 16.15 shows one of the more complex assemblies.

12   Warning lamp systems – switches and sensors

1   A wide variety of switches and sensors are employed to check the

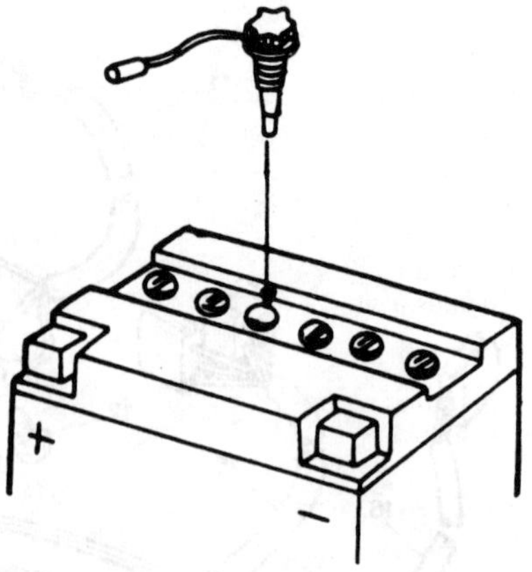

Fig. 16.16 Battery electrolyte level sensor (Sec 12)

status or condition of the various parts of the engine and electrical system, and also to control safety features like starter lockout circuits. The type of sensor varies according to its function, but most are little more than switches. The most common types likely to be encountered are discussed below.

Starter lockout switches (neutral, clutch and side stand)

2   Refer to Chapter 15.

Brake light switches

3   Refer to Chapter 14.

Battery level switch

4   These are normally used in conjunction with a computer monitor circuit to warn of low electrolyte level in the battery, and are particularly useful where the battery is awkwardly located and thus difficult to check visually.

A lead electrode is fitted to one of the battery cells, and when in contact with the electrolyte produces a reference supply of about 9 volts (Fig. 16.16). As long as this voltage is detected by the microprocessor, the warning lamp remains off, but if the level drops below the bottom of the electrode, the warning lamp comes on to indicate that topping up is

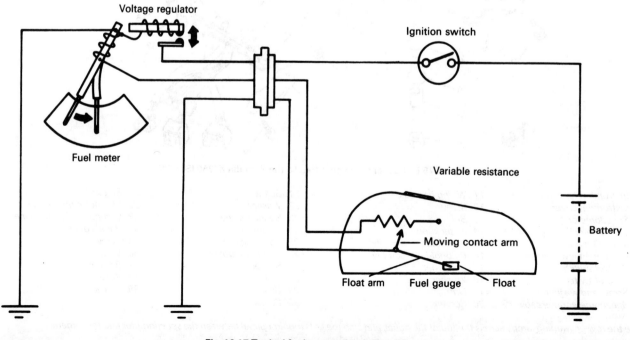

Fig. 16.17 Typical fuel gauge circuit (Sec 12)

required. Note that this is not applicable to maintenance-free (MF) batteries.

Oil and water temperature senders and switches

5   Some machines are equipped with oil temperature gauges which warn when the engine temperature reaches a dangerous level. The sender unit is a device known as a thermistor which has a resistance that varies according to its temperature. The sender is connected to a meter mechanism which indicates the temperature on the instrument panel. On liquid-cooled engines a similar arrangement is used to monitor the coolant temperature.

6   A fan switch operating on coolant temperature is used on liquid-cooled motorcycles, following automobile practice.

Fuel, oil and brake fluid level switches

7   These are float-type switches designed to warn of low fuel, oil or hydraulic fluid level by lighting the appropriate warning lamp in the instrument panel. The switch has one fixed contact and a moving contact fitted to the base of the float. As the level drops, the contacts close, earthing (grounding) the warning lamp.

Fuel gauge circuit

8   A float-operated sender unit is used in conjunction with a fuel gauge to give a precise indication of the amount of fuel remaining in the tank. A float is attached to the end of a wire arm and moves up and down with the fuel level.

As the float position changes in accordance with the fuel level it operates a variable resistance known as a rheostat, comprising a number of turns of resistance wire wound round a flat former. The moving contact blade sweeps along the windings, thus determining the overall resistance in the circuit. This resistance is measured by the gauge meter mechanism which can then be calibrated to show the corresponding fuel level (Fig. 16.17).

---

13   Electrical connections

---

1   Motorcycle wiring suffers from a harsh environment and where connections are made care must be taken to ensure weather proofing. Fitting any add-on electrical equipment may involve connecting into existing wiring; good electrical and physically strong connections are important. A sudden failure of lighting, ignition or an alarm system can be dangerous, especially at speed or in a fast lane.

2   Three types of connection are used for most add-on or changes to motorcycle wiring.

   (a)   Self stripping (Scotchlok) connectors.
   (b)   Soldered joints.
   (c)   Crimped joints.

Self stripping (Scotchlok) connectors

3   These may be used for wiring-in accessories into an existing circuit without the need for cutting the original run-wire (Fig. 16.18).

Slot the run-wire into the through channel and push the accessory (tap) wire into the blind hole as far as it will go. **Do not** remove any insulation. Squeeze the blade down with engineer's pliers until it is flush with the top of the Scotchlok body. The blade will then have sheared through the insulation of both run and tap wires and be in contact with the inner copper conductors. A firm grip is achieved by the unique spring compression action of the blade. Snap over the hinged cover and the connection is complete.

Soldered joints

4   The soldered joint is reliable when made properly and is the surest way of making an electrical connection. Solder is an alloy of tin and lead. When melted between two metals to be joined, it will wet both surfaces and form a solder joint when cooled below the solidifying temperature

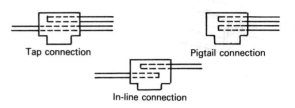

Tap connection   Pigtail connection

In-line connection

Three ways of using a Scotchlok connector

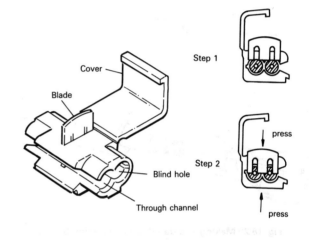

Cover

Blade

Step 1

press

Step 2

Blind hole

press

Through channel

Step 3

H.26748

Fig. 16.18 How to fit a Scotchlok connector (Sec 13)

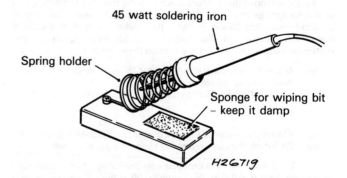

45 watt soldering iron

Spring holder

Sponge for wiping bit – keep it damp

H26719

Fig. 16.19 A soldering iron is essential (shown complete with stand) (Sec 13)
For larger jobs use a 60 watt iron (or larger)

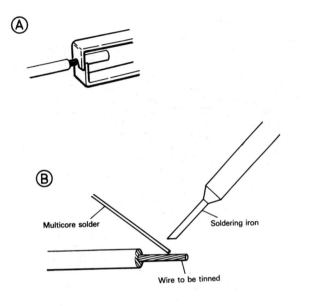

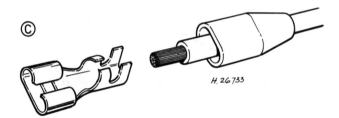

Fig. 16.20 Making a soldered connector joint (Sec 13)

A   Use wirestrippers to remove insulation – be careful not to cut any
     wire strands
B   Put solder on the work – not on the iron
C   Connector prepared for soldering

of about 183°C (360°F), depending on the type of solder chosen. The
solder forms an alloy with the metal parts to be joined and gives a good
stable low resistance joint, providing the following conditions are
achieved.

    (a)   The joint metal surfaces are clean of dirt and oxide.
    (b)   The temperature of both metals to be joined is high enough for
         the solder to flow freely and wet the surfaces.

5   Final cleaning of the surfaces is achieved by the use of soldering flux
which, for light electrical work, is already in the solder wire in the form of
a rosin-based core. **Never** use acid flux (Bakers fluid) with electrical
equipment because of the danger of subsequent corrosion. For
motorcycle connector soldering you need the following.

    (a)   An electric soldering iron of at least 45 watt rating with a stand
         as shown (Fig. 16.19).
    (b)   A reel of 18 SWG Multicore solder – either Savbit or 60/40 type.

6   Soldering hints.

    (a)   Always put solder to the joint and not on the soldering iron bit.
    (b)   Do not get the joint so hot that the wire insulation melts!

7   Fig. 16.20 illustrates the procedure for soldering a Lucar connector
on a cable. First make sure the soldering bit is tinned with solder and
remember to wipe it occasionally on a damp sponge.

Slide the insulating cover on the cable. Strip off about ¼inch (6.4 mm) of
insulation from the wires to be joined by the connector (Fig. 16.20, part

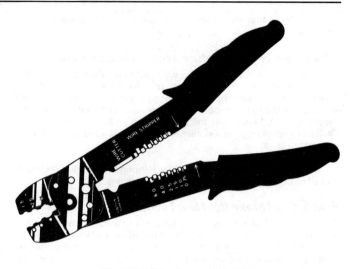

Fig. 16.21 Crimping tool (Sec 13)

A). Clean the exposed wires with a penknife or abrasive paper and tin
lightly with solder (Fig. 16.20, part B). For spade connectors, scrape
clean and tin the channel in which the wire will lie. Lay the wire in place
and reheat the joint, flooding wire and tag with solder so that it flows.

Do not use any more solder than is necessary so that the grips can be
bent over the soldered area. If the connector has grips for the insulation,
bend them over with pliers and slide on the insulating cover (Fig. 16.20,
part C).

Crimped connections

8   A quick and widely used method of joining wires to connectors,
crimping consists of pressing the connector sleeve (or wings) down
onto the wire by a simple hand tool. This method achieves the same
result as soldering but with lower reliability. Note that when fitting
alarms which disable ignition, it is better to use soldered joints because
of the small chance of accidental circuit failure due to corrosion.

9   Making a satisfactory crimped joint depends on cleanliness of wires
and connectors. It is essential to remove oxide film and dirt by scraping
both the wire and the connector until bright, abrasive paper or a
penknife being the usual means involved.

10   Spade (Lucar) connectors are available in both insulated and
non-insulated types and it is important to use the correct crimping tool.
Lucas market separate tools for the two types. Tools are also available
from auto accessory dealers, and are usually for insulated connectors
(Fig. 16.21).

11   Fig. 16.22 illustrates the crimping procedure. Insulated terminal
connectors require that 5 mm (about ¼inch) of wire insulation be
stripped back. Crimp firmly over the wire and then over the insulation as
shown in part A.

Non-insulated spade connectors will have two pairs of wings, one for
gripping the wires and the other for the wire insulation (part B). Do not
forget to slide a PVC cover over the wire before the crimping operation.
Using the correct part of the tool, crimp down the wings over the wire
and then over the insulation. In this operation it may be necessary to
bend the wings over separately, finishing off with a squeeze over both
wings when they have been correctly located. It is common practice to
use the PVC cover for non-insulated spade terminals but there is also a
total cover 'clikfit' type (part C).

Weather protection

12   Where joints are exposed to the weather, additional protection is
afforded by the application of silicone-based grease. This applies to
crimped, soldered or Scotchlok joints. 3M, the makers of Scotchlok
connectors, also supply Scotch 23 self-fusing tape which is moisture
sealing and will mould to the shape of the protected object – in this case
one of the joints described above.

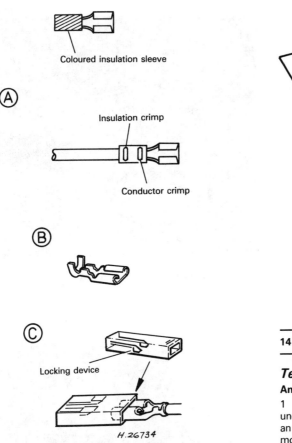

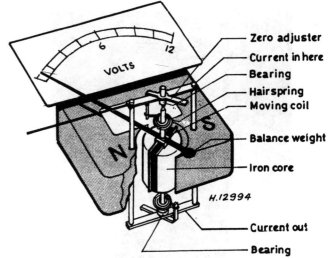

Fig. 16.23 Moving coil instrument of a typical analogue meter
(Sec 14)

Fig. 16.22 Blade-type crimping connectors (Sec 13)

A   Insulated blade connector
(female)
B   Non-insulated blade
connector (female)

C   Clikfit sleeve – insulates full
range of $\frac{1}{4}$ in (6.4 mm)
connectors crimped or soldered.

14   Test equipment

Test meters

Analogue meters

1   The traditional meter has a pointer which indicates on a scale underneath the measured value of volts, amperes or ohms. This type is an analogue meter and usually incorporates a moving-coil type of movement (Fig. 16.23).

The moving coil is like a small electric motor which turns when current is passed through it and is restrained by coiled hairsprings. The greater the current, the greater the deflection of the pointer which is attached to the coil.

2   A moving coil is deflected by direct current only and can be scaled as a voltmeter by adding a resistor in series, this being called a multiplier.

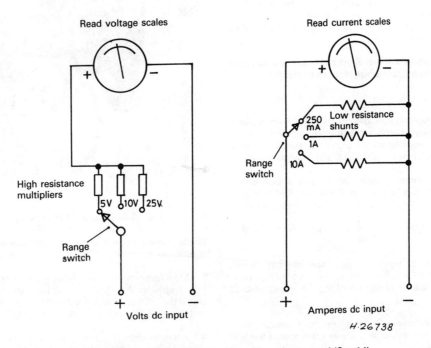

Fig. 16.24 Multi-range testmeter (dc volts and amperes) (Sec 14)

Fig. 16.25 General purpose multimeter (Sec 14)

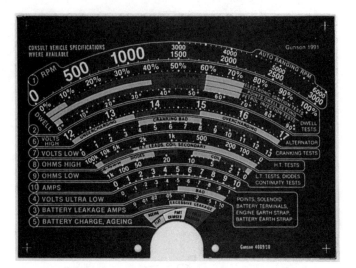

Fig. 16.26 Gunson Testune analogue multimeter scale (Sec 14)

To make the moving coil instrument into an ammeter, the terminals are bridged by low value resistors known as shunts. Several ranges of voltage and current measurements can be obtained by switching in different values of shunts and multipliers (Fig. 16.24).

To measure alternating voltage or current a small rectifier may be switched in across the moving coil terminals, this converting the incoming alternating current into a form of direct current. The scale is then calibrated in volts or amperes ac.

Digital meters

3   All electrical quantities can be measured by instruments which display the result in figures. Such instruments are called digital meters and, in general, are more accurate than analogue meters (Fig. 16.27).

4   The test voltage or current is sampled by the meter input circuits at the rate of about two times per second and measured in terms of clock pulses. Most digital meters use seven segment liquid-crystal displays, the seven segments being electronically switched to give any number between 0 and 9 (see Fig. 2.45).

A valuable feature of the digital voltmeter is the high input resistance of the order of 10 megohms (10 million) which is much higher than that of an analogue meter.

Multimeters

5   It is inconvenient to have separate meters for volts, amperes and ohms. Combined multipurpose meters are nearly always used and can measure at least the three major quantities plus other special features such as dwell angle. They may be in both digital and analogue types.

Such meters are known under various names and abbreviations including multimeter, VOM (voltage-ohm-milliampere), DMM (digital multimeter) and AVO (a trade name meaning amperes, volts, ohms).

Examples of analogue and digital multimeters are shown in Figs 16.25 to 16.27.

6   Analogue multimeters particularly need special care when switching from one range to another. The rotary switch may pass through current ranges – amperes – before reaching the desired voltage range.

If the test prods have been left connected to a live circuit, this can mean the rapid end to an expensive instrument. **Always** disconnect the test leads before changing ranges.

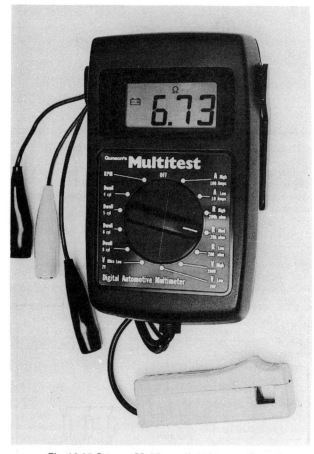

Fig. 16.27 Gunson Multitest digital meter (Sec 14)

Digital meters have some protection against overload but it is safe practice to disconnect the meter whether analogue or digital.

7   Ideal for motorcycle general purpose testing and at low cost is the Altai testmeter (Fig. 16.25) available from electronics stores in the US and in the UK from AO Services (0895-449336). This multimeter has dc and ac voltage ranges, 250mA and 10A dc current and ohms ranges.

8   A comprehensive analogue instrument is the Gunsons Testune which covers a wide range of dc volts including an expanded scale of

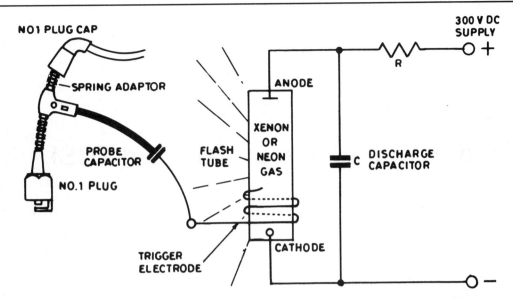

Fig. 16.28 Operation of a typical stroboscope (Sec 14)

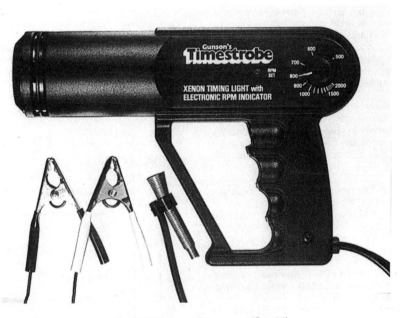

Fig. 16.29 Xenon stroboscope (Sec 14)

12 – 17 volts for accurate measurements of alternator and regulator performance. It measures rpm, dwell, ohms and battery leakage which makes it a most useful tool (Fig. 16.26).

9 Digital testmeters can be more expensive, but good value is the Gunson Multitest which has features not easily found elsewhere. In addition to voltage ranges 0 – 2V, 0 – 20V and 0 – 200V it is also capable of reading starter motor currents up to 200A with the external shunt provided. An inductive pick-up for measurements of engine rpm comes with the meter. This clips round an HT lead, requiring no disconnection for rpm measurement (Fig. 16.27).

Stroboscopes (timing lights)

10 Stroboscopes for ignition tuning are high intensity flashing lamps, the flash rate being controlled by an ignition spark. With the engine running the stroboscope is pointed towards the timing marks and has the effect of freezing the motion so that the marks appear to be stationary. The timing adjustment is then made to align the rotating timing mark with the fixed mark on the engine case.
Accelerating the engine will enable the full automatic advance to be checked. If the rotating mark appears to move backwards up to full advance then all is well.

11 One type of stroboscope is illustrated diagrammatically in Fig. 16.28. A fraction of the spark plug voltage is passed to the control grid of the xenon or neon tube by the probe lead and a capacitor. The main discharge electrodes of the tube are fed from a capacitor charged up from a high voltage dc supply. When the spark pulse reaches the control grid this is sufficient for the gas in the tube to break down, allowing current to flow through until the capacitor C is discharged.

The current flow gives rise to an intense flash of light over a period of only microseconds. Xenon gives a whitish light, and is more intense than the red neon type of lamp, but the advantage is paid for in a higher cost.

It is recommended that the xenon stroboscope should be chosen as neon types give a much lower light intensity and tend to present a blurred image. The Gunson Xenon 'Timestrobe' stroboscope shown in Fig. 16.29 is a good example of low cost equipment that will stand rugged treatment in a workshop.

Chapter 17
Braking and traction control (ABS and TCS)

Contents

1 Anti-lock Braking System (ABS)

1   The purpose of the Anti-lock Braking System (ABS) is to provide maximum braking when required, but also to prevent wheel skid. Maximum braking force between the road surface and tyre will be present just short of the point of skidding; when a tyre skids across a surface the rider loses directional control because turning requires a sideways (lateral) force between tyre and road surface – this is not present when skidding. The almost inevitable result is that the rider will come off and add to the accident statistics.

2   The single-track vehicle (ie motorcycle or bicycle) is not balanced in itself and only remains stable at low speeds due to the force exerted by the rider on the handlebars, and at higher speeds due to the gyroscopic effect of the two wheels – especially the front wheel. Whenever the wheels stop turning for more than 0.5 seconds, the motorcycle will suddenly become unstable.

3   Most riders instinctively know that when the front brake is applied (by hand) and the rear brake (by foot) there is a proper proportion of braking and the right total amount of braking in all situations. *Those who do not learn this quickly are at risk!*

It is known that one in ten riders falls off due to overbraking, but that many accidents (statistics unknown) are due to insufficient braking in an emergency. It is estimated that only about 70% of maximum possible braking is used by most riders on the straight and 60% when cornering.

4   ABS braking allows the rider to apply the brakes as hard as he can without risking either wheel locking up – **providing** he is riding straightahead. On treacherous road surfaces with low frictional coefficients, eg wet roads, gravel, sand or diesel oil, ABS has a far superior performance than the most skilled rider. Additionally, traversing a change from a dry to wet surface requires a sudden but precise alteration of brake pressure – ABS achieves this, but many riders do not.

Cornering is a different matter and even with ABS full application of brakes is not possible. When the bike and rider lean in round a corner, the tyre contact point with the road moves over, away from the tyre centre line. If the rider brakes in this situation, the motorcycle automatically moves upwards from its inclined position and tries to run straightahead. Given these circumstances, full braking is impossible.

2 Principles of ABS braking

1   All systems have toothed wheels on both front and back axles, sometimes attached to brake discs. A fixed sensor on each assembly counts the teeth passing and the sensor voltages are fed into an Electronic Control Unit (ECU).

2   Usually when reaching the skidding point during braking, one of the wheels will have a different rotational speed from the other. The ECU reads the difference in rotational speed of front and back wheels; when there is no speed difference, the ECU takes no action.

Where a difference of more than 30% occurs, the ECU activates one of two pressure modulator units which are hydraulically connected to the braking system. The pressure modulator reduces the hydraulic brake pressure on the wheel just going into the skid condition until there is no further sign of wheel locking, then increases the pressure again up to locking point.

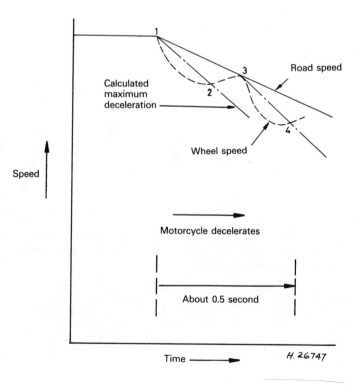

Fig. 17.1 Overbraking sequence with ABS – speed diagram (Sec 2)

1   *Skid imminent – wheel speed falls below calculated maximum possible deceleration rate. Pressure on brake reduces and wheel speeds up*

2   *At point 2 wheel speed corresponds to maximum deceleration and pressure modulator de-activates*

3   *If the rider continues to overbrake cycle repeats*

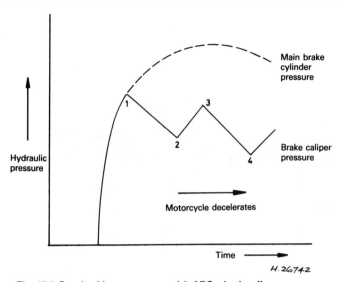

Fig. 17.2 Overbraking sequence with ABS – hydraulic pressures (Sec 2)

1   *Skid detected – modulator reduces pressure*
2   *Modulator de-activates – wheel speed deceleration ideal*
3   *If applied brake pressure is too high, slip (skid) may recur – the process is repeated at a rate of 3 to 8 cycles per second depending on frictional value of road surface (ie slipperiness)*

This process repeats 3 – 8 times per second for as long as the rider maintains the brake lever pressure and the speed does not fall below a certain point (4 km/h or 2.5 mph in the case of BMW) (Figs. 17.1 and 17.2).

3   Another, less common, condition may arise where the rider applies both brakes evenly so that both wheels go into the skid (lock-up) state simultaneously. To meet this state the ECU road memory has a programme for the maximum deceleration short of skidding. When the wheels slow down quicker than this figure due to locking-up action, ABS is applied to both wheels.

4   Automobiles with ABS can exhibit a vibration which is felt on the footbrake pedal. Some motorcycle systems have a one-way valve in the hydraulic system which prevents this sensation.

5   Different manufacturers' designs vary but the essential feature is the same. When the rider manually applies enough brake pressure to take a wheel up to the skidding point, the pressure modulator will reduce the braking force at the brake disc. It will then re-apply it up to skid point, reduce it again, etc., until the motorcycle is brought down to the speed required (often this is standstill). This produces the **maximum possible deceleration** and removes the danger of skidding.

6   Correct tyre sizes and inflation pressures are important on any motorcycle fitted with ABS. The front and rear wheel sensors detect wheel speed difference and if, for example, one tyre had very low pressure, this could give a false reading to the ECU.

3   Current designs

1   At the time of writing, current models with ABS are the BMW K-series, the Honda ST1100 ABS-TCS and the Yamaha FJ1200A and GTS1000A.

2   ABS braking was first fitted on production cars as far back as 1978, and soon motorcycle design engineers began experimental work to see if the benefits could be applied to two-wheeled vehicles. The first working system based on hydraulic/mechanical principles was developed in Britain.

German work followed later using electronic/hydraulic units developed by BMW, FAG and Hella and known as the FAG-Kugelfischer system. This system first appeared on BMW K-series motorcycles in 1988 and is undergoing constant development (Fig. 17.3).

Japanese systems have subsequently been introduced, and have appeared on the Honda ST1100 ABS-TCS and Yamaha FJ1200A and GTS1000A.

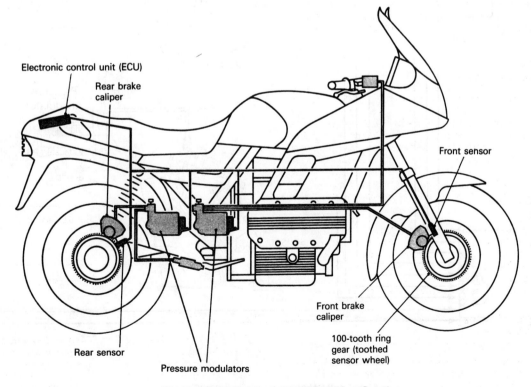

Fig. 17.3 BMW K-series with ABS braking (Sec 3)

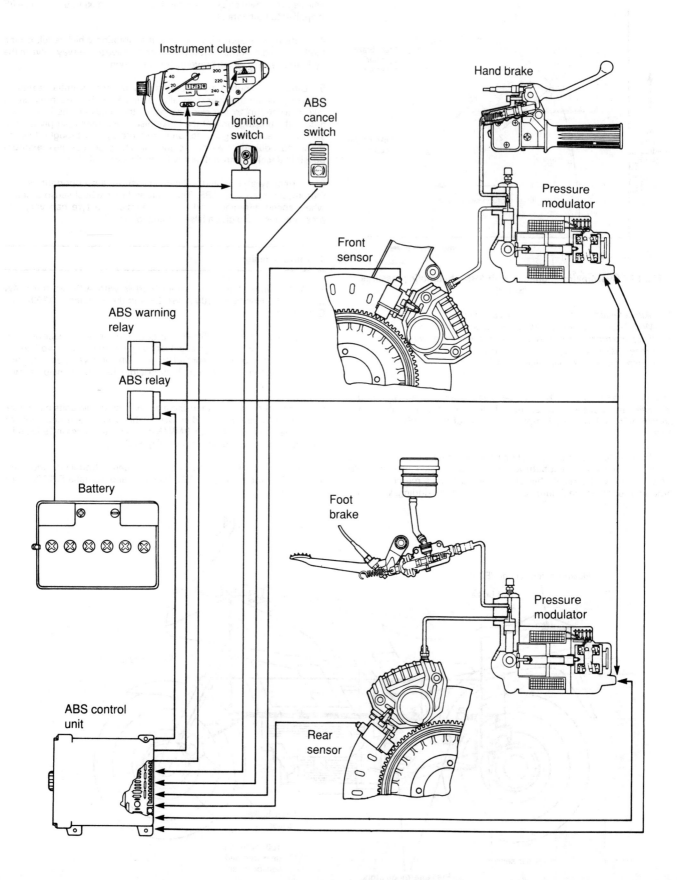

Fig. 17.4 BMW ABS operating circuit (Sec 4)

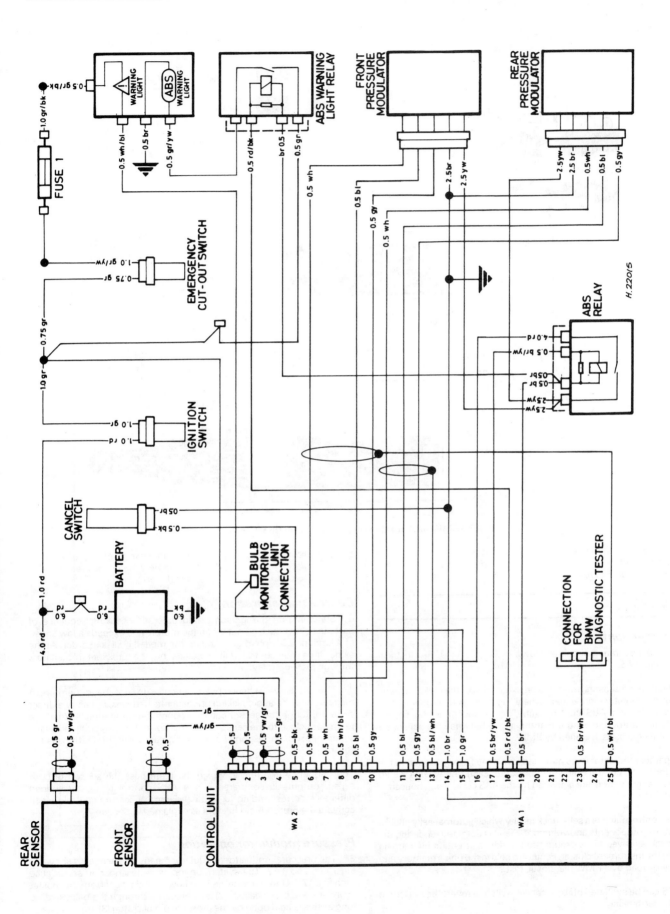

Fig. 17.5 BMW ABS electrical circuit (Sec 4)

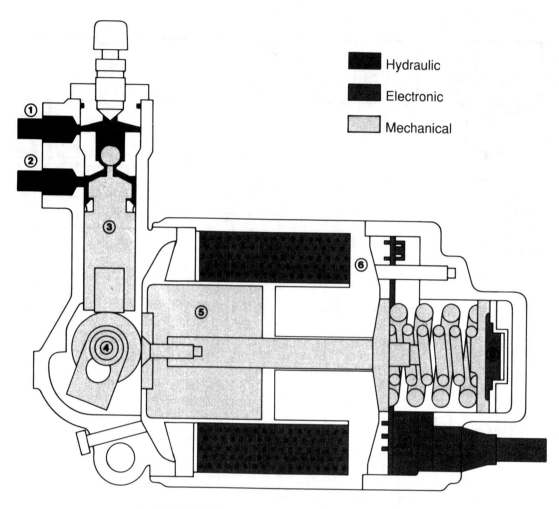

Fig. 17.6 BMW ABS pressure modulator in section (Sec 4)

1	*Fluid connection from brake master cylinder*	3	*Piston*
2	*Fluid connection to brake caliper*	4	*Idler rollers*

5	*Solenoid core*	7	*Output powerstage of control unit*
6	*Solenoid*	8	*Piezo element (detecting pressure of springs)*

4   BMW ABS

ABS components

1   The ABS operating circuit is shown in Fig. 17.4 and the electrical circuit in Fig. 17.5.

2   Wheel speed sensors, mounted on extensions of the brake calipers, continually monitor individual wheel speeds and transmit this information to the ABS control unit. The sensors must be set up carefully if disturbed to ensure that the airgap between the sensor tip and toothed ring is as specified by BMW.

3   Separate modulator units mounted low in the frame, just above the rider's footrests, control brake fluid pressure. Each unit weighs 3.8 kg (8.4 lb). The modulators are activated by the ABS control unit housed in the tail fairing.

4   The control unit has a self-check facility which automatically checks the system components and voltage; if a fault is detected rendering the system inoperative, this is brought to the rider's attention by warning lamps in the instrument cluster. Faults are held in the unit's memory and can only be read by a BMW diagnostic tester.

5   ABS can be switched off by a cancel switch to revert the system to normal rider-braking.

Control unit operation

6   Switching on the ignition produces a self checking sequence of flashing lights which go out when the motorcycle exceeds a low speed of 4 km/h or 2.5 mph (depending on the model) if all is in order. At the same time the control unit switches on the pressure modulators through the ABS relay.

7   The inductive wheel speed sensors do not have permanent magnets so as to avoid picking up magnetic particles, but carry a direct current through the sensor coil to produce the same effect. When the teeth pass close to the sensor the direct current has an added ac wave superimposed, corresponding to the rate at which the teeth pass the sensor.

The frequency (the rate at which the teeth pass the sensor) of both sensor outputs is compared in the ABS control unit. Any sudden difference corresponding to skid condition causes the control unit to activate the pressure modulators as explained in Section 2.

Pressure modulator operation

8   The pressure modulator (modulator means 'to change') is shown in Figs. 17.6 and 17.7. The system operation is described in accordance with Fig. 17.6. Under normal use the flow of brake fluid from the master cylinder (1) to brake caliper (2) is unhindered through the ball valve, so long as this is held open by the pressure pin of piston (3).

When skid conditions are detected by the sensors, the output power stage (7) receives signals from the control unit and switches on current through solenoid (6). The core (5) moves axially (like the core of a starter solenoid) to the right, against spring pressure. The idling rollers (4) move to the right and the piston (3) moves down, closing the ball valve. This removes any subsequent pressure pulsation through the brake lever.

As the piston moves down, the volume applied to the brake caliper (2) increases, reducing the pressure. The drop in pressure allows the wheel to accelerate again at a rate determined by the tyre's grip on the road

surface. Increase of wheel speed is notified by the wheel sensor to the control unit which switches off the modulator solenoid (6). The coil springs force the solenoid core (5) to the left, lifting piston (3) to the original position. If the applied brake pressure by the rider is still too high, the action repeats.

Piezo element (8) is a quartz crystal which produces a voltage proportional to pressure. The signals generated by spring pressure on the piezo crystal check that the solenoid is working and contribute to the self checking of the system.

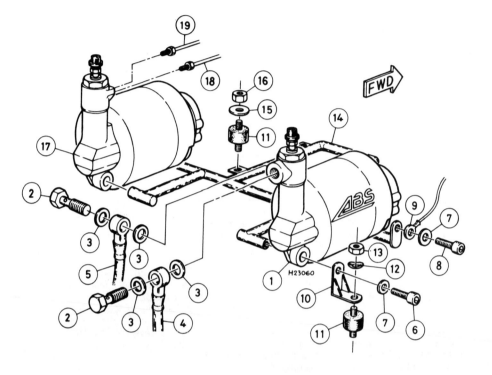

1 Rear brake modulator
2 Union bolt
3 Sealing washer
4 Hose to rear master cylinder
5 Hose to rear caliper
6 Allen screw
7 Washer
8 Allen screw
9 Earth lead
10 Rear bracket
11 Rubber mounting
12 Lock washer
13 Nut
14 Mounting bracket
15 Washer
16 Nut
17 Front brake modulator
18 Pipe to front master cylinder
19 Pipe to front caliper

Fig. 17.7 BMW ABS pressure modulators (Sec 4)

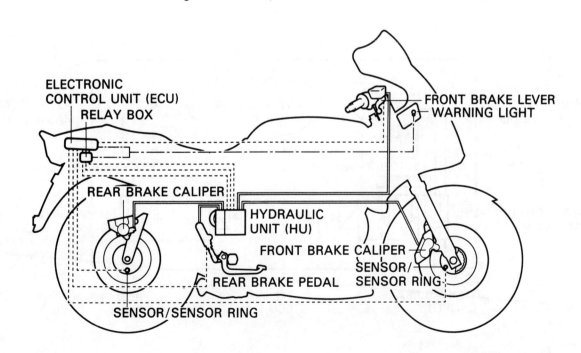

Fig. 17.8 ABS component location on the Yamaha FJ1200A (GTS1000A similar) (Sec 5)

5 Yamaha ABS

ABS components

1   The location of ABS components is shown in Fig. 17.8 and, in common with other systems, the heavier components are fitted roughly mid way between the front and rear wheel.

2   Hall effect sensors and toothed rotors (termed 'sensor rings') are located within the hubs (Fig. 17.9). When refitting a wheel it is not necessary to check the sensor to sensor ring gap since these will not have been disturbed.

3   Brake fluid pressure is modulated by an hydraulic unit (HU) which contains a motor driving two pumps, one for the front brake lever circuit and one for the rear brake pedal circuit (Fig. 17.10).

A buffer chamber is incorporated in the front and rear circuits of the hydraulic system; these chambers store brake fluid from the brake calipers when pressure is released. The fluid is then returned to the brake line.

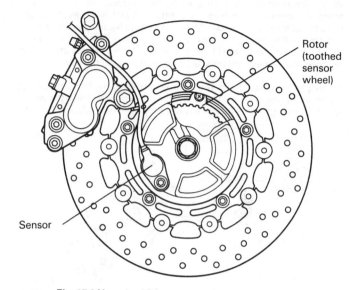

Fig. 17.9 Yamaha ABS sensor and rotor units (Sec 5)

ECU operation

4   The ECU checks first that the system is working correctly. Coded flashing signals are given to indicate all correct, or any one of several fault conditions. Its second function is to determine the running state of the motorcycle. Memory in the ECU can store information on faults which can be retrieved when the system is connected to a diagnostic tester.

The final function is to determine whether braking force should be increased or decreased, a task carried out continuously whether the rider is applying the brakes or not.

5   If when braking, the front and rear wheel speed differs from the optimum pre-determined braking speed programmed into the ECU, the ECU activates the hydraulic unit to regulate the brake fluid pressure at the calipers. Decisions on this are made by the ECU every 8 milliseconds.

Hydraulic Unit (HU) operation

6   During normal braking, the master cylinder pressurizes the brake caliper directly (Fig. 17.11).

7   When ABS operates, the solenoid valve opens releasing brake fluid to the buffer chamber. The flow control valve is sucked over to the right because of the pressure difference on either side of the orifice. The flow control valve cuts off the caliper passage on the left side of the orifice and, as the movement continues, the passage to the right of the orifice opens, so depressurizing the caliper (Fig. 17.12).

8   When the danger of skid is past, pressure is re-applied to the caliper at a graduated rate. The ECU switches off the current to the solenoid valve, shutting off the buffer chamber, the contents being circulated by the pump. The flow control valve moves over to the left, re-pressurizing to a specified amount by the metering edge (Fig. 17.13).

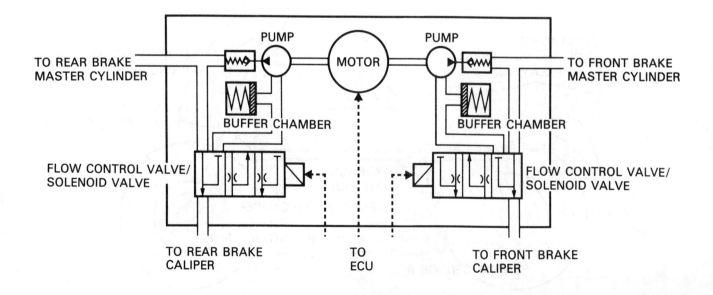

Fig. 17.10 Yamaha ABS hydraulic unit (HU) (Sec 5)

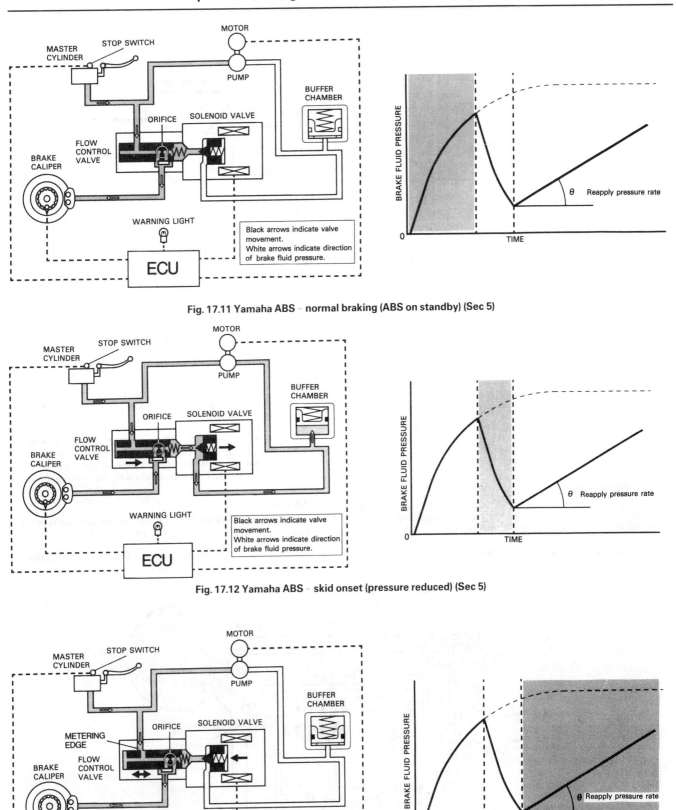

Fig. 17.11 Yamaha ABS – normal braking (ABS on standby) (Sec 5)

Fig. 17.12 Yamaha ABS – skid onset (pressure reduced) (Sec 5)

Fig. 17.13 Yamaha ABS – pressure reapplied at graduated rate (Sec 5)

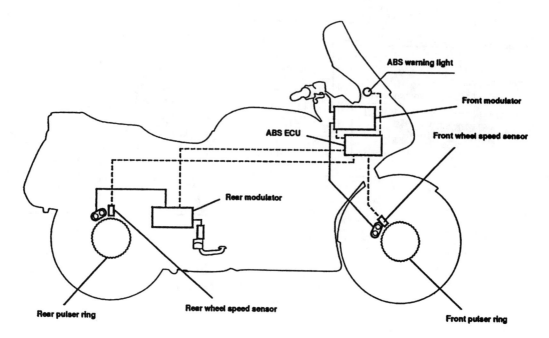

Fig. 17.14 ABS component location on the Honda ST1100 (Sec 6)

6   Honda ABS

1   The only Honda model featuring this system at the time of writing is the ST1100. It has a combined ABS braking and TCS traction control system, known as ABS-TCS. The ABS function is described in this section, but refer to Section 7 for details of TCS.

ABS components

2   The Honda system employs an ECU controlling two separate, self-contained, pressure modulators which are maintenance free. The location of ABS equipment is shown in Fig. 17.14.

Each modulator features two compact, high speed solenoid valves (IN

and OUT) for quick and precise hydraulic pressure control. A pump and motor pressurise the modulator with a fluid which is kept separate from the brake fluid in the calipers.

At start-up the ECU carries out a diagnostic hydraulic pressure check; errors are signalled to the rider by a coded flashing lamp in the instrument cluster. There is fail-safe provision in the event of pump failure which is referred to in Honda literature as the 'back-up' mode.

Operation

3   Other systems work on the principle of pressure decrease and pressure increase to the brake caliper of a slipping wheel.

On standby mode (Fig. 17.15) the master cylinder is connected directly

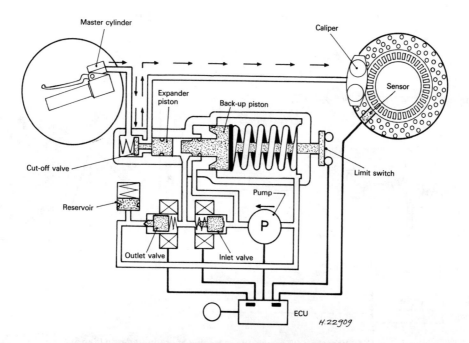

Fig. 17.15 Honda ABS on standby mode (Sec 6)

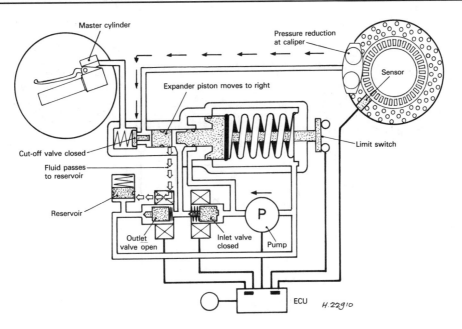

Fig. 17.16 Honda ABS on pressure decrease mode (skidding threshold) (Sec 6)
Outlet valve opens – expander piston moves to the right – pressure to caliper reduces – cut-off valve closes – master cylinder isolated from caliper

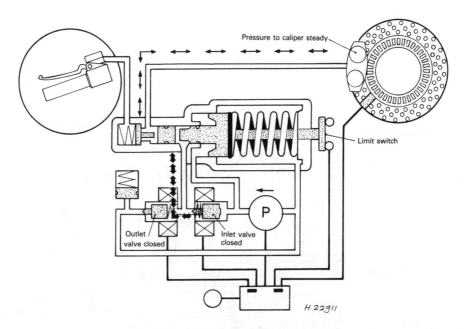

Fig. 17.17 Honda ABS on hold mode (Sec 6)
Both valves closed holding caliper pressure steady

to the brake caliper. Up to the onset of skidding the brakes are rider controlled. Honda use **3-stage** working, described as follows.

Pressure DECREASE mode

4   When the ECU detects the onset of skidding it reduces hydraulic pressure to the brake caliper by simultaneously closing the inlet valve and opening the outlet valve (Fig. 17.16). Loss of pressure on the right side of the cylinder valve moves it to the right, closing the cut-off valve. This de-pressurizes the pressure in the brake caliper line.

Pressure HOLD mode

5   Following a pre-determined decompression period the outlet valve closes and the hydraulic pressure remains steady but lower than that pressure which causes skidding. This allows recovery of wheel speed (Fig. 17.17).

Pressure INCREASE mode

6   The ECU will detect the recovery of wheel speed and once this is attained, it signals the opening of the inlet valve and closing of the outlet valve. Pump pressure forces the expander valve to the left, so repressurizing the brake caliper line (Fig. 17.18).

Pressure loss protection – BACK-UP mode

7   If there is a loss of pressure in the pumped system due to leakage, pump failure, or simply when the rider switches off ignition, the back-up piston under force of a strong spring pushes the cut-off valve open and normal rider-operated braking now takes place. The limit switch opens, signalling this condition to the ECU.

When the rider starts the engine again, unless the pump pressure builds up to close the switch within 5 seconds, the ECU opens the outlet valve,

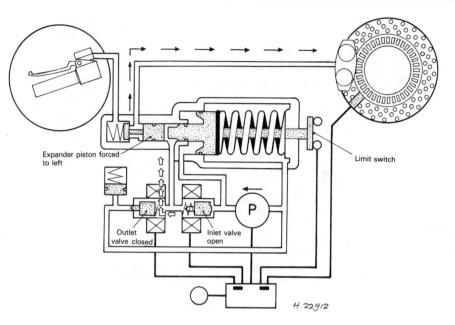

Fig. 17.18 Honda ABS on pressure increase mode (Sec 6)

When wheel speed recovers, inlet valve opens – outlet valve closes. Pump pressure forces expander piston to left-repressurizing brake caliper line

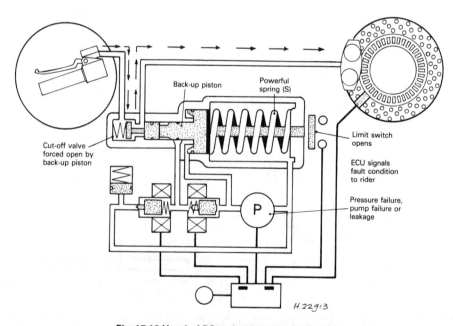

Fig. 17.19 Honda ABS on back-up mode (Sec 6)

If pump pressure fails, the back up piston is forced left by springs. The back up piston pushes the expander piston to the left, thus opening the cut-off valve – rider has control of braking

allowing the pressure to drop completely. The back-up piston moves to the left, opening the cut-off valve. ABS switches off and a warning light comes on (Fig. 17.19).

7 Honda TCS

Description

1 Traction slip is, in a sense, the converse of skidding. With traction slip the driving wheel will accelerate faster than the friction between tyre and road surface can cope with. The result is wheel spin without appreciable movement of the motorcycle.

While this may be caused by a rider opening the throttle too fast, it is also possible for it to occur on a slippery road. In either case, riding stability is affected and it is an additional hazard the rider can do without.

2 Honda have produced the first traction control system for a motorcycle. It is a simple system using certain common components from the ABS and has the main aim of suppressing tyre slip, leaving the rider with an ample margin of control.

TCS reduces the engine power by retarding the ignition timing when traction slip is detected. The retardation is regulated by the ECU so that the rear wheel has adequate traction for the particular road surface condition (Fig. 17.20).

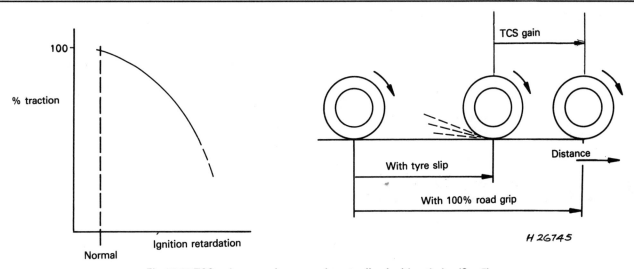

Fig. 17.20 TCS reduces engine power by retarding ignition timing (Sec 7)

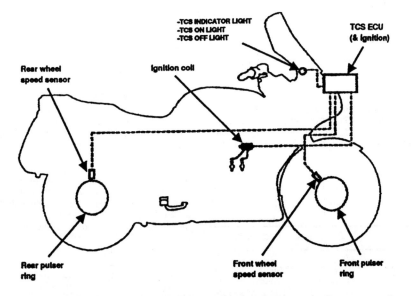

Fig. 17.21 TCS component location on the Honda ST1100 (Sec 7)

TCS components

3   Fig. 17.21 shows the location of components on the ST1100 ABS-TCS equipped motorcycle. Note that TCS uses the same Hall-effect wheel speed sensors and toothed rings (pulser rings) as the ABS system.

The ECU is combined with the ignition control unit, which is logical since the ECU will put ignition retard signals into the ignition control unit when wheel spin is detected. Repetition sampling rate is approximately 100 operations per second. The ECU calculates rear tyre slip and the engine running condition to determine how much ignition retardation is required. The result is the correct control of engine torque to keep tyre slip within the desired limits.

4   A 'TCS-ON' light in the instrument panel comes on when ECU is applying retardation. It may be regarded as a hint to the rider to adjust his acceleration level.

Chapter 18 Theft deterrents

Contents

1 Introduction

1   Every year an increasing theft rate of motorcycles occurs and owners look to means of prevention. In the UK, statistics show that a motorcycle is stolen every 7 minutes.

2   Electronic alarm systems have reached a high degree of sophistication and can protect against bike movement and accessory theft. Each of the alarm protection products will have an individual specification, the sophistication being reflected in the price; one of the systems will be described.

2 The Datatool alarm

1   This system consists of a kit (Fig. 18.1) which can easily be installed by the owner. At the heart of the system is a control unit which monitors all the alarm functions (Fig. 18.2). It can be mounted in any secure position where it is not visible or easily reached (Fig. 18.3).

2   The alarm is set into operation (armed) by an infra-red transmitter carried by the rider. On board is an infra-red receiver and when the rider presses the transmitter button, the turn signals will flash twice and the light emitting diode (LED), mounted on the motorcycle, will flash continuously.

3   To dis-arm the alarm (ie to switch it off) the rider presses the transmitter, the turn signals flash once and the LED turns off. If the rider loses the transmitter an over-ride key facility is provided.

The transmitter must be pointed at the receiver and be within 0.5 – 2.5 metres (1.5 – 8.0 ft). Like such transmitters for TV control, the 3-volt lithium battery's life is high, being about one year.

Although the current demand of the alarm is low, it will drain the battery over a long period, as the graph for a 14 ampere-hour battery shows in Fig. 18.4. The alarm always draws current except when turned off by the manual over-ride key.

4   An additional feature is a security loop of 4 metres in length which may be threaded through valuables such as panniers, radio, etc; attempted removal of these items will break the loop, setting off the alarm. Any attempt to move the motorcycle, start it with a key, 'hot-wire' the ignition, or cut the security loop will trigger the alarm.

If the power supply is cut (such as if the battery supply lead were cut) or the alarm disconnected, the internal 110 dB siren will sound continuously and the ignition will be disabled.

Once the alarm is triggered, the turn signals will flash, the bike horn will sound intermittently, the internal siren will sound and the ignition will be disabled. After 30 seconds this all stops and the alarm will automatically reset to the armed condition. The LED will light continuously (not flashing) to show the rider that the alarm has been set off while he/she was away.

Fig. 18.1 Datatool alarm kit components (Sec 2)

Fig. 18.2 Microchips and internal circuitry illustrate complexity of alarm control unit (Sec 2)

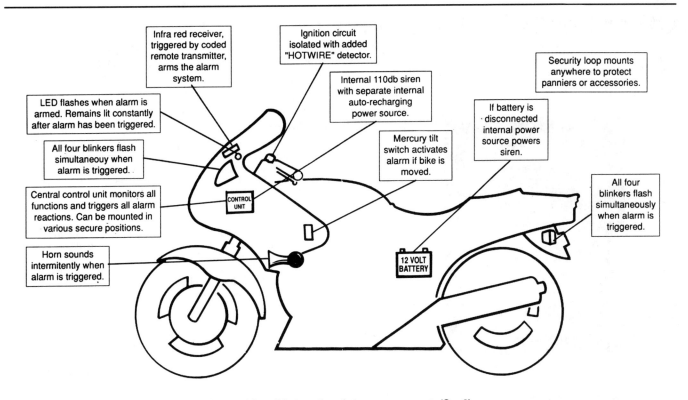

Fig. 18.3 Possible location of alarm components (Sec 2)

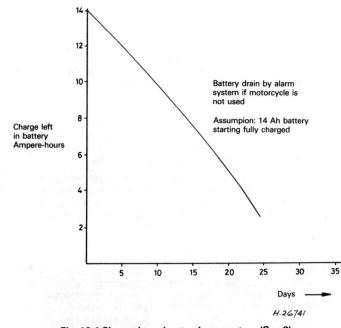

Fig. 18.4 Charge loss due to alarm system (Sec 2)

5   The movement sensor consists of a mercury switch mountable on the motorcycle by velcro pads. Any movement causes the mercury to bridge two contact spikes, setting off the alarm. The mercury switch is mounted at 45° to the direction of travel, so that it will function with the motorcycle on its main or side stand. Sensitivity is increased by adjusting the angle to the horizontal – the more to the horizontal, the higher the sensitivity. Other manufacturers use a movement sensor of the ball bearing and cup type. With movement in any direction the ball moves to contacts round the side of the cup.

3   General alarm installation notes

1   Fitting an alarm to a motorcycle will depend upon the particular machine and manufacturer's advice should be followed. The decisions to be made before installation include routing the alarm cables and where to make connections. Avoid running near exhaust or other hot spots and secure all cables.

2   Connectors should be soldered if possible; a failed connection can cause the ignition to cut out, and if this happens in the fast lane at speed, the possible hazard is obvious. It pays to seal connectors against weather with silicone-based grease.

4   Datatag system

1   Mitsui Machinery Sales, the UK Yamaha importers, have developed Datatag, a sophisticated security marking system which uses a coded microchip device buried into the equipment to be protected. The microchip is coded with a unique identification number and when interrogated by an electronic scanner, will give positive identification of ownership.

2   The device is a transponder which has no batteries but is activated when a hand-held scanner is passed over it. A signal is emitted from the microchip which is read as the identity number on the scanner. A laser etching process ensures that the code number cannot be erased or changed. No two chips will have the same code since the 10 character coding allows the use of 500 billion numbers.

The small size of the transponders allows them to be inserted into a variety of components and the scanners can read through almost any material.

Other books in the Haynes range

In addition to the comprehensive range of Haynes Motorcycle Owners Workshop Manuals, readers will find the three books detailed below of interest especially if they are taking an educational course in this subject.

Motorcycle Basics Manual
Book No. **1083**

Quite a large proportion of motorcycles, mopeds and scooters in everyday use are ridden by owners who have little understanding of how their motorcycle works. Many are quite content to remain in this state of blissful ignorance, having their motorcycle serviced at regular intervals as and when the need occurs, or repairs carried out when problems necessitate taking the motorcycle off the road. Not everyone has the ability or inclination to look after these matters themselves and it is well that they are aware of their own limitations.

If, however, the correct mental approach is adopted it will often be found that a complicated looking assembly is nothing more than a number of relatively simple basic units bolted together to make up a single compact unit. These individual units are described in ten chapters accompanied by over 150 illustrations. Complicated technical terminology has been kept to a minimum and used only where considered necessary, but to help readers even further, a basic glossary of technical terms is included.

Topics covered include: basic and improved 2- and 4-stroke engine types, engine designs and layouts, fuel and exhaust systems, ignition systems, lubrication and cooling systems, wheels, brakes and tyres, suspension, steering, frames and electrical systems.

Motorcycle Workshop Practice Manual
Book No. **1454**

This manual will enable the DIY motorcycle mechanic to undertake with sufficient knowledge and confidence repair or overhaul work on his or her motorcycle. Although not intended as a substitute for the experience gained from years spent working on motorcycles, the reader will benefit from the wealth of information given by the author, who has a long involvement with motorcycling and has written many titles in our Owners Workshop Manual range. Having worked in similar conditions himself, the author is able to appreciate the poor facilities and often limited resources of the DIY mechanic and consideration has therefore been given to these factors in the manual.

The text is illustrated with over 300 line drawings and its six chapters cover the subjects of: the workshop; tools; workshop techniques; engine and transmission; frame and suspension; and electrics and ignition. In addition, a glossary of technical terms is included to take the mystery out of technical jargon.

Typical examples of the numerous topics covered are, cylinder head overhaul, dealing with engine seizure, removing damaged fasteners, repairing accident damage, bearing removal, making alternatives to service tools, plating, riveting, welding, reboring, painting, frame coatings, welding and electrical testing.

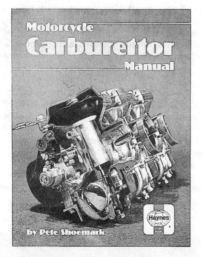

Motorcycle Carburettor Manual
Book No. **603**

There can be few motorcyclists who have not been confronted by carburation problems in one form or another. The number of symptoms which can be attributed to some sort of carburettor malfunction is just short of infinite, and this often leads to some tentative screwdriver twiddling on the part of the owner in the vain hope that this will resolve the problem. Unfortunately, unless they are very lucky indeed, this will only add another discrepancy and will often mask the true cause of the original problem. Given that many motorcycles possess four or more carburettors, this can lead to a very interesting tangle which can take hours to sort out.

This manual sets out to overcome such problems, first by giving the reader a sound knowledge of the simple principles which govern the way a carburettor functions, and then by examining in detail the more practical aspects of tuning and the correction of maladjustments. In addition to this the overhaul of the main types of carburettor is discussed in detail as is the practical use of tuning aids and equipment by which greater accuracy can be obtained.

The manual is divided into thirteen chapters covering the theory of carburation, development history, carburettor types, overhaul, tuning and also includes a fault diagnosis section.

Index